'Both timely and authoritative . . . The subject of archives and libraries is one of permanent importance in the understanding a nation has of itself, and touches not only high politics but also information technology and life-and-death drama. I can think of no one better qualified to write about it than Richard Ovenden. I enjoyed *Burning the Books* immensely'   PHILIP PULLMAN

'A stark and important warning about the value of knowledge and the dangers that come from the destruction of books. Vital reading for this day and age'   PETER FRANKOPAN

'Like an epic film-maker, Richard Ovenden unfolds vivid scenes from three millennia of turbulent history, to mount passionate arguments for the need to preserve the records of the past – and of the present. This urgent, lucid book calls out to us all to recognise and defend one of our most precious public goods – libraries and archives'   MARINA WARNER

'*Burning the Books* is fascinating, thought-provoking and very timely. No one should keep quiet about this library history'   IAN HISLOP

'A magnificent book – timely, vital and full of the most incredible tales, a manifesto for our humanity and its archives'
PHILLIPE SANDS

'"Dangerous souvenirs" is what Richard Ovenden calls the books salvaged by ex-monks under the nose of Henry VIII. Now as then, books need friends. This fascinating book will help to find them'
ALAN BENNETT

Richard Ovenden has been Bodley's Librarian (the senior executive position of the Bodleian Libraries, University of Oxford) since 2014. Prior to that he held positions at Durham University Library, the House of Lords Library, the National Library of Scotland and the University of Edinburgh. He moved to the Bodleian in 2003 as Keeper of Special Collections, becoming Deputy Librarian in 2011. He was educated at the University of Durham and University College London and holds a professorial fellowship at Balliol College, Oxford. He is a fellow of the Society of Antiquaries, the Royal Society of Arts and a member of the American Philosophical Society. He was appointed OBE in the Queen's Birthday Honours 2019.

Richard serves as Treasurer of the Consortium of European Research Libraries, President of the Digital Preservation Coalition and as a member of the Board of the Council on Library and Information Resources (Washington, DC).

Also by Richard Ovenden

John Thomson (1837–1921): Photographer

A Radical's Books *(with Michael Hunter,*
Giles Mandelbrote and Nigel Smith)

Burning the Books

A History of Knowledge Under Attack

RICHARD OVENDEN

JOHN MURRAY

First published in Great Britain in 2020 by John Murray (Publishers)
An Hachette UK company

1

A CIP catalogue record for this title is available from the British Library

Hardback ISBN 978-1-529-37875-7
Trade Paperback ISBN 978-1-529-37876-4
eBook ISBN 978-1-529-37878-8

Typeset in Bembo MT Pro by Palimpsest Book Production Ltd,
Falkirk, Stirlingshire

Printed and bound in Great Britain by Clays Ltd, Elcograf S.p.A.

John Murray policy is to use papers that are natural, renewable and recyclable
products and made from wood grown in sustainable forests. The logging and
manufacturing processes are expected to conform to the environmental
regulations of the country of origin.

John Murray (Publishers)
Carmelite House
50 Victoria Embankment
London EC4Y 0DZ

www.johnmurraypress.co.uk

For Lyn

Contents

'Wherever they burn books, they will also, in the end, burn human beings.'

Heinrich Heine, 1823

'Those who do not remember the past are doomed to repeat it.'

George Santayana, 1905

Nazi book-burnings in Berlin, 10 May 1933.

Introduction

I N BERLIN, ON 10 May 1933, a bonfire was held on Unter den Linden, the capital's most important thoroughfare. It was a site of great symbolic resonance: opposite the university and adjacent to St Hedwig's Cathedral, the Berlin State Opera House, the Royal Palace and Karl Friedrich Schinkel's beautiful war memorial. Watched by a cheering crowd of almost forty thousand a group of students ceremonially marched up to the bonfire carrying the bust of a Jewish intellectual, Magnus Hirschfeld (founder of the ground-breaking Institute of Sexual Sciences). Chanting the 'Feuersprüche', a series of fire incantations, they threw the bust on top of thousands of volumes from the institute's library, which had joined books by Jewish and other 'un-German' writers (gays and communists prominent among them) that had been seized from bookshops and libraries. Around the fire stood rows of young men in Nazi uniforms giving the Heil Hitler salute. The students were keen to curry favour with the new government and this book-burning was a carefully planned publicity stunt.[1] In Berlin, Joseph Goebbels, Hitler's new minister of propaganda, gave a rousing speech that was widely reported around the world:

> No to decadence and moral corruption! Yes to decency and morality in family and state! . . . The future German man will not just be a man of books, but a man of character. It is to this end that we want to educate you . . . You do well to commit to the flames the evil spirit of the past. This is a strong, great and symbolic deed.

Similar scenes went on in ninety other locations across the country that night. Although many libraries and archives in Germany were left untouched, the bonfires were a clear warning sign of the attack on knowledge about to be unleashed by the Nazi regime.

★

Knowledge is still under attack. Organised bodies of knowledge are being attacked today, as they have been attacked throughout history. Over time society has entrusted the preservation of knowledge to libraries and archives, but today these institutions are facing multiple threats. They are targets for individuals, groups, and even states motivated to deny the truth and eradicate the past. At the same time, libraries and archives are experiencing declining levels of funding. This continued decline in resources has combined with the growth of technology companies, which have effectively privatised the storage and transmission of knowledge in digital form, taking some of the functions of publicly funded libraries and archives into the commercial realm. These companies are driven by very different motives from the institutions that have traditionally made knowledge available for society. When companies like Google have digitised billions of pages of books and made them available online, and when free online storage is provided by firms like Flickr, what is the point of libraries?

Just at the time that public funding is under extreme pressure we find that democratic institutions, the rule of law and open society are also under threat. The truth itself is under attack. This is, of course, no new thing. George Orwell pointed this out in *Nineteen Eighty-Four*, and his words ring disconcertingly true today as we think about the role that libraries and archives must play in defence of open societies: 'There was truth, and there was untruth, and if you clung to the truth even against the whole world, you were not mad.'[2] Libraries and archives have become central to the support of democracy, the rule of law and open society as they are bodies that exist to 'cling to the truth'.

The notion that there could exist 'alternative facts' was famously suggested by Kellyanne Conway, US Counselor to the President, in January 2017. She was responding to criticism of Trump's assertion that the crowd that had attended his inauguration ceremony was larger than the crowd at Barack Obama's five years before, when images and data showed the opposite to have been the case.[3] It was a timely reminder that the preservation of information continues to be a key tool in the defence of open societies. Defending the truth against the rise of 'alternative facts' means capturing those truths, and the statements that deny them, so that we have reference points that societies can trust and rely on.

Libraries are crucial for the healthy functioning of society. While I have worked in libraries for more than thirty-five years, I have been a user of them far longer, and have seen the value they bring. This book has been motivated by my own sense of anger at recent failures across the globe – both deliberate and accidental – to ensure that society can rely on libraries and archives to preserve knowledge. The repeated attacks on them over the centuries need to be examined as a worrying trend in human history and the astonishing efforts made by people to protect the knowledge they hold should be celebrated.

The revelation that landing cards documenting the arrival into the UK of the 'Windrush generation' had been deliberately destroyed by the Home Office in 2010 shows the importance of archives. The government had also begun to pursue a 'hostile environment' policy on immigration, which required the Windrush migrants to prove their continued residence here or be deported.[4] Yet they had been guaranteed citizenship under the British Nationality Act 1948 and had come in good faith to the UK, which faced severe labour shortages after the Second World War. By spring 2018, the Home Office had admitted to the wrongful deportation of at least eighty-three of these citizens, eleven of whom had since died, prompting a public outcry.

I was struck by the absurdity of a policy, instigated and aggressively promulgated by a government department (under the leadership of Theresa May, who had become prime minister by the time the situation came to light) that had destroyed the main evidence that would have enabled many of the people to prove their citizenship.[5] Although the decision to destroy the records was made before the implementation of the policy and was probably not malicious, the Home Office's motivation to persist with the hostile treatment may have been. I wrote an op-ed in the *Financial Times*[6] pointing out that the preservation of knowledge of this kind was vital for an open, healthy society, as indeed it has been since the beginning of our civilisations.

For as long as humans have gathered together in organised communities, with a need to communicate with one another, knowledge has been created and information recorded. In the earliest communities, this took the form, as far as we know, of oral information, and the only permanent record that survives is in the form of images: paintings made on the walls of caves, or the scratches of symbols on stones. We know nothing of the motivation behind these marks; anthropologists and archaeologists can only make educated guesses.

By the Bronze Age, communities were becoming better organised and more sophisticated. As groups of nomads settled, and began to establish fixed communities, involved in farming and early industry, they also began to develop hierarchies of organisation, with governing families, tribal chiefs and others who led the rest of the community.

These communities, from around 3,000 BCE onwards, began to keep written records. From these earliest archives, and in the documents found in them, we know a surprising amount of detail about how those societies operated.[7] In other documents people began to record their thoughts, ideas, observations and stories. These were preserved in the earliest libraries. This process of organising knowledge soon required the development of specialised skills, which included the recording of knowledge and techniques for copying. Over time these tasks resulted in the creation of professional roles – loosely similar to those of the librarian or archivist. 'Librarian' comes from the Latin word *librarius*, from *liber* meaning 'book'. The term 'archivist' is from the Latin *archivum*, which refers to both written records and the place where they are kept. The origins of this word derive from the Greek *archeia* meaning 'public records'. Libraries and archives were not created or run with the same motivation as those in the modern world, and it is dangerous to draw analogies between these ancient collections and those of today. Even so, these civilisations created bodies of knowledge and developed skills to organise them, many of which we recognise today, such as catalogues and metadata.[8]

The roles of librarian and archivist were often combined with others, such as priest or administrator, becoming more distinct and visible in ancient Greece and Rome, where libraries were more publicly available, and the belief that access to knowledge is an essential element of a healthy society began to take hold.[9] A list of the names of the men who held the post of head librarian of the Great Library of Alexandria during the third and second centuries BCE survives – many of these figures were also recognised as the leading scholars of their time, such as Apollonius of Rhodes (whose epic poem about Jason and the Golden Fleece inspired the *Aeneid*) and Aristophanes of Byzantium (inventor of one of the earliest forms of punctuation).[10]

Storehouses of knowledge have been at the heart of the development of societies from their inception. Although the technologies of creating knowledge, and the techniques for preservation have altered radically, their core functions have changed surprisingly little. Firstly, libraries and archives collect, organise and preserve knowledge. Through gift, transfer and purchase they have accumulated tablets, scrolls, books, journals, manuscripts, photographs and many other methods of documenting civilisation. Today these formats are expanded through digital media, from word-processing files, to emails, web pages and social media. In antiquity and the medieval period the work of organising libraries had sacred connotations: the archives of the ancient kingdoms of Mesopotamia were often kept in temples, and King Philippe Auguste (also known as Philip II) of France established the 'Trésor des Chartes' (the treasury of charters). This was at first a 'mobile' collection, but by 1254 came to be stored in a purpose-built suite of rooms at the holy site of the Sainte-Chapelle in Paris.[11]

Through developing and publishing their catalogues, providing reading rooms, sponsoring scholarship, by publishing books, staging exhibitions, and more recently through digitisation, libraries and archives have been part of the broader history of disseminating ideas. The creation of national libraries from the eighteenth century and public libraries from the nineteenth century onwards massively expanded the role that these institutions played in transforming society.

At the heart of this is the idea of preservation. Knowledge can be vulnerable, fragile and unstable. Papyrus, paper and parchment are highly combustible. Water can just as easily damage them, as can mould created through high humidity. Books and documents can be stolen, defaced and tampered with. The existence of digital files can be even more fleeting, owing to technological obsolescence, the impermanence of magnetic storage media, and the vulnerability of all knowledge placed online. As anyone who has encountered a broken web link has discovered, there can be no access without preservation.

Archives are different from libraries. Libraries are accumulations of knowledge, built up one book at a time, often with great strategic purpose, while archives document directly the actions and decision-making processes of institutions and administrations, even of governments. Libraries often hold some of this material as well – the printed *Journal of the House of Commons*, for example – but archives are by their nature full of material, often mundane in its character, not intended to be read by a mass audience. But where libraries deal with ideas, ambitions, discoveries and imaginings, archives detail the routine but vital stuff of everyday life: land ownership, imports and exports, the minutes of committees and taxes. Lists are often an important feature: whether they are lists of citizens recorded in a census, or lists of immigrants arriving on a boat, archives are at the heart of history, recording the implementation of the ideas and thoughts that may be captured in a book.

The flip side of this, of course, is that the significance of books and archival material is recognised not only by those who wish to protect knowledge, but also by those who wish to destroy it. Throughout history, libraries and archives have been subject to attack. At times librarians and archivists have risked and lost their lives for the preservation of knowledge.

I want to explore a number of key episodes from history to highlight different motivations for the destruction of the storehouses of knowledge, and the responses developed by the profession to resist it. The individual cases that I focus on (and I could have chosen dozens of others) tell us something about the period in which the events took place and are fascinating in their own right.

The motivations of states that continue to erase history will be considered in the context of archives. As knowledge is increasingly created in digital form, the challenges that this reality poses for the preservation of knowledge and for the health of open societies will be examined. The book will end with some suggestions for how libraries and archives could be better supported in their current political and financial contexts, and as a Coda I will suggest five functions that these institutions have for society, to highlight their value, for the benefit of those in positions of power.

Libraries and archives themselves destroy knowledge daily. Duplicate books are routinely disposed of when only one copy is needed. Smaller libraries are often subsumed into a bigger unit, a process that usually results in the knowledge being maintained by the bigger library but sometimes, by accident or design, unique materials are lost. Archives are designed around a process called appraisal, a system of disposal and retention. Not everything can or should be kept. Although this can sometimes seem outrageous and incomprehensible to historians, the idea that every document should be kept is economically unsustainable. Much of what is destroyed in such processes is information that is already held elsewhere.

The processes of selection, acquisition and cataloguing, as well as of disposal and retention, are never neutral acts. They are done by human beings, working in their social and temporal contexts. The books and journals that sit on library shelves today, or are made available through our digital libraries, or the documents and ledgers that are in our archives, are there because of human agency. The past behaviour of humans involved in the creation of collections was, therefore, subject to bias, prejudice and personality. Most libraries and archives have great omissions in their collections, 'silences' that have often severely limited how the historical record treats, for example, people of colour, or women. Anyone using those collections today must be aware of those contexts. Readers of this book are similarly encouraged to bear these historical contexts in mind and to remember that in the past people did things differently.

In examining the history of libraries and the way their collections have evolved over time we are, in many ways, telling the story of the survival of knowledge itself. Every individual book that exists now in these institutions, all the collections that together build up into larger bodies of knowledge, are survivors.

Until the advent of digital information, libraries and archives had well-developed strategies for preserving their collections: paper. The institutions shared the responsibility with their readers. All new users of the Bodleian, for example, are still required to formally swear 'not to bring into the Library, or kindle therein, any fire or flame', as they have done for over four hundred years. Stable levels of temperature and relative humidity, avoidance of flood and fire, and well-organised shelving were at the heart of preservation strategies. Digital information is inherently less stable and requires a much more proactive approach, not just to the technology itself (such as file formats, operating systems and software). These challenges have been amplified by the widespread adoption of online services provided by major technology companies, especially those in the world of social media, for whom preservation of knowledge is a purely commercial consideration.

As more and more of the world's memory is placed online we are effectively outsourcing that memory to the major technology companies that now control the internet. The phrase 'Look it up' used to mean searching in the index of a printed book, or going to the right alphabetical entry in an encyclopaedia or dictionary. Now it just means typing a word, term or question into a search box, and letting the computer do the rest. Society used to value the training of personal memory, even devising sophisticated exercises for improving the act of memorising. Those days are gone. There are dangers in the convenience of the internet, however, as the control exercised by the major technology companies over our digital memory is huge. Some organisations, including libraries and archives, are now trying hard to take back control through independently preserving websites, blog posts, social media, even email and other personal digital collections.

'We are drowning in information, but are starved of knowledge,' John Naisbitt pointed out as early as 1982 in his book *Megatrends*.[12] A concept of 'digital abundance' has since been coined to help understand one important aspect of the digital world, one which my daily life as a librarian brings me to consider often.[13] The amount of digital information available to any user with a computer and an internet connection is overwhelmingly large, too large to be able to comprehend. Librarians and archivists are now deeply concerned with how to search effectively across the mass of available knowledge.[14]

The digital world is full of dichotomies. On the one hand the creation of knowledge has never been easier, nor has it been easier to copy texts, images and other forms of information. Storage of digital information on a vast scale is now not only possible but surprisingly inexpensive. Yet storage is not the same thing as preservation. The knowledge stored by online platforms is at risk of being lost, as digital information is surprisingly vulnerable to both neglect as well as deliberate destruction. There is also the problem that the knowledge we create through our daily interactions is invisible to most of us, but it can be manipulated and used against society for commercial and political gain. Having it destroyed may be a desirable short-term outcome for many people worried about invasions of privacy but this might ultimately be to the detriment of society.

I am lucky enough to work in one of the world's greatest libraries. Formally founded in 1598, and first opened to readers in 1602, the Bodleian in Oxford has enjoyed a continuous existence ever since. Working in an institution like this I am constantly aware of the achievements of past librarians. The Bodleian today has well over 13 million printed volumes in its collection, plus miles and miles of manuscripts and archives. It has built up a broad collection including millions of maps, music scores, photographs, ephemera and a myriad other things. This includes petabytes worth of digital information such as journals, datasets, images, texts, emails. The collections are housed in forty buildings dating from the fifteenth to the twenty-first century, which have a fascinating history in themselves.

The Bodleian's collection includes the First Folio of Shakespeare (1623), the Gutenberg Bible (c.1450), as well as manuscripts and documents from around the world – the late Ming Period Selden Map of China, or the illuminated masterpiece the *Romance of Alexander* from the fourteenth century, for example. These items have fascinating histories that tell the story of how they have passed through time and now sit on the shelves of the Bodleian. The Bodleian is in fact really a collection of collections, and the stories of how these collections came to be in the Bodleian have helped to build its fame over the past four hundred years.[15]

My own education, up to the age of eighteen, was transformed by being able to use my home town of Deal's public library. In that building I discovered the joys of reading. At first this was escape through science fiction (especially Isaac Asimov, Brian Aldiss and Ursula K. Le Guin), and then I read Thomas Hardy and D. H. Lawrence, but also authors from beyond Britain: Hermann Hesse, Gogol, Colette and many more. I found I could borrow vinyl records and discovered there was more to classical music than Tchaikovsky's *1812 Overture*: Beethoven, Vaughan Williams, Mozart. I could read the 'serious' newspapers and the *Times Literary Supplement*. All for free – crucially important as my family were not wealthy and there was little money to buy books.

The library was (and is) run by local government, free for users of the majority of its services, and funded from local taxation under legal provisions that were first set out by the Public Libraries Act of 1850. There was political opposition to the idea at the time. As the bill worked its way through Parliament, the Conservative MP Colonel Sibthorp was sceptical of the importance of reading to the working classes, on the grounds that he himself 'did not like reading at all and had hated it while at Oxford'.[16]

The system of public libraries that the Act inaugurated replaced a patchwork of endowed libraries, parish libraries, collections in coffee houses, fishermen's reading rooms as well as subscription libraries and book clubs, which were products of the 'age of improvement' and the concept of 'useful knowledge'. This term grew out of the ferment of ideas in the eighteenth century. The American Philosophical Society was started by a group of prominent individuals, including Benjamin Franklin, in 1767, for 'promoting useful knowledge'. In 1799, the Royal Institution was founded 'for diffusing the knowledge and facilitating the general introduction of useful mechanical inventions and improvements'. Both organisations had libraries to support their work.

Libraries were a key part of a wider movement to broaden education, for the benefit of the individual, but also for society as a whole. A century or more later Sylvia Pankhurst, the inspirational champion of women's rights, wrote to the director of the British Museum requesting admission to the Reading Room of the library: 'as I desire to consult various government publications and other works to which I cannot obtain access in any other way.' At the foot of her letter of application she cited her object of study: 'to obtain information on the employment of women'.[17]

The Public Libraries Act made it possible for local authorities to institute public libraries and pay for them through 'rates' (as local taxation was then called), but this system was entirely voluntary. It was not until 1964 that the Public Libraries and Museums Act made it a *duty* for local authorities to provide libraries, and the system retains a strong place in the general consciousness today as a cherished service, part of the national infrastructure for public education.[18]

Despite this, public libraries in the UK have borne the brunt of the pressure that successive governments have placed on budgets available to local authorities.[19] Local authorities have had to make very tough decisions on how to manage, many of them targeting libraries and county record offices. As of 2018/19 there are 3,583 public libraries in the UK compared with 4,356 in 2009/10: 773 have closed. Libraries in many communities have also come to depend increasingly on volunteers to remain open as the number of people employed in the sector fell to less than 16,000.[20]

The preservation of knowledge is a critical struggle all over the world. In South Africa, following the collapse of the apartheid regime, the approach taken to help heal a society, riven by the violence and oppression of the previous century, was to 'faithfully record the pain of the past so that a unified nation can call upon that past as a galvanising force in the large tasks of reconstruction'.[21] A Truth and Reconciliation Commission was established as a way of 'addressing their difficult past'.[22] The commission was there to support the transitioning of society in a peaceful way, while at the same time coming to terms with – and confronting – the recent history and its impact on society and on individual citizens. There were political and legal aspects to the commission, but also historical, moral and psychological aims; one of the aims in the Promotion of National Unity and Reconciliation Act was to establish 'as complete a picture as possible of the nature, causes and extent of gross violations of human rights'. This was undertaken in partnership with the National Archives of South Africa, whose staff were intimately involved in ensuring that the past could be properly addressed, and the record would be available for people. However, the emphasis in South Africa was not to open up state archives to encounter the 'nature, causes and extent' of what had gone wrong, as has been the case in East Germany following the collapse of communism in 1989, but rather on the hearings themselves, where the testimonies created a deep oral history, which has formed a new archive.

Officials in South Africa's apartheid regime destroyed documents on a massive scale. The Truth and Reconciliation Commission was hampered all along by this; in their final report they devoted an entire section to the destruction of records. They put it bluntly: 'The story of apartheid is, amongst other things, the story of the systematic elimination of thousands of voices that should have been part of the nation's memory.' The report placed blame on the government: 'The tragedy is that the former government deliberately and systematically destroyed a huge body of state records and documentation in an attempt to remove incriminating evidence and thereby sanitise the history of oppressive rule.' The destruction highlighted the critical role that these records played: 'the mass destruction of records . . . has had a severe impact on South Africa's social memory. Swathes of official documentary memory, particularly around the inner workings of the apartheid state's security apparatus, have been obliterated.'[23] In Iraq, as we shall see in chapter 12, many of the key records were not destroyed but removed to the United States, where some still remain. Their return could form part of another process of national 'truth and reconciliation' in that country so ravaged by civil war.

Libraries and archives share the responsibility of preserving knowledge for society. This book has been written not just to highlight the destruction of those institutions in the past, but also to acknowledge and celebrate the ways librarians and archivists have fought back. It is through their work that knowledge has passed down from one generation to the next, preserved so that people and society can develop and seek inspiration from that knowledge.

In a famous letter of 1813, Thomas Jefferson compared the spread of knowledge to the way one candle is lit from another: 'He who receives an idea from me', wrote Jefferson, 'receives instruction himself without lessening mine; as he who lites his taper at mine, receives light without darkening me.'[24] Libraries and archives are institutions that fulfil the promise of Jefferson's taper – an essential point of reference for ideas, facts and truth. The history of how they have faced the challenges of securing the flame of knowledge and making it possible to enlighten others is complex.

Individual stories in this book are instructive of the many ways knowledge has been attacked throughout history. Jefferson's taper remains alight today thanks to the extraordinary efforts of the preservers of knowledge: collectors, scholars, writers, and especially the librarians and archivists who are the other half of this story.

Austen Henry Layard sketching at Nimrud.

I

Cracked Clay Under the Mounds

THE ANCIENT GREEK general and historian Xenophon, writing in his most famous work, the *Anabasis* or *Persian Expedition*, recounted the dramatic story of how he led a stranded army of 10,000 Greek mercenaries out of Mesopotamia and back to Greece. Xenophon described the army passing through the centre of what is now Iraq and pausing at a spot on the banks of the River Tigris, at a place he referred to as Larisa.[1] Surveying the landscape, Xenophon noted an immense deserted city with towering walls. From here they marched further along to another city, Mespila, that Xenophon states 'was once inhabited by the Medes'. It was here, according to Xenophon, that Medea, the king's wife, had sought refuge while the Persians were besieging their empire. The Persian king was unable to take the city, Xenophon reports, until Zeus 'rendered the inhabitants thunderstruck'.[2]

What Xenophon was looking at, in this ancient landscape, was the remains of the cities of Nimrud (Larisa) and Nineveh (Mespila). These cities were at the heart of the great Assyrian Empire and flourished under the rule of the famed and formidable King Ashurbanipal. After Ashurbanipal's death, Nineveh was destroyed by an alliance of Babylonians, Medes and Scythians in 612 BCE. Xenophon confuses the Assyrians (who had inhabited the city) and the Medes (who took it) with the Medes and the Persians, the major eastern power at his time of writing.[3]

I find it astonishing to think that Xenophon viewed these great mounds more than two millennia ago; that the ruins were already many centuries old when he saw them, with the events that destroyed the cities already obscure even to that great historian. The Greeks saw themselves as the pioneers of libraries and by the time Xenophon was writing the Greek world had a vibrant book culture, in which libraries played an important part. Xenophon would surely have been excited to have learned of the magnificent library preserved deep in the soil below, that would one day reveal the story of its ancient founder, Ashurbanipal.

It would take a further twenty-two centuries before the great library of Ashurbanipal would be discovered and the full history of this empire (and of its predecessors and neighbours) could be unravelled, both from archaeology of many Assyrian sites excavated since but especially from the documents found in these digs.

Writing feels like such a recent technology in the long story of humanity that it is tempting to assume our most ancient civilisations relied primarily on oral communication to pass on knowledge. These civilisations, centred around the area we know today as Turkey, Syria, Iraq and Iran, left large and impressive physical remains – buildings and objects above the ground and uncovered in archaeological digs – but they also left behind documents that give us clear evidence that the written record existed alongside oral communication in the centuries before the civilisations of Egypt, Mycenae, Persia, and eventually Greece and Rome. This written record is highly revealing of these cultures. The peoples of Assyria and their neighbouring civilisations had a well-developed culture of documentation and have passed down to us a rich intellectual inheritance.

In the middle of the nineteenth century, the lands that Xenophon described at the turn of the fifth and fourth centuries BCE became the subject of great interest to rival European imperial powers. This interest was to help recover the cultures of knowledge developed in these civilisations, revealing not only some of the earliest libraries and archives on the planet, but also evidence of ancient attacks on knowledge.

The British presence in this region was originally due to the activities of that engine of imperial expansion, the East India Company, which mixed trade with the enforcement of military and diplomatic power. One of its key employees in the region was Claudius James Rich, a talented connoisseur of oriental languages and antiquities, considered by his contemporaries to be the most powerful man in Baghdad, apart from the local Ottoman ruler, the Pasha; 'and some even questioned whether the Pasha himself would not at any time shape his conduct according to Mr. Rich's suggestions and advice, rather than as his own council might wish'.[4] In pursuit of gratifying his 'insatiable thirst for seeing new countries',[5] Rich had even managed to enter the Great Mosque at Damascus in disguise, which would have been a tall order for a Western visitor at the time.[6] Rich travelled extensively throughout the region and made detailed studies of its history and antiquities, building a collection of manuscripts, which were purchased by the British Museum after his death. In 1820–1 Rich first visited the site of Nineveh, and the great mound of Kouyunjik (as it was called in Ottoman Turkish), which was at the heart of the Assyrian city. During this visit, Rich unearthed a cuneiform tablet that had been preserved from Ashurbanipal's palace. This tablet was the first of tens of thousands that would be discovered on the site.

Rich sold his collection of amateurishly excavated artefacts to the British Museum, and the arrival of the first cuneiform tablets in London triggered a flurry of excited interest in the region, and speculation about what treasures might be in its soil. The collection was seen in London by Julius Mohl, the secretary of the French Asiatic Society, who also read Rich's published accounts. Mohl immediately encouraged the French government to send its own expedition to Mesopotamia, so that they could compete with Britain for the glory of French scholarship. A French scholar, Paul-Émile Botta, was dispatched to Mosul as consul, with enough funds to make his own excavations, beginning in 1842. These were the first serious excavations to be made in the area and their publication in Paris in a sumptuously illustrated book, *Monument de Ninive* (1849), furnished with illustrations by the artist Eugène Flandin, made them famous among European elites. We do not know exactly where and when, but its pages were at some point turned with a growing sense of wonder by an adventurous young Briton named Austen Henry Layard.

Layard grew up in Europe, in a wealthy family, and spent his early years in Italy where he read avidly, being most strongly influenced by the *Arabian Nights*.[7] He developed a love for antiquities, fine arts and travelling, and as soon as he was old enough he embarked on extensive journeys across the Mediterranean, through the Ottoman Empire, eventually visiting the country we now call

Iraq, at first with an older Englishman named Edward Mitford, and then alone. Having reached the city of Mosul, Layard met Botta who told him about his own discoveries in the mound of Kouyunjik, and it may have been there that he saw a copy of the *Monument de Ninive*.[8] So Layard was inspired to begin digging, using a workforce made up of local people that reached over a hundred and thirty at its height, and despite scientific archaeology being in its infancy at the time his efforts were astonishingly professional and productive. Layard's digs were at first financed privately by Stratford Canning, the British ambassador in Constantinople, as the excavations became an aspect of rivalry between France and Britain. Over just six years a team of workers from local tribes were overseen and supported by Hormuzd Rassam, a Chaldean Christian from Mosul, and brother to the British vice consul. The two became close friends as well as colleagues. From 1846 Rassam served as secretary and paymaster for Layard's digs, but he was also intellectually engaged with the enterprise. Rassam's role in these sensational excavations has received less attention than it deserves, partly because he lacked the cunning to promote himself with prompt publications on his findings and partly because some of his successes were undermined by racist detractors, and his final years were marred by legal disputes and disillusionment. Rassam enabled Layard's excavations to be a great success through his organisational abilities, but he also contributed to the interpretation of cuneiform, and after Layard returned to Britain to pursue a political career, Rassam continued to oversee major archaeological digs in Iraq, funded by the British Museum.[9]

As the digs progressed, they discovered enormous chambers filled with clay tablets. Layard and his team had discovered not just fragments of knowledge from the Assyrian Empire but the institution at its very heart: the great library of Ashurbanipal. Some 28,000 tablets would be brought back to the British Museum; thousands more are now in other institutions.[10]

Up to a foot high, clay tablets filled the chambers, some broken into fragments but others miraculously preserved intact over millennia. One chamber, 'guarded by fish gods', Layard wrote, 'contained the decrees of the Assyrian kings as well as the archives of the empire'.[11] Many were historical records of wars, he surmised, as 'some seem to be Royal decrees, and are stamped with the name of a king, the son of Essarhaddon; others again, divided into parallel columns by horizontal lines, contain lists of the gods, and probably a register of offerings made in their temples.'[12] Particularly remarkable were two fragmentary clay sealings, bearing the royal signets of an Egyptian king, Shabaka, and an Assyrian monarch (probably Sennacherib). Layard suggested they may have adorned a peace treaty. Discoveries such as this would begin a process of grounding legendary events in documentary evidence. Investigation into the language, literature, beliefs and organisation of these ancient civilisations continues to this day.

I have been lucky enough to handle some Mesopotamian clay tablets and see for myself the pioneering ways ancient communities documented knowledge. I have examined a variety of clay tablets preserved in the Ashmolean Museum in Oxford, which show the sophistication developed by these cultures. The first to come out of the storage drawers in the museum were small oval tablets from a site at Jemdet-Nasr in southern Iraq. The tablets were highly practical, their shape designed to fit easily in the palm of the hand. Information was scratched into the clay while it was still moist. It is likely that these tablets, which held administrative information mostly about quantities of produce being traded (one tablet shows an image of donkeys, preceded by the number seven, for example, which referred to 'seven donkeys'), would have been discarded after use as they were found as fragments piled in a corner of a room. Other tablets have been found as waste materials being used to patch a wall or some other part of a building in need of repair. Often throughout history records of this kind have only been preserved by accident. Ancient Mesopotamia was no exception.

Far more exciting were the clay tablets that had not been discarded but preserved and used again. I marvelled at slightly larger tablets, which contained more densely packed inscriptions. These square tablets are known as 'library' documents as they contain literary or cultural texts on topics ranging from religion to astrology, and were designed to be kept for reading over long periods. One of the literary tablets even has a colophon, which is where the scribe records the details of the document itself – what the text was, who the scribe was, and where and when he worked (it was almost always men who did the copying). These details, akin to the title pages of modern books, show that the tablets were intended to be kept with others, as the specific colophon helped to distinguish the contents of one tablet from another. This is the earliest form of metadata.

The surviving tablets show that there were other kinds of archival documents too, records of administrative and bureaucratic activity. A group of very small tablets, which looked a lot like the breakfast cereal 'shredded wheat', were 'messenger' documents. They provided proof of identity of a messenger who had come to either collect or deliver goods of some kind. They were small because they needed to be portable; they were kept by a messenger in a pocket or a bag and handed over on arrival. It is unclear why these were kept and not used for building repairs, but it may well have been for future reference.

Thanks to almost two centuries of archaeology we now know that these ancient peoples had a sophisticated culture, fostering libraries, archives and scribes. As the earliest civilisations formed, moving from nomadic to settled existence, so too did the sense that a permanent record of communication and of storing knowledge was required. When Ashurbanipal's library was in operation, the tablets used then – heavy and cumbersome – required chambers such as those Layard discovered for storage so that copies could be made or information retrieved. Over time, scholars have uncovered evidence from the tablets of cataloguing and arrangement.

In 1846 Layard began to ship material back to Britain, and his finds became an instant sensation when they were revealed in London. Public pressure, fuelled by news reports, helped to change the view of the board of the British Museum, which agreed to fund further expeditions, partly spurred on by politicians who saw the success of the excavations as a victory over their French rivals. Layard became a national hero – nicknamed the 'Lion of Nineveh' – and was able to build a career as a writer and politician thanks to his new-found fame. The discovery of the library of Ashurbanipal was perhaps his most important find. The sculptures, pottery, jewels and the statuary (now on display in the great museums of London, Berlin, New York and Paris) were aesthetically stunning, but deciphering the knowledge contained in the collections was to truly transform our understanding of the ancient world.

From studying these excavated tablets, we now understand that the Royal Library of Ashurbanipal was perhaps the first attempt to assemble under one roof the entire corpus of collectable knowledge that could be assembled at the time. Ashurbanipal's library consisted of three main groups: literary and scholarly texts, oracular queries and divination records, and letters, reports, census surveys, contracts and other forms of administrative documentation. The mass of material here (as in many of the other ancient libraries discovered in Mesopotamia) concerned the prediction of the future. Ashurbanipal wanted the knowledge in his library to help him decide when was the best time to go to war, to get married, to have a child, to plant a crop, or to do any of the essential things in life. Libraries were necessary for the future because of the knowledge they collected from the past, to put into the hands of the decision-makers, the most important decision-maker in Nineveh being Ashurbanipal.[13]

The literary texts embraced a wide range of subjects from the religious, medical and magical, to the historical and mythological, and were highly organised, arranged in a subject sequence with tags attached to them, which we might today regard as catalogue records or even as metadata. These were kept as a permanent reference resource, whereas the archival materials were retained on a more temporary basis as a means of settling legal disputes over land and property.[14] Among the most important discoveries made by Layard and Rassam at Nineveh were a series of tablets that contain the text of one of the world's earliest surviving works of literature, the Epic of Gilgamesh. Several different series of tablets were found at Nineveh showing the ownership of this same key text over multiple generations, all preserved together, passed down from one generation of kings to the next, even with a colophon claiming it was written in Ashurbanipal's own hand.

From the archaeological finds of the contents of Mesopotamian archives and libraries, and from the study of the texts on the tablets unearthed, we can identify a distinct tradition of organising knowledge and even the identities of professionals with responsibilities for these collections. Unlike today, where the professional roles of archivist and librarian are quite distinct, these lines are less easy to observe in ancient communities. Libraries such as Ashurbanipal's reveal a desire to manage information and also give us a sense of how valuable knowledge was to rulers and how they were determined to acquire it by any means.

The scholarship of the last forty years on the Royal Library of Ashurbanipal has determined that it was built up not just by scribal copying but also by taking knowledge from neighbouring states. Our understanding of this comes from a variety of sources excavated in recent decades and was not apparent to Layard or the early pioneers of cuneiform. The tablets that reveal these acts of forced collection are perhaps the earliest forerunner of what we now call displaced or migrated archives (to which we will turn in chapter 11), a practice that has been taking place for millennia. A large number of the surviving tablets from Ashurbanipal's library came through this route.[15]

Our understanding of this practice has been expanded through the discovery of tablets excavated at many other sites in the region, such as Borsippa in what is now southern Iraq. In the first millennium BCE, Borsippa was part of the Babylonian Empire, subjugated by Assyria. Tablets excavated there preserve later copies of a letter originally sent from Nineveh to an agent, Shadunu, who was charged to visit a group of scholars in their homes and to 'collect whatever tablets are stored in the temple in Ezida' (the temple of Nabu, especially dedicated to scholarship, at Borsippa).[16] The desiderata are named quite specifically, which suggests that Ashurbanipal knew what might have been available in the collections of private scholars.[17] Ashurbanipal's instructions were clear and uncompromising:

> . . . whatever is needed for the palace, whatever there is, and rare tablets that are known to you and do not exist in Assyria, search them out and bring them to me! . . . And should you find any tablet or ritual instruction that I have not written to you about that is good for the palace, take that as well and send it to me . . .[18]

This letter corroborates evidence from other tablets in the British Museum, that Ashurbanipal both seized and also paid scholars to give up their tablets, or to copy some of their own tablets and others in the famous collection at Borsippa well known for its sophisticated scribal tradition.

A small group of accession records survive, which help us get a broader sense of the way these seizures helped to build Ashurbanipal's great library at Nineveh (and also confirm the sense that the library was very carefully organised and managed). The scale is something that is immediately surprising. Of the 30,000 tablets that are known to survive from Ashurbanipal's library, the group of accession records suggests an intake at one time of around 2,000 tablets and 300 ivory or wooden writing boards. This was an immense single accession and the materials ranged over thirty genres from astrological omens to medical recipes. The provenance of the material is not recorded in every case but it is clear that the tablets came from private libraries in Babylonia. Some of them seem to have been 'gifted' by the scholars who owned them, perhaps to curry favour with the royal authorities in Nineveh, perhaps to give up some material so that the rest of their libraries could be left. The only dates that are identifiable point to 647 BCE, mere months after the fall of Babylonia during the civil war between Ashurbanipal and his brother Shamash-shumu-ukin. The conclusion is clear: he used the military victory as an opportunity to enlarge his own library through the enforced sequestration of knowledge.[19]

But Ashurbanipal's library was soon to suffer a similar fate. His victory over Babylonia would provoke a burning desire for revenge, and this was wreaked on Ashurbanipal's grandson Sin-shar-ishkun, who succeeded his father in 631 BCE. The Babylonians allied with the neighbouring Medes, whose forces besieged Nineveh in 612 BCE, eventually taking the city and unleashing a torrent of destructive force, which would encompass the collections of knowledge, including the library formed by Ashurbanipal. Although Layard's work uncovered remarkable feats of preservation and acquisition, everywhere he dug there was also evidence of fire and violence. The excavations revealed layers of ash, objects were found to have been deliberately smashed inside rooms, and some of the discoveries of human remains were particularly horrific for later archaeologists at nearby Nimrud, who found bodies, their limbs still shackled, that had been thrown down a well.[20]

While the destruction of Ashurbanipal's library at the fall of Nineveh was a catastrophic act, the precise details of what happened are unclear. The major library and archival collections may simply have been swept up in the general destruction of the palace complex. Fires and looting were widespread across the site, and we cannot tell whether the library was specifically targeted, although evidence does survive of the smashing of specific tablets (such as diplomatic treaties).[21] At the Temple of Nabu in Nimrud, for example, sealed tablets of the vassal treaties of Esarhaddon, father of Ashurbanipal, were found smashed to pieces on the floor, left there as the battle raged around the great city, not to be found until two and a half millennia later.[22]

The Royal Library at Nineveh is the most celebrated collection of its kind from the Mesopotamian civilisations, but it was not the earliest. More than five thousand tablets have been found at Uruk in southern Iraq and date from the fourth millennium BCE, and are mainly concerned with economics, but also with naming things. A thousand years later we have evidence from Syria, in the ancient site of Ebla (south of the modern city of Aleppo), that there were scriptoria and library/archive rooms, including brick benches to help sort through tablets. Although there was no specific architectural expression of libraries as separate buildings, from this period there is growing evidence of the emergence of curatorial techniques for managing information, including different modes of storage. These include devices such as wooden shelves or stone pigeonholes found in the archive room of the Temple of Nabu at Khorsabad (the former capital of Assyria until it was moved to Nineveh), and shelves in the Temple of Shamash in the Babylonian city of Sippar, which were used to help sort collections of tablets, implying that their number had become so numerous that special techniques were required to help sort and manage their collection.[23] The use of metadata (in the form of labels and other ways of describing the contents of the tablets) to aid retrieval of information and scribal copying alongside the storage of texts was also a feature of innovation throughout the civilisations of Mesopotamia. The necessity to keep knowledge safe and to enable the sharing of it through copying has very ancient roots, coterminous with civilisation itself.

Direct evidence of the libraries and archives of the ancient world is scarce and the nature of the societies that developed these collections is so different from ours that it is dangerous to draw too many close parallels. Despite these caveats I think it is possible to suggest some broad patterns.

The libraries and archives of Mesopotamia, especially the library

of Ashurbanipal, show that the ancient world understood the importance of accumulating and preserving knowledge. These civilisations
developed sophisticated methods: organising clay tablets, adding
metadata to help with storage and retrieval as the size of collections
grew. The copying of texts was also supported, for dissemination
among the small elite groups in the royal households who were
allowed access to them.

These collections were often formed by the rulers who thought
the acquisition of knowledge increased their power. The forced
collection of clay tablets from neighbouring and enemy states
deprived those enemies of knowledge and made them weaker. As
many of the texts were concerned with predicting the future,
capturing tablets would not only help you make better predictions
but it would also mean your enemy would be worse at understanding
the future.

From Ashurbanipal's library we have a sense of what it preserved
for the benefit of successive generations, as tablets were passed on
from father to son, including those of the Epic of Gilgamesh. There
was an understanding even then that the preservation of knowledge
had a value not just for the present but for the future. The survival
of the collections themselves is accidental. The civilisations fell and
did not endure. Their libraries and archives, even those designed
to persist, have only been discovered in recent centuries, and then
only through scholars at the dawn of archaeology.

The poet Virgil holding a scroll, seated between a lectern for writing, and a 'capsa' (or book box) for holding scrolls, early fifth century.

2

A Pyre of Papyrus

A s we think about the legacy of ancient libraries in the public consciousness, there is one legendary library whose fame has outlasted all others: Alexandria. Despite the fact that it existed far later than those in Mesopotamia, and that no material evidence survives from the library itself, Alexandria is the archetypal library of the Western imagination, and is still often referred to as the greatest library ever assembled by the great civilisations of the ancient world.

Despite the fact that our knowledge of the Library of Alexandria is patchy, to say the least – the primary sources being few, mostly repeating other sources now lost or too distant to verify – the idea of a truly universal library, a single place where the entire knowledge of the world was stored, has inspired writers and librarians throughout history. We do know that there were in fact two libraries in ancient Alexandria, the Mouseion and the Serapeum, or the Inner and Outer Libraries. The Mouseion was a temple to the muses – nine Greek sister goddesses who presided over human creativity and knowledge, everything from history to epic poetry to astronomy – and is where we get our term 'museum' from. The Mouseion was, however, far from a museum: it was a living library, full of books (in the form of scrolls) and scholars.

The Mouseion was a great storehouse of knowledge, a place for scholars to come and study. The building was located in the Royal Quarter, the Broucheion, close to the palace, giving a clear indication of its importance.[1] Strabo, the Greek historian and geographer, writing in the first few years of the Christian era, highlighted the importance of royal patronage for the library, and described it as having a shared dining space where the king would sometimes join the scholars.[2] These scholars read like a roll call of the great thinkers of the ancient world, including not just Euclid (the father of geometry) and Archimedes (the father of engineering) but Eratosthenes who was the first person to calculate the circumference of the earth with remarkable accuracy. Many of the intellectual breakthroughs that modern civilisation is based on can be traced to their work.

An offshoot of the library was held in the Serapeum, a temple to the 'invented' god Serapis. Ancient writers disputed whether Ptolemy I or II had introduced the cult of Serapis to Egypt, but archaeological evidence demonstrates that the temple was founded by Ptolemy III Euergetes I (246–221 BCE).[3] The foundation of this library legitimised it further. Like the Mouseion it was built to impress. Roman historian Ammianus Marcellinus described it as 'so adorned with extensive columned halls, with almost breathing statues, and a great number of other works of art, that next to the Capitolium [Rome's central temple], with which revered Rome elevates herself to eternity, the whole world beholds nothing more magnificent'.[4]

The Library of Alexandria grew steadily following its foundation, according to a curious document known as the *Letter of Aristeas*, written around 100 BCE. This document tells us that within a short period from its foundation the library grew to 500,000 scrolls, and that the addition of the Serapeum brought greater capacity. The Roman historian Aulus Gellius in his compendium *Attic Nights* gave a figure of 700,000 volumes, split across the two libraries. John Tzetzes got a little more precise – librarians tend to feel much happier with precise counts of their collections – stating that the Mouseion held 490,000 volumes and the Serapeum 42,800. We must treat the ancient estimates of the size of the collection with extreme caution. Given the extent of the surviving literature from the ancient world, the numbers quoted for the library cannot be realistic. While these estimates need to be looked at sceptically, they make it clear that the library was enormous, much bigger than any other collection known at the time.[5]

What can be said concerning the role that the Library of Alexandria played in the ancient kingdom? Was it more than just a storehouse of knowledge? While we know practically nothing about how the library operated, it seems that together with the evident ambition to acquire and preserve knowledge, there was a desire to encourage learning too. Aphthonius, writing in the fourth century CE, speaks of 'storehouses . . . open to those eager to study, an encouragement for the entire city to gain wisdom'.[6] It may be that the 'legend' of Alexandria has as much to do with the accessibility of the knowledge it contained as the size of the collection. We know from the Roman historian Suetonius that the Emperor Domitian at the end of the first century CE sent scribes to Alexandria to copy texts that had been lost in various Roman library fires.[7] The large size of the two libraries, and the resident community of scholars of the Mouseion, and the liberal access policy, combined to create an aura around the library that placed it at the centre of scholarship and learning.

When the Library of Alexandria has been discussed, more often than not it is the cautionary tale of its destruction that is invoked – that towering library, said to contain a vast ocean of knowledge, razed to the ground in a fiery blaze. In some ways the destruction of the library has become as important, if not more, to its legacy as its existence. This is made clear when we realise that the classic story of Alexandria, consumed by one catastrophic inferno, is a myth. In fact it is a collection of myths and legends (often contradicting one another) that the popular imagination continues to cling to.

One account, perhaps the best known, is the story told by Ammianus Marcellinus who in his *History* (written around CE 380–390) declared that the 'unanimous testimony of ancient records declares that 700,000 books, brought together by the unremitting energy of the Ptolemaic kings, were burned in the Alexandrine war, when the city was sacked under the dictator Caesar'.[8] Another ancient writer, Plutarch, gives us more detail about the burning. After an Alexandrian mob had turned against the Romans, Caesar was forced to barricade himself in the palace quarter near the dockyards. An attempt was made to 'cut him off from his navy', and 'he was forced to fend off the danger with fire, and this, spreading from the dockyards, destroyed the great library'. We get a slightly different take from Dio Cassius who, in his *Roman History* (written circa CE 230), tells us that although 'many places were set on fire' it was the storerooms in the dockyards rather than the

Mouseion (library), both those of 'grain and books, said to be great in number and of the finest', that were destroyed.[9]

This myth – that Caesar was responsible for the destruction in some way – has had to compete through history with others. By CE 391, Alexandria had become a Christian city, and its religious leader, the Patriarch Theophilus, lost patience with the pagan occupiers of the Serapeum and destroyed the temple. In CE 642 the Muslim occupation of Egypt saw the occupation of Alexandria for the first time, and one account of the destruction of the library attributes its demise to deliberate destruction by Amr (the Arab military leader who had conquered the city) on the orders of the Caliph Omar. This account ascribes a perverse logic to the Caliph: 'If these writings of the Greeks agree with the book of God, they are useless, and need not be preserved,' so the account tells us: 'if they disagree, they are pernicious, and ought to be destroyed.' This legend describes the orders of the Caliph being 'executed with blind obedience', the scrolls being distributed to Alexandria's four thousand baths, where they were used as fuel to heat the water, taking six months to exhaust the supply.[10]

What the ancient historians all agree on, is that the library was destroyed. The weight of their opinions helped to propagate the myth. That propulsion was greatly speeded in the late eighteenth century with the publication of volume III of Edward Gibbon's great epic *The History of the Decline and Fall of the Roman Empire*, which includes the most vivid passage about the destruction of the library that had yet appeared in the English language. This passage would make the loss of Alexandria the powerful symbol for barbarity that it still is today. 'The valuable library of Alexandria was pillaged or destroyed; and near twenty years afterwards, the appearance of the empty shelves excited the regret and indignation of every spectator whose mind was not totally darkened by religious prejudice,' he wrote, emphasising the loss of the 'compositions of ancient genius' and lamenting that so many works had 'irretrievably perished'.[11]

What these myths all have in common is that they mourn the library as a victim of barbarity triumphing over knowledge. These stories have encouraged the symbolisation of Alexandria: the telling and retelling of the myths has led to its name being almost always invoked as metaphor, either to capture the desire to amass universal knowledge or to convey the loss of great amounts of knowledge. But what really happened to the Library of Alexandria? And is there more we can learn from its destruction, and its existence, behind the myth?

The fact that the library failed to exist beyond the classical period is unquestioned. Exactly why is less clear. Caesar himself reported the burning of Alexandria as an accidental consequence of his war against his great rival Pompey, in 48–47 BCE. Ships bringing enemy troops had been docked in the harbour, close to a series of warehouses, and Caesar's troops torched them. In the conflagration that followed, a number of nearby warehouses were destroyed. Following the city's instructions that all incoming ships should be searched for books, which were required to be copied for the library, it is feasible that these seized books had been temporarily stored in the dockside warehouses. Material damage was done to the collections of the library, but it was not its end. This ties in with the account of the geographer Strabo who did much of his own research some decades after the events of 48–47 BCE using sources from the library.[12]

Both libraries were very fragile. The Serapeum seems to have suffered a fire at some point around CE 181 and again in 217 but was rebuilt, although there is no indication whether the fire affected the library or just the temple complex.[13] In CE 273 the Emperor Aurelian recaptured Alexandria after it had been occupied by the insurgent rebellion of Palmyra, destroying the palace complex and almost certainly inflicting damage on the library (although no ancient writers confirm this explicitly), but if this is a true record (and over a century later the area had still not been rebuilt) then it is possible that the Library of the Serapeum may have outlived the Mouseion.[14]

Gibbon's profound statement about the loss of the library was the result of a great deal of careful reading around the subject, and his judgement on the most likely cause of the destruction can enlighten us. He dismissed the idea that the destruction of the library could be blamed on the Muslim conquerors of Egypt, and the instruction of Caliph Omar. This version of events had been reported by some early Christian writers (such as Abulpharagius), especially the evocative story of the scrolls being fuel for the thousands of hot baths in the city. Gibbon knew that this account had evoked a strong response in the scholars who had encountered it and 'deplored the irreparable shipwreck of the learning, the arts, and the genius, of antiquity'.[15] The Enlightenment sceptic was scathing in his analysis of that account: it was scarcely logical that the Caliph would burn Jewish and Christian religious books, which were also considered holy texts in Islam. Moreover the story was implausible on practical grounds as 'the conflagration would have speedily expired in the deficiency of materials'.[16]

For Gibbon, the Library of Alexandria was one of the great achievements of the classical world and its destruction – which he concludes was due to a long and gradual process of neglect and growing ignorance – was a symbol of the barbarity that overwhelmed the Roman Empire, allowing civilisation to leach away what was being re-encountered and appreciated in his own day. The fires (whether accidental or deliberate) were major incidents in which many books were lost, but the institution of the library disappeared more gradually both through organisational neglect and through the gradual obsolescence of the papyrus scrolls themselves.

A manuscript by the medical scientist Galen, found relatively recently in a monastery library in Greece, contains a previously unknown account of a fire in CE 192 in the imperial library in Rome. The library, known as the Domus Tiberiana, was on the Palatine Hill in the heart of the city. The fire destroyed the original scrolls that contained a famous Greek scholar's edition of the works of Homer, one of the most influential authors of the classical world (and perhaps of all time).[17] What is important is that these scrolls had been brought to Rome from the Library of Alexandria as booty. Seized by Lucius Aemilius Paullus, father of the famous Roman general Scipio, from the defeated King Perseus of Macedon in 168 BCE this was the first great collection of papyrus scrolls to be brought back to Rome, and it had a profound effect on the literary life of the city.[18]

Papyrus was first used in Egypt as a writing material. It was derived from the papyrus rush, from which the pith could be extracted from the stem. Layers of the pith were laid on top of one another, fused together using water, dried in the sun, and then smoothed to enable the surface to take a form of ink. The sheets of papyrus were normally joined together and wrapped around a wooden rod to form a scroll (loosely termed *liber* in Latin, from where we derive the word 'library'). Papyrus itself would be replaced by a more durable technology – parchment, developed in the western Mediterranean and then across Europe and then by paper, brought to the West from Asia through the agency of Arab craftsmen and traders, but for four centuries papyrus was the dominant writing medium.

One of the problems with papyrus was how easily it could be set on fire. Being made from dried organic matter, wrapped tightly around a wooden rod, it is inherently flammable, and when placed in a library of similar materials, these weaknesses become potentially disastrous. Most surviving papyrus was found as waste material, in rubbish heaps in Egypt (like the famous site of Oxyrhynchus) or as cartonnage – material used to wrap mummified bodies. The number of surviving libraries of papyrus scrolls is tiny, with the most famous being at Herculaneum – where the 'Villa of the Papyri' was discovered in the middle of the eighteenth century sealed under the tsunami of volcanic ash that came out of nearby Mount Vesuvius in CE 79. Eventually over 1,700 scrolls were excavated there, most charred or completely fused by the heat of the eruption. Enough of them are readable for us to know that the collector behind the library must have been fascinated by Greek philosophy (especially that of Philodemus).[19] The fragile scrolls are still being unrolled and deciphered, most recently via X-ray: in 2018 it was announced that part of Seneca's famous lost *Histories* had been discovered on one of them.

The environment papyrus is stored in is crucial to its long-term preservation. The climate of the coastal port of Alexandria was humid, which would have affected the older scrolls, encouraging mould and other organic decay.[20] Other large library collections of papyrus (such as that at Pergamon in present-day Turkey) went through a process of recopying texts from papyrus scrolls onto parchment, a writing material based on treated animal skin. This was a kind of technological migration of knowledge from one format to another.

A lack of oversight, leadership and investment spread over centuries seems to have been the ultimate cause of the destruction of the Library of Alexandria. Rather than highlighting the cataclysmic nature of barbaric ignorance triumphing over civilised truth, Alexandria is a cautionary tale of the danger of creeping decline, through the underfunding, low prioritisation and general disregard for the institutions that preserve and share knowledge. In contrast, Pergamon, Alexandria's great rival, developed and maintained its collections.

Modern scholarship dates the foundation of the library at Pergamon to the end of the third century BCE, although ancient writers, like Strabo, dated its foundation to early on in the second century BCE, and attributed the foundation to King Eumenes II (197–160 BCE) of the Attalid dynasty.[21] Pergamon was the library that most threatened the reputation of Alexandria as the greatest library of the ancient world, with this rivalry based not only on the nature and size of its holdings, but on the role played by the scholars who worked as part of the library itself.[22] According to several ancient writers the rivalry became a matter of state, triggering competition between their two kings Ptolemy V (204–180 BCE) and Eumenes.[23] The two libraries each had their own star scholars: Alexandria had Aristarchus, the famous commentator on the works of Hesiod. He was rivalled by Pergamon's brilliant Crates of Mallos, the commentator on Homer. Like Alexandria, no specific remains can help us locate the physical site of this library, and its decline seems to have been closely related to the decline of the Attalid dynasty, which had linked the prestige of the library to their own status. Once the Attalid kingdom was taken over by the Romans in 133 BCE, the library ceased to be so crucially bound up with the state, and its own decline began.

The Library of Alexandria helps us understand the ideals of a library, as it created a template, which many other libraries in subsequent centuries have sought to emulate (even though the details of exactly what the library was like is obscure). From Alexandria we learn of the power of linking a great collection to the service of a community of scholars who were able to share knowledge and to develop new knowledge through their studies. Strabo did his geographic research at Alexandria, and referred to the librarians and scholars as a 'synodos', or community, of thirty to fifty learned men (women do not appear to have been included). The community was international: many came from Greece, which ruled Alexandria, but Roman scholars copied and commentated on Greek poetry and drama there.

The leadership of the institution was very important in its success. Five of the first six librarians were among the most important writers from the classical world: Zenodotus, Apollonius Rhodius, Eratosthenes, Aristophanes and Aristarchus.[24] Around 270 BCE the librarianship passed to Apollonius Rhodius who wrote a great epic, the *Argonautica*, and who is reputed to have encouraged a young scholar named Archimedes of Syracuse to come and work in the Mouseion. During his time there Archimedes observed the rising and falling of the level of the River Nile, and invented the engineering device known as the 'screw' that still bears his name.[25] The mathematician Euclid was invited to join the community at Alexandria, and he is thought to have compiled his famous *Elements of Geometry*, arguably the foundation of modern mathematics, while there, and he may also have taught his follower, Apollonius of Perga. The librarians and scholars of Alexandria did more than preserve knowledge, they standardised the texts, adding their own ideas to make new knowledge. What was created at Alexandria was what could not be destroyed in the fire and the long process of neglect: an approach to learning that we now call scholarship.

It is hard to prove the direct link between the libraries of the ancient world and those of subsequent generations, but it is possible to detect a common human practice of organising and preserving knowledge. There is no direct line of professional practice for librarians from Alexandria or Nineveh. No manuals were created, no pithy sayings have been passed down. What survives is more of an ethos – the ethos that knowledge holds great power, that the pursuit of gathering and preserving it is a valuable task, and that its loss can be an early warning sign of a decaying civilisation.

As I walk around the Bodleian today, there are constant reminders of the history of the practice of librarianship. Across the twenty-eight libraries that form the Bodleian you can see the evolution of practical methods to preserve and share knowledge. We continue to use these buildings, many of which were designed as libraries long ago (some more than six centuries ago), a fact that continues to inspire all of us who work there. These buildings now have electric lighting, central heating, computers, Wi-Fi and other aids to learning, but the process of innovation had its origins almost two thousand years before the founding of the Library of Alexandria.

When we examine the physical legacy of ancient libraries, it is truly remarkable what has survived. In the late 1940s, for example, a young goatherd named Muhammed edh-Dhib discovered a group of pottery vessels in the Qumran Caves in the Judaean desert. Inside these vessels were hundreds of scrolls containing the oldest surviving copies of texts of almost every book of the Hebrew Bible. An archaeological excavation dated the occupation of the site surrounding the cave complex to between circa 100 BCE and CE 70, while the manuscripts were written between the fourth century BCE and CE 70 (the destruction of the Second Temple of Jerusalem). Known as the Dead Sea Scrolls their fragile and fragmentary state belies their remarkable survival. We have no real understanding of exactly how these documents came to be stored (or perhaps 'hidden') in the caves of Qumran, but the consensus is that they were purposefully hidden by a Jewish religious group, now thought to be the Essenes, during the Roman suppression that followed the First Jewish Revolt in CE 66–73. The desert location and the way this archive was stored ensured its preservation. Most of the Dead Sea Scrolls were written on parchment, although a small number were written on papyrus. The parchment documents are more durable.

A key lesson from Alexandria is that its demise would become a warning for subsequent societies. The commonly held view, encouraged by Edward Gibbon, has been that 'dark ages' followed the collapse of the Roman Empire. Historians today are clear that there was no 'dark age' following the destruction of the Library of Alexandria. Any darkness that still persists is due to a lack of evidence of the preservation of knowledge. Knowledge continued to be gathered and learning flourished across Europe, Asia, Africa and the Middle East in continuation of the work undertaken at Alexandria and other centres. The learning of the Greek world would be most powerfully preserved through Arab culture, and through the power of copying and of translation. Major communities in Arabic centres of learning, such as Tabriz in modern-day Iran, would enable the transmission of Greek culture and science, much of which would come back to the West through re-translation into

Latin, and through the cultural exchange in cosmopolitan cities like Toledo in al-Andalus (as Muslim Spain was called).[26]

As the Library of Alexandria decayed during the first centuries of the first millennium CE, the knowledge of the ancient world continued to be preserved through the agency of libraries. Evidence from one of these early libraries can be found in a mosaic on the tomb of the Empress Galla Placidia at Ravenna, in the chapel built specifically to house her tomb in CE 450. It shows a cupboard for storing books, which holds two shelves, each containing separate books lying flat, the four volumes being labelled for each of the Evangelists. The cupboard stood on stout legs raising it up from the floor (perhaps to protect the contents from flooding).[27]

The Capitular Library in Verona in northern Italy has its origins in the cathedral scriptorium. The oldest book associated with the library dates to CE 517, and was written by one Ursicinus, who held a minor order in the cathedral, but the library holds books that are at least a century older, when it is just possible that Alexandria may still have had some remnant of its former glory. It is very likely that these books were copied in its scriptorium from books brought for the purpose of building its collection. In the sixth century in the desert of Sinai, a religious community built a monastery dedicated to St Catherine, and formed a library that housed biblical manuscripts of tremendous importance, especially the celebrated Codex Sinaiticus, the earliest and most complete manuscript of the Bible in Greek, dating from the first half of the fourth century. The library continues to preserve manuscripts and printed books for the use of its own community and other scholars to this day.

Many key works were, however, lost during the period we now call 'Late Antiquity' (the period from roughly the third to the eighth centuries), and we know this through the occasional ghostly traces of them in later books, or from chance finds of fragments of papyri, where previously unknown texts have been found by archaeological digs over the last 150 years. These discoveries of papyri have also revealed better versions of the texts of classical authors that were known in the Middle Ages. Johannes Lydus at Byzantium in the sixth century had more complete texts of Seneca and Suetonius than have passed down to us. The North African Bishop St Fulgentius in the fifth century, and St Martin, Archbishop of Braga in Portugal in the sixth century, cited (or indeed plagiarised) texts from Petronius and Seneca that have not survived to join the corpus of Latin writers today.[28]

The best example of literary loss is the Greek poet Sappho, who was born on the island of Lesbos in the seventh century BCE, and who was such an important cultural figure in the ancient world that Plato referred to her as 'the tenth muse'. Famous for her love poetry addressed to women, the English terms 'sapphic' and 'lesbian' are derived from her own name and the name of her home island. Name-checked by everyone from Horace to Ovid, and so popular that the scholars of Alexandria compiled not one but two nine-book critical editions of her poems, her work only survives in fragments of the texts. The single complete poem we have comes from an anthology of Greek lyrics and the rest have been pieced together from quotations found painted on potsherds and on papyrus found in rubbish heaps, especially one at Oxyrhynchus in Egypt. Poem 38 is a fragment that simply reads 'you burn me'. As with the Library of Alexandria, there are competing theories as to why the works of such a key writer have not survived. The most popular has long been that the Christian Church deliberately destroyed them on moral grounds. Writers in the Renaissance even claimed that Sappho's works were burned in Rome and Constantinople in 1073 on the orders of Pope Gregory VII. In reality, Sappho's works (in an obscure Aeolic dialect hard to read) were probably lost when the demand was insufficiently great for them to be copied onto parchment when the bound codex superseded the use of papyrus scrolls. The rubbish heap at Oxyrhynchus, excavated in 1897 by the Egypt Exploration Society, provides us with over 70 per cent of surviving literary papyri.

As Christianity became established, books and libraries spread across Europe and the Mediterranean world. Even in Britain, at the very edge of the Roman Empire, we assume from scraps of evidence that there were libraries (the poet Martial, who died early in the second century, commented sarcastically that his works were read even in Britain). In major centres like Constantinople (which had been known as Byzantium, until refounded in CE 330) the spirit of Alexandria lived again when an imperial university was refounded by Emperor Theodosius II in c.425 and a new clerical academy was established.[29] In the sixth century the scholar and statesman Cassiodorus retired from the court of King Theodoric of Italy to become a monk; he established a monastery in Vivarium in Calabria and built up an important library. The scriptorium there was a significant intellectual source, and at least two books were copied and sent to the early Christian community at the Abbey of Monkwearmouth–Jarrow in northern England. One was the *Commentary on the Psalms* by Cassiodorus himself (an eighth-century copy is now in the Cathedral Library at Durham) and the other was a copy of the Bible. It was later copied in the scriptorium at Monkwearmouth–Jarrow, making a book now known as the Codex Amiatinus, which was sent back to Rome as a gift. It never reached the city and is now in the Laurentian Library in Florence. The Codex Amiatinus even contains a painting of a library, complete with bookcase, books and with the Prophet Ezra busy writing next to it.[30]

During this period knowledge was copied and disseminated outside the Christian world by Islamic and Jewish communities. In the Jewish faith, the copying of the Old Testament and other sacred texts was so important that religious laws grew up to govern how the written word was to be handled.[31] Across the Islamic world, although the oral tradition of memorising the Quran was still dominant, the book became an important intellectual mechanism for spreading the holy book as well as other ideas. Islamic communities learned how to make paper from the Chinese and, according to the thirteenth-century encyclopaedist Yaqut al-Hallawi, the first paper mill in Baghdad was established CE 794–5, and enough paper was produced there for the bureaucrats to replace their parchment and papyrus records.[32] This mass availability of paper (less fragile than papyrus and much cheaper than parchment) enabled Muslims to develop a sophisticated book culture; as a result, libraries, paper-sellers and booksellers became a common sight in Baghdad where traders in books and paper were renowned as men of learning. This culture soon spread to other cities across the Islamic world.

From Islamic Spain to the Abbasid kingdom in Iraq libraries sprang up. There were great libraries in Syria and Egypt, over seventy libraries in Islamic Spain, and thirty-six in Baghdad alone, the first public collection in this great city being assembled during the reign of al-Mansur (754–75), the founder of Baghdad or his successor Harun al-Rashid (786–809). Harun's son, the caliph al-Mamun, established the House of Wisdom, founded in the eighth century as a library and an academic institute devoted to translations, research and education, attracting scholars from all over the world from many cultures and religions. Here the spirit of Alexandria ruled again and teachers and students worked together to translate Greek, Persian, Syriac and Indian manuscripts. Under the caliph's patronage the scholars at the House of Wisdom were able to study Greek manuscripts brought from Constantinople as well as translate the works of Aristotle, Plato, Hippocrates, Euclid, Ptolemy, Pythagoras, Brahmagupta and many others. Other libraries were created in succeeding centuries, such as the House of Knowledge, built in 991 by the Persian Sabur ibn Ardashir. It held over ten thousand volumes on scientific subjects but was destroyed during the Seljuq invasion in the middle of the tenth century.[33]

One commentator, the Egyptian encyclopaedist al-Qalqashandī, reported that 'the library of the Abbasid caliphs in Baghdad . . . included books beyond measure that were valuable beyond anything else'. These libraries were to suffer damage, both deliberately and indirectly during the invasion of the Mongols in the thirteenth century.[34] Islamic scholars also created their own sophisticated scholarship, especially in the sciences, and the collecting of books of Islamic science by European libraries over a thousand years later would help stimulate the creation of new scientific approaches.[35]

By the seventh century in northern Europe there were many more monasteries and many of them had libraries. These collections were small. In Britain, the early Christian communities at Canterbury, Malmesbury, Monkwearmouth–Jarrow and York had enough books to be termed library collections, but few of the books in these islands survived the Viking invasions.[36]

In the early ninth century, the monks of Iona, an island community established by St Columba, were massacred by the Vikings and their important scriptorium was destroyed. One theory is that the famous illuminated manuscript known as the Book of Kells was in fact written on Iona and moved to Kells through fear of Viking raids.[37] One book that survived the Viking incursions, the world-famous Lindisfarne Gospels (now in the British Library), originated in the Christian community of Lindisfarne in the eighth century, and around a hundred and fifty years later left the island when the community moved to a safer location on the mainland, taking the book and the body of their spiritual leader St Cuthbert with them. The book is most famous today as a work of early Christian art, with paintings inside of spectacular beauty and intricacy, but it was important in its day as a powerful symbol of the Christianisation of northern Europe.

A century after it left the island of Lindisfarne the great book – lavishly bound with precious metals, stones and jewels – came to rest with its religious community at Durham. Here, in the mid tenth century, Aldred, a monk later to be associated with Durham's sister community at Chester-le-Street, added an Old English gloss to the Latin text of the Gospels, effectively the earliest rendering of the New Testament in the English language. He added a colophon that records a tradition about the book: it was written by Eadfrith, Bishop of Lindisfarne (c.698–722), bound by Aethilwald, the successor bishop (who died in 740), and Billfrith adorned the cover with gold, silver and gems. In the twelfth century, the Durham monk Symeon recognised that the book, 'preserved in this church', was as much of a treasure as the body of St Cuthbert itself.[38]

The Bodleian has two books that were in a library in Constantinople at this period, and they are the earliest surviving complete copies of Euclid's *Elements* and Plato's *Dialogues*. Both were in the library of Bishop Arethas of Patras in the late ninth century.

By the time of the Norman invasion in 1066, the largest collections, such as that at Ely, were just a few hundred volumes strong, much smaller than their counterparts in the Islamic world. Most of the libraries in England before the Norman Conquest were small enough to be kept in a few strong chests or cupboards, and only a small number of monastic houses had library rooms. Peterborough Abbey, for example, founded in the seventh century, has a surviving list of books gifted to it by Bishop Aethelwold of Winchester (who refounded the abbey in 970). It lists only twenty books.[39] The Venerable Bede tells us that Pope Gregory the Great sent many books to Augustine at Canterbury in the early seventh century, but these may have been service books and Bibles, and the only explicit reference to a library by Bede refers to that at Hexham, in Northumberland, which evidently comprised histories of the passions of the martyrs as well as other religious books.[40]

Libraries continued to exist following the end of the ancient civilisations, although none of the libraries from Greece, Egypt, Persia or Rome continued in an unbroken line. Through the act of copying new libraries were soon established to house the new books created. A few of these new Christian libraries – like those of St Catherine's Monastery, or the Capitular Library in Verona – have continued since they were first begun in the last years of the ancient world. Many more established in the following centuries have also endured. They created a pattern for a flourishing of knowledge and engendered a network of institutions that was to support the societies of the West and of the Middle East throughout the Middle Ages.

The legend of Alexandria generated the idea that libraries and archives were places where new knowledge could be created – which is what we see with the Mouseion's mixture of books and scholars. Alexandria's fame spread across the ancient world, and has been passed down through history, inspiring others to emulate its mission to gather and organise the world's knowledge: the preface to *The Life of Sir Thomas Bodley*, published in 1647, boasted that the great library he had set up surpassed even the 'proud fame of the Aegyptian Library'.[41] The legacy of Alexandria has also been an inspiration to librarians and archivists in their fight to protect and save knowledge.

St Dunstan kneeling at the foot of Christ. From St Dunstan's
Classbook, late tenth century.

3

When Books Were Dog Cheap

I N MEDIEVAL ENGLAND one man travelled the length and breadth of the country, from monastery to monastery, on a mission commissioned by King Henry VIII. Travelling alone and on horseback, John Leland cut a striking solitary shape against the backdrop of the turbulent Tudor period, and his journey was to give us the last possible glimpse of the contents of the monastic libraries before they were destroyed in the name of the Reformation.

Leland had been born into a changing world. Education and knowledge had been controlled by the Catholic (a term that also means 'universal') Church for over a millennium. A network of monasteries and religious orders maintained the libraries and the schools. England was still recovering from a long and bloody civil war, a new royal family – the Tudors – were on the throne and there was growing restlessness across Europe over the Church's wealth and power. A new intellectual movement, humanism, which encouraged the learning of languages and the study of classical authors, had created an intellectual ferment that offered new ways of looking at the world. A questioning of assumptions by interrogating the sources of ideas was taking hold in the elites of Europe. The key English humanists (Thomas More, adviser to the king and author of *Utopia*, and John Colet, the Dean of St Paul's Cathedral) wanted to teach a new generation of scholars who would spread this message. Although Leland had been orphaned as a child, his adoptive father enrolled him as one of the first pupils at John Colet's refounded school, where he was taught Latin and Greek. These schools were very different to those that had come before, as they encouraged their pupils to read the classics as well as the scriptures and Catholic writers.

After studying at Cambridge, Leland became tutor to the son

of Thomas Howard, the 2nd Duke of Norfolk, and then went on to Oxford where he was perhaps associated with All Souls College. Although not rich or of noble blood, Leland was as clever and ambitious as his patron Cardinal Wolsey, and with his encouragement he then skipped across the Channel to Paris, to move in the circles of some of the greatest intellectuals of the time, including the learned Guillaume Budé, the royal librarian, and the brilliant François du Bois, professor of rhetoric. Encouraged by these men, he worked on his poetry and immersed himself in the humanist method of scholarship, seeking out and studying sources in manuscript.[1]

When Leland came back from France in 1529 Wolsey was no longer in favour, and like his new patron Thomas Cromwell he had to find a way to survive in the dangerous climate of Henry VIII's court, a place of intrigue, back-stabbing, condemnation and execution.

At this time Henry VIII was building up arguments against the Catholic Church. At first these were focussed on finding a way to divorce his queen, Catherine of Aragon, and marry the beautiful young courtier Anne Boleyn. His best advisers used theological arguments to back up his case, but what began with a divorce appeal then escalated into a more fundamental battle over the authority of the Pope in England. The debates were increasingly overshadowed by an audacious sense of opportunism. If he could pull it off, Henry could seize control not only of religious authority in his realm but also the massive wealth that the Catholic Church had built up over the preceding centuries. This was England's version of the phenomenon we now call the Reformation, which had begun in Germany in 1517, with a powerful reforming movement led by Martin Luther, and which spread throughout Europe during the sixteenth century. Leland and Cromwell were both determined to be a central part of this.

Henry was only the second ruler of the Tudor dynasty, and without a male heir his grip on the throne was fragile. Manipulating the past became a vital weapon in these battles. Manuscript histories and chronicles found in the libraries of the monastic houses became highly prized evidence of ancient English independence from papal authority, especially before the Norman Conquest. Even the stories of mythical British figures like King Arthur were dragged into the debates. The contents of these libraries could therefore hold the key to unlocking Henry's future. Leland jumped at the chance to use his scholarly talents to support his position in the court. He became a particular expert on King Arthur and wrote two works proving his historical veracity. He became known as 'antiquarius', which was not an official position but was a suitable term for someone who was deeply interested in the past.

The king's plans gradually came to fruition. Anne Boleyn was given a triumphal entry into London on 31 May 1533, and was crowned queen in Westminster Abbey the following day. For this glittering occasion, brilliantly stage-managed by Thomas Cromwell, Leland even penned official Latin celebratory verses that referred eight times to the king's hopes for Anne's fertility. It wasn't, however, for his poetry that Henry wanted Leland to work for him. Following the coronation he was given, so Leland later recalled, 'a most gracious commission . . . to peruse and diligently search all the libraries of monasteries and colleges' in the country.[2] Through this commission, Leland took an active role in the king's 'great matter', the arguments in support of the annulment of his marriage to Catherine of Aragon and the legitimacy of his new wife, Anne Boleyn. From these debates would come the formal separation of England from papal authority and the assertion of the king and not the Pope as the supreme authority of the Church in England.

Over the course of his extraordinary journey, Leland pored over the books he found on the shelves of more than a hundred and forty libraries. He was a fervent researcher, documenting the books he examined and writing up notes of what he had encountered at the end of every trip. After his death, his friends tried to put these notes in order. This was not easy. In 1577, the historian John Harrison reported that they were 'motheaten, mouldy, and rotten', and that his books were 'utterly mangled, defaced with wet, and weather, and finally imperfect through want of sundry volumes'. His frustration at trying to make sense of such a jumble rings off the page: 'his annotations are such and so confounded, as no man can (in a manner) pick out any sense from them.'[3]

The notes were neatly bound up when they came (very conveniently for me) into the Bodleian in the eighteenth century, but were originally just a mass of papers covered in Leland's handwriting, with layers of crossing out and corrections, some showing signs of having been folded up, some stained and water damaged, others torn and worn. Although Leland only listed the books that he found particularly interesting, they reveal a mass of detail of what was destroyed, which helps us to identify the original home of many books that have survived, sometimes as a direct result of Leland's activities. His notes also give a good deal more personal insight into the libraries he travelled to, often on long journeys, planned out in advance with orderly lists and sometimes even with rough maps to help find his route.

We take it for granted that we would use a map to navigate around the countryside, but Leland's journey took place thirty years before Christopher Saxton produced the first printed maps of England. The notes show signs of his detailed preparations, lists of libraries to consult, and even small sketches of localities, to help organise his time efficiently. There is a map of the Humber estuary, showing a cluster of monasteries in Lincolnshire and Yorkshire that he visited in 1534.[4]

What Leland was attempting to chart was the rich store of knowledge spread across almost 600 libraries of medieval Britain, from which there are more than 8,600 surviving volumes. The medieval collections ranged from the handful of service books owned by the smaller parish libraries, to the large, highly organised collections of books in the libraries of the religious orders. One of the most renowned libraries of medieval England was that of the Benedictine Abbey of St Augustine at Canterbury, which held almost 1,900 volumes when the last of the medieval catalogues of its contents was compiled (between 1375 and 1420, with additions between 1474 and 1497). Only 295 of these books are known to survive today.[5] The library at St Augustine's was large by medieval standards and its catalogue included books that had been written at, or given to, the abbey from as far back as the late tenth century. Most of the books were works on religion, either biblical texts, or commentaries on the Bible by later theologians (for example, the Venerable Bede) or the works of the Church Fathers. The library allowed its monastic community to read across the range of human knowledge: from history (both ancient and modern historians) to science (including astronomy, mathematics, geometry) and medicine, and there was a major section on the works of that great polymath of the ancient world, Aristotle. The catalogue had smaller sections on poetry, books on France, grammar, on canon law, logic, the lives of saints, and on letters.

Glastonbury, in the west of England, as one of the greatest monastic houses in the country, was for Leland an eagerly antici-pated destination. Not only was the abbey the site of the tomb of King Arthur (and therefore of great interest to Henry's political argument), but it also had one of the country's most famous libraries. Leland vividly described his first visit: 'I had hardly crossed the threshold, when the mere sight of the most ancient books left me awestruck, stupefied in fact, and because of this I stopped in my tracks a little while. Then, having saluted the genius loci, I exam-ined all the bookcases for some days with the greatest curiosity.'[6] Leland's notes refer to just forty-four books, which were mostly consistent with the key targets of his antiquarian searches. The great chroniclers of English history were consulted: William of Malmesbury, Gerald of Wales, Geoffrey of Monmouth, and the Dominican Nicholas Trevet. But he also looked closely at many ancient manuscripts: copies of the works of Alcuin, the Venerable Bede and Aelfric, as well as works by the Church Fathers such as St Augustine or Gregory of Nazianzus. They had been preserved at Glastonbury for centuries. Some of these books were of central concern to Henry's political campaign, but others were purely of interest to Leland's own antiquarian projects, especially his great work *De uiris illustribus* (*On Famous Men*), a compilation of accounts of all the main writers of Britain. His entry for Geoffrey of Monmouth confirms that he consulted the confirmatory charters from Henry II, as well as inscriptions in stone, but it was manu-scripts like Geoffrey's *Life of Merlin* which he read most 'avidly' in the library at Glastonbury.[7]

Glastonbury was, in Leland's words, 'the most ancient and at the same time the most famous Abbey in our whole island'. Leland recounted later how, 'wearied by the long labours of research I was refreshing my spirits thanks to the kindness of Richard Whiting [the abbot] . . . a most upright man and my particular friend'.[8] Leland was given astonishing access to the libraries and monasteries he visited, and one can picture some of his hosts enjoying conversations about Britain's past with their learned visitor. We get a glimpse of this at Glastonbury through one later entry in *De uiris illustribus*, where he describes seeing a manuscript of a work by John of Cornwall, as Whiting was guiding him through the shelves: 'the book was actually in my hands and my first taste of it had pleased me greatly', when the abbot 'called my attention elsewhere', and Leland 'forgot to seek it out again'.[9]

Some of the books that Leland saw there have survived and the Bodleian holds some of the greatest. The most famous of the Glastonbury books is known as St Dunstan's Classbook, a composite volume, with parts dating from the ninth, tenth and eleventh centuries, which were brought into England from the Celtic cultures of Wales and Brittany.[10] The manuscript is made up of four distinct elements. Each part looks and feels very different, from the style of the script to the parchment it is written upon: some parts feel like suede – soft, thick and almost velvety to the touch – whilst others are much thinner and crackly, revealing different traditions of making parchment in the early Middle Ages.

This book provides a rare glimpse into a period of British history for which comparatively few signs of intellectual life survive. The first and oldest part is a book of grammatical writings of an ancient writer called Eutyches (a text known as *De verbo*), with commentaries in Latin and Breton of the ninth and tenth centuries, showing its connection to European ideas. The second part, written in the second half of the eleventh century, is an Old English homily on the finding of the true cross, and the third and fourth parts written in Wales in the ninth century include an anthology of useful knowledge and a famous Roman poem on the art of seduction, the *Ars amatoria* of Ovid, with Welsh glosses (annotations that help explain the text). We cannot be certain when these individual sections were gathered together, but there is a drawing that shows St Dunstan, successively Bishop of Worcester and London and finally Archbishop of Canterbury from 959 to 988, on the opening leaf – he kneels at the feet of Christ in the drawing, begging for his protection, which, according to a later inscription, was the work of the saint himself.[11] St Dunstan was one of the most influential figures in the early English Church, leading it during a period known for the influence of European monastic ideas in England, especially the reform of the Benedictine movement.

Thanks to the survival of the medieval catalogues from Glastonbury we know that this volume was present in the abbey's library in 1248, and we also know that it was in the custody of one of the monks, Brother Langley, in the fifteenth century. It was also one of the forty books that Leland swooned over when he visited in the 1530s, and he recorded it in his notebook as 'The Grammar of Eutyches, formerly of Saint Dunstan'.

But the days of the Classbook's residence and that of its neighbours on the shelves of the library were numbered. In 1534 the Act of Supremacy made Henry VIII the head of the Church in England, and marked the formal separation of the authority of the Pope from the religious life of England and Wales. From this point onwards the monasteries began to be dissolved formally, most significantly after 1536 with the passing of the Act for the Court of Augmentations (which created the machinery for handling former monastic properties) and the Act for the Dissolution of the Lesser Monasteries. After a short respite, when some of the larger houses assumed they would escape, Thomas Cromwell's scheme moved into overdrive, and in 1539 the Act for the Dissolution of the Greater Monasteries was passed, allowing the final great institutions to be targeted for visitation, and either voluntarily surrendered or suppressed. One of these 'Greater Monasteries' was Glastonbury, which was to become the site of one of the last and most violent acts of the English Reformation.

Over the summer of 1539 the surviving financial records of the abbey record the natural rhythm of this great community continuing in the way it had for centuries: food was bought for the refectory, the grounds were maintained and watercourses cleared, and the seventy-year-old abbot continued to preside over the institution.[12] Perhaps Whiting thought his abbey might be spared, due to his friendship with Leland and as he had not stood in the way of the Reformation in Parliament (where he sat in the House of Lords), and had subscribed, like many of his fellow abbots, to the oath accepting the Royal Supremacy. But Glastonbury was a famously rich abbey and the king's appetite for increasing his wealth was prodigious. Cromwell sent commissioners to the abbey in September

1539 circulating accusations that Whiting knew not 'God, neither his prince, neither any part of a Christian man his religion'. He was examined at his house at Sharpham Park on 19 September where the commissioners declared that evidence was found of his 'cankered and traitorous heart'. But when Whiting would not surrender the abbey voluntarily, the visitors of the commission searched the abbey and 'found' incriminating documents condemning the royal divorce as well as money that had been hidden. This was all the commissioners needed. Whiting was tried at the neighbouring town of Wells on 14 November 1539, the main charge levied against him being that of the 'robbing of Glastonbury church'. The following day he was dragged through the streets before being taken up to the Tor, where 'he asked Gods mercy and the king for his great offenses', and hanged. His body was butchered, one quarter of it taken and displayed for all to see at Wells, another to Bath, the rest at Ilchester and Bridgwater. His head was placed on the abbey gate at Glastonbury itself.

This bloody process brought about the destruction of the abbey. Within a few days it had been plundered, and every nook and cranny had been searched.[13] All the property of the abbey was put up for sale: silverware such as candlesticks and chalices, vestments and church equipment like organs, but also more mundane items: the cooking equipment, crockery and cutlery, even glasses, beds, tables and paving slabs. Lead from the roof and metal from the bells were especially valuable.

The books went quickly. Leland's notes are our only account of the library on the eve of the Reformation, but based on the early catalogues and a broader representation of losses at other houses we can estimate that perhaps a thousand manuscripts were destroyed. Only about sixty remain that are identifiably from Glastonbury, in thirty contemporary library collections around the world, but it is highly likely that there are more, as many manuscripts lack the marks that can pin them to a specific medieval library.

What played out on Glastonbury Tor was just a fraction of the violence and destruction that the Reformation would bring to the British Isles and Europe. In Britain alone, tens of thousands of books were burned or broken up and sold as scrap; in the words of the seventeenth-century writer and historian Anthony Wood: 'books were dog cheap and whole libraries could be had for an inconsiderable nothing.'[14]

In Europe, too, the Reformation afflicted the libraries of the monastic and other religious communities. In Lower Saxony monastic buildings were torn down, and all moveable properties including books were carried away by fleeing Catholic monks and priests. The Peasants' War of 1525 saw many libraries and archives targeted by peasant bands because they contained feudal charters and tax rolls that kept the peasants in bondage. Here the Reformation was the trigger for broader social movements to be unleashed, the documented past being one of the targets. The sixteenth-century German historian Johann Letzner researched in the town of Walkenried and lamented the loss of the library when it was burned down in the 1520s. Precious volumes from the monastery library had been used to provide stepping stones for muddy paths. Cyriakus Spangenberg described manuscripts being stuffed down a monastery well in 1525. In Calenburg, Letzner noted that citizens burned books owing to their association with the old religion.[15]

John Bale, Leland's successor, in his published account of Leland's *The laboryouse journey*, went into more detail:

> To destroy all without consideration, is and will be unto England for ever, a most horrible infamy. A great number of them which purchased those superstitious mansions, reserved of those library books, some to rub their boots. Some they sold to the grocers and soap sellers, and some they sent to overseas to the bookbinders, not in small number, but at times whole ships full, to the wondering of the foreign nations . . . What may bring our realm to more shame and rebuke, than to have it known abroad, that we are despisers of learning?[16]

Evidence of the losses through deliberate destruction can be found from fragments of the books that have survived in bookbindings from the period. Before the mechanisation of book production in the middle of the nineteenth century, books were bound by hand and those hand-made bindings were often strengthened by waste paper or parchment in the part of the book known as the 'pastedown'. This was often reused material from discarded books.

The practice of reusing old books in unusual ways had gone on in the Middle Ages, with some (typically service books – books needed by priests to perform religious services) broken up and either sold or reused when they became outdated or too worn for daily use. Parchment leaves were reused to strengthen more than books. An Icelandic 'manuscript' now in the University of Copenhagen was found being used as a stiffener for a bishop's mitre.

The Reformation created a massive amount of new material for bookbinders who were for the most part concentrated in the major centres of book production. In England this meant London, Oxford and Cambridge, and the practice of using manuscript fragments in bindings has been studied in greatest detail at Oxford.[17] Between 1530 and 1600 binders used printed waste material from outdated or overused books, especially those used by university students. As the Reformation moved with unstoppable force we find evidence of the effect of this on book collections in the bindings of later books, many of which remain on the shelves of libraries in Oxford today. Service books were rarely used as pastedowns in Oxford before 1540, but from the 1550s they become frequent. Studies made on surviving bindings from this period show service books, biblical commentaries, lives of the saints, works of canon law, scholastic theology, the Church Fathers and medieval philosophy all turned into binders' waste.

Thanks to the careful keeping of college accounts in Oxford we even have some detailed examples. At All Souls College, a famous printed edition of the Bible, made in Antwerp 1569–73, was given to the college library in 1581. The Plantin Bible is a large, eight-volume work and the Oxford bookbinder Dominic Pinart, who was paid by the college to repair it, required a lot of parchment to support the structures of its leather-bound covers. Between thirty-six and forty leaves were removed from a large-format thirteenth-century commentary on the book of Leviticus that had been given to the college in the fifteenth century. More of these leaves are also to be found in the binding of a book Pinart constructed for Winchester College. Bizarrely, no other leaves were used, and the disfigured manuscript still remains in the college library today.[18]

It was not just the libraries of the former monasteries that were destroyed and dispersed, other kinds of books were also singled out for destruction. These were the now illegal service books of the Catholic Church: missals, antiphonaries, breviaries, manuals and other books that had long been used by priests and others for the proper observance of the complex services of divine worship in the unreformed medieval church. These books began to be destroyed in monasteries and churches during the early phases of the Reformation, but following the passing of the 1549 'Acte for the abolishinge and putting awaye of diverse bookes and images', state sponsorship of this destruction intensified.

This is not to say that there was no resistance to this destruction and censorship. An antiphonary (a large service book with musical notation used by choirs) made for the parish church of St Helen's Ranworth still survives today. It had been carefully adapted to comply with the new religious laws of censorship that would have dominated the lives of the parish priest, the churchwardens and other officials of St Helen's. According to the 1534 Act, references to the English saint Thomas Becket (whose martyrdom had been the result of his disobedience to the English king) needed to be removed from the calendar: a section of all service books which detailed the dates throughout the years when each saint and other important religious festivals should be commemorated (these were often adapted to include local saints). The Ranworth Antiphonary had 'erased' the entry for St Thomas with the very faintest of diagonal lines, leaving it easy to continue to read the words. Once Mary Tudor took power and reimposed Catholicism, the text for St Thomas was rewritten back into the antiphonary.[19]

While the losses during the Reformation were great, the cases of survival – only five thousand or more books are known to survive today from the libraries of the medieval monasteries of the British Isles – are vivid testaments to how individuals can resist the destruction of knowledge. In some cases, these were the monks, nuns, friars and canons forced to leave their monasteries and who occasionally took the most precious books with them. In York, Richard Barwicke, a former monk at the Benedictine abbey, took books from the abbey library with him, bequeathing them to a secular friend. William Browne, the last prior of Monk Bretton in Yorkshire, took 148 books with him when the Benedictine house was dissolved. At the time of his death in 1557 Philip Hawford, the last abbot of the Benedictine house at Evesham in Worcestershire, owned 75 books, mostly acquired when he was a monk.[20] Even the most famous medieval manuscript of them all, the Book of Kells, now the greatest treasure of Trinity College Dublin, was in all likelihood removed from St Mary's Abbey at Kells by Richard Plunket, the last abbot. They were dangerous souvenirs, particularly in the most intensely Protestant period of the Reformation, when decoration and colour, statuary and religious iconography were stripped out of churches across northern Europe.

St Dunstan's Classbook survived by coming into the ownership of the Renaissance collector Thomas Allen. Allen gathered books from dissolved monastic libraries throughout the country. One Oxford bookseller seems to have acquired many old manuscripts, as 'in the reign of King Edward VI there was a cart load of MSS [manuscripts] carried out of Merton College library when religion was reformed . . . Mr Allen told him that old Garbrand the bookseller . . . bought them of the College . . . Mr Allen bought some of them of him.' Presumably Garbrand Harkes (he is known to have been active from the 1530s to at least the 1570s) may have been able to source manuscripts from further afield for his regular customers.[21]

Other Glastonbury manuscripts were available at the end of the sixteenth century for collectors to snap up, even in remote parts of the country. By 1639, James Ussher, the scholarly Archbishop of Armagh, had seen the enormous *Magna Tabula* of Glastonbury Abbey, a vast wooden folding panel, which has parchment sheets of text pasted onto its boards, at Naworth Castle, in a remote corner of Cumbria, very close to Hadrian's Wall. The *Magna Tabula* contains legends of the founding of Glastonbury Abbey by Joseph of Arimathea (Jesus's supposed uncle) and accounts of the saints buried there, and seems to have been made to stand in the abbey church for the monks and other worshippers to see and read. Even closed it measures over two feet by three feet and is one of the Bodleian's heaviest manuscripts (the library's book-fetchers groan whenever a scholar asks to see it). It cannot have been easy to transport it from Glastonbury to Naworth, telling evidence that the trade in old books in early modern England was not only determined but remarkably effective.[22]

One significant figure responsible for preserving some of these books from destruction was the same man who had been upholding the king's demands, John Leland. In his *The laboryouse journey* he recounted how he had 'conserved' monastic books, and in his poem 'Antiphilarchia' he reported fitting out the royal libraries at Greenwich, Hampton Court and Westminster with new shelves to accommodate the collections from the dissolved monasteries, some of which he had found. A number of books, many now regarded as cultural treasures, were identified by Leland for the Royal Library. A ninth-century Gospel now in the British Library, with close associations to the Anglo-Saxon King Athelstan, for example, was one of a group of books he acquired from St Augustine's Abbey, Canterbury for the king.[23] This book's Anglo-Saxon royal associations are clear, but it is harder to see why the twelfth-century copy of an obscure commentary on Matthew's Gospels by Claudius of Turin, which had been seen by Leland in Llanthony Priory in 1533–4, had also been identified for acquisition for the king's library at Westminster.[24]

Leland may have chosen books during his visits and had them transferred almost immediately, but it is more likely that they remained *in situ* until the commissioners visited the monasteries. Most of the books that survive in the Royal Collection (which are for the most part now in the British Library in London) leave no specific indication that they passed through Leland's hands, but he certainly had a major role in preserving them.[25] There is a glimpse of how it might have worked in a letter concerning the great library of the Benedictine abbey at Bury St Edmunds in Suffolk. Just five days after the formal Dissolution on 4 November, Leland came back to Bury to 'see what books be left in the library there, or translated thence into any other corner of the late monastery'.[26] We also know that at least 176 volumes were in Leland's personal library when it was seen by his friend and successor John Bale, and Bale probably only listed part of the collection.

Although Leland was responsible for some of the dispersals he was horrified at the destruction. He wrote to Thomas Cromwell, his sponsor, that 'now Germans perceiving our . . . negligence, do send daily young scholars hither, that spoil [the books], and cut them out of libraries, returning home and putting them abroad as monuments of their own country'.[27] But the full impact of the

Dissolution on the libraries and the realisation of how far he had strayed from his humanist beginnings may only have sunk in in the decade or so following the intense phase of his journeys and after he had fallen from favour at court in his mid-forties. A letter survives 'dolorously lamenting his sudden fall'.[28]

In 1547 John Leland went mad. He collapsed into a frenzied state, his small dwelling in the grounds of the former Carthusian priory in London, known as the Charterhouse, turned into a disordered mess, his papers strewn around it. Friends came to help, but it was too late. Leland had fallen deeply 'into madness or insanity from a sudden striking down of his mind, from an imperfection of the brain, from frenzy from affliction, melancholy or from any other moderate disposition of the spirit'. On 21 February 1547, just a few weeks after the death of Henry VIII, he was officially declared insane, 'upon that day he became demented and remained so ever since'. An official document in 1551 recorded that he had been 'mad, insane, lunatic, furious, frantic'.[29] He may have been susceptible to mental illness. We have no way of reconstructing the decline of his mental state, but for such a bookish person the understanding that his own work had played a part in so much destruction may have been too much to bear. By April 1552 Leland was dead but the Reformation ploughed on.[30]

The devastation was not just limited to the destruction of texts of the old religion and the institutions that housed them. The medieval archives of the monastic and other religious houses also suffered. They had been retained mainly for the legal and administrative ease they provided to the new owners of the properties who were keen to collect rents from tenants. The possession of title deeds was vital in organising rent collection or in the subsequent sale of property. In the 1520s, one precursor to the Reformation was the suppression of two Oxford religious houses, the monastery of St Frideswide and the Augustinian abbey at Osney. Both were closed and some of their properties transferred to form Cardinal College, which began altering old buildings and putting up new ones in 1525. The new college had been a 'present' from Henry VIII to Cardinal Wolsey. After Wolsey's fall from favour in 1529, Cardinal College went through a period of further change and became a Protestant establishment, Christ Church, in 1546, and the old priory church of St Frideswide became the new Cathedral Church of Oxford. The new administrators of Christ Church were determined to maintain an organisational grip on the extensive land holdings that they now possessed. The contents of the muniment rooms of the two abbeys must have been transferred to a central record store at some point in the 1520s, where the title deeds and other documents began to be sorted. This process had resulted in an accumulation of documents in a room off the cloisters at Christ Church where they were consulted by the antiquarian Anthony Wood in the middle of the seventeenth century.

The process of sorting the title deeds and other records of land ownership had resulted in some documents being deliberately neglected: 'And because the nembers thereof have not the Lands, which those Evidences concern, they take no care of the Evidences, but lay them in a By-place expos'd to weather, and thereby are much perished and become not legible.'[31] Wood had a free rein to help himself to materials he found there, and among the documents he preserved were at least two, possibly three, of the original thirteenth-century official copies of Magna Carta, the most import-ant political document of medieval England.

The original agreement that was sealed on the field of Runnymede following the final meeting of King John and the English barons in June 1215 does not survive. What does survive is a series of copies made by official state scribes in the Royal Chancery (the legal administration of the English monarchs), which had the king's seal attached to them, and carried the same legal power as if they were the original itself. These documents were issued periodically throughout the thirteenth century, sent to the counties, to be read aloud by the king's representatives, the sheriffs. The sheriffs then looked for safe places to store and preserve the documents. In Oxfordshire, the nearest place of safekeeping was at Osney Abbey. It was from Osney Abbey that engrossments of the 1217 and 1225 Magna Carta were transferred with the rest of the monastic archive to Cardinal College in the 1520s.[32]

As Magna Carta had nothing to do with land ownership, the engrossments had been transferred to a pile of unwanted documents. Anthony Wood instantly saw the significance of the documents and preserved them; they eventually found their way to the Bodleian

Library. Thanks to the preservation of the engrossments of Magna Carta by individuals like Wood, and by institutions like the Bodleian, the significance of its text became a key part of the constitutional arguments in favour of democracy and the rule of law in the seventeenth and eighteenth centuries, still a strong influence on our ideas of good government today.

The European Reformation of the sixteenth century was in many ways one of the worst periods in the history of knowledge. Hundreds of thousands of books were destroyed, and countless others dislocated from the libraries they were housed in, many for centuries. The archives of the monasteries that were in the front line of the Reformation have not been studied to the same extent, but as the account of Magna Carta shows huge numbers of archival documents were destroyed. The monks and nuns who had performed the roles of librarian and archivist were powerless to hold back the force of the Reformation, and so the task of preservation fell to a group of individuals who, in the words of the seventeenth-century writer John Earle, were 'strangely thrifty of times past' and who would typically be 'an admirer of the rust of old monuments' who was 'enamoured of wrinkles and loves all things (as the Dutch do cheese) for being mouldy and worm-eaten'. These individuals were antiquaries, and according to Earle a typical antiquary was of the kind who likes to pore over a manuscript 'everlastingly, especially if the cover be all moth-eaten'.[33] They were deeply interested in the past and anxious to collect the remnants of the libraries. Their motivations were often partly driven by their Catholicism (as in the case of Lord William Howard) but sometimes by their Protestantism (Leland after all was motivated to support Henry's arguments for the divorce and for the split from Rome). What united them was a passion for the past, and for the recovery of ideas and knowledge. They formed networks, which meant they could copy each other's books, and even formed a society in 1607; initially short-lived it was refounded a century later, and still exists today as the Society of Antiquaries. These individuals helped preserve a substantial portion of the knowledge of the medieval period. Their work was to trigger the creation of many of the most important modern libraries, and furthered the professions of librarian and archivist.

Sir Thomas Bodley (1545–1613). Portrait by an unknown artist, c.1590s.

4

An Ark to Save Learning

A S THE LIBRARIES of monasteries either closed or lacked the supporting framework of funds to run them, gaps appeared in the preservation of knowledge. Individuals played an important part in bridging them. One of the most important people to try to fill these gaps was Sir Thomas Bodley. The greatest English intellectual of the period, Francis Bacon, described Bodley's contribution – the creation of the library that still bears his name – as 'an ark to save learning from the deluge'.[1] The deluge that Bacon was referring to was, of course, the Reformation. By the time the religious upheavals had swept through Oxford its university library had grown in size and quality to be a major institutional collection, one of the largest outside the monasteries.

The first sense of a university library in Oxford had emerged four centuries earlier with the concept of loan chests: where money could be borrowed in return for books – valuable objects – being deposited. The religious orders were important in developing the culture of libraries in the city and the emergent university. The city's earliest organised libraries were founded in the twelfth century by the Augustinian Order, which established the Abbey of Osney and the Priory of St Frideswide, and in the thirteenth by the Cistercians, who established the Abbey of Rewley. These houses all had libraries, although they were not part of the university. The mendicant orders (religious men and women who travelled and lived in cities, focussing on studying and preaching) were much more integrated with the university, especially the Dominican and Franciscan friars, and both of their houses in Oxford had libraries.[2] The Dominicans also had a *librarius* – a member of the community responsible for the care and use of their books. The wealthier colleges soon began to develop their collections in imitation of the practices of the friars, who from the late thirteenth century had developed a system of organising their collections so that some of the books became a 'circulating' collection, from which the students (novice friars) could have books assigned to them, and were allowed to keep them in their rooms for personal use. Alongside this remained the common library, which became the reference collection, which was kept in a specially identified room where books could be consulted silently, and where they were often chained to library furniture. The first indication of this practice in Oxford was in the thirteenth century at the Franciscan convent, where the library of the convent (*libraria conventus*) was kept separately from that of the students (*libraria studencium*).[3] This 'two collection' approach was soon adopted by the colleges of the university. We see this expressed formally in new statutes at University College in 1292, but it can also be seen at Oriel, Merton, Exeter, Queen's, Balliol, Magdalen and Lincoln colleges. Although it is tempting to identify the physical room as 'the library', it was actually the sum of both collections that made the library.[4]

The university (as opposed to the individual colleges, halls and convents) book collections in the loan chests began to grow so much that by the early fourteenth century a new, purpose-built library room was needed to house the books. A structure was proposed adjacent to the University Church (where the loan chests were kept) but between 1439 and 1444 the library was doubled in size by five spectacular gifts of books from Humfrey, Duke of Gloucester, the younger brother of Henry V, bringing works of humanistic learning for the first time to join the scholastic texts already in the medieval library. Here were ancient writers like Plato, Aristotle and Cicero, but also the works of the French humanist Nicolas de Clamanges and translations of Plutarch by the Italian humanist Leonardo Bruni.[5] The university authorities immediately decided to adapt a new building project already underway (the magnificent medieval room known today as the Divinity School), and added another storey above it to house the university library. The new library room was designed both to house the collections and to make them available to the scholars of the university. The stone structure of the space is miraculously unchanged today, and still operates as a library room, despite the astonishing changes in the city and the university since the middle of the fifteenth century.[6]

The books in this room, known today as Duke Humfrey's Library, were chained to ensure that such valuable volumes would remain in place for others to use, and the library became a central place for learning. Those students and researchers who use the library today can still see the stone window and roof corbels, featuring heads of humans and animals, in a working environment that opened up for use four years before Christopher Columbus landed on the American continent.

The scholars of the medieval university library had their access to its collections brutally disrupted. In 1549–50, the commissioners of King Edward VI visited the university and, although we do not know the exact circumstances, by 1556 no books remained, and the university elected a group of senior officers to arrange the sale of the furniture. It has been estimated that 96.4 per cent of the original books in the university library were lost.[7] Just a handful of books and the shadows made by the original fifteenth-century shelves on the stone piers remain today.

What happened to the books? Anthony Wood, writing more than a century after these events in his *History and Antiquities of the Universitie of Oxford* (1674), suggested that 'some of those books so taken out by the Reformers were burnt, some sold away from Robin Hoods pennyworths, either to Booksellers, or to Glovers to press their gloves, or Taylors to make measures, to Bookbinders to cover books bound by them, and some also kept by Reformers for their own use.'[8]

Just eleven volumes have survived. In the Bodleian's stacks just three remain today: a copy of John Capgrave's *Commentary on the Book of Exodus*, the *Letters* of the classical author Pliny the Younger (copied in Milan around the year 1440) and a copy of the *Works* of Nicolas de Clamanges, given to the university in 1444.[9]

But out of this destruction grew one of the most distinguished libraries in the world. In the newest part of the Bodleian, the Weston Library, there hangs a sixteenth-century painting of the man responsible, Sir Thomas Bodley. Stare at Bodley's portrait today and you can see the raffish charm of the man. He is dressed in fine clothes, his beard is well trimmed, and there is a definite gleam in his eye.

Born into a wealthy family in 1547, his childhood was still marred
by the violence and uncertainty of the Reformation. His parents
had so fully embraced Protestantism that all the Bodleys were forced
into exile when Mary Tudor took the throne and reintroduced
Catholicism to England in 1553. On her death the family returned
and Thomas came up to Magdalen College Oxford, graduating in
1566, and for the next thirty years he combined a successful career
as a merchant in Exeter (helped considerably by his marriage to a
rich widow whose fortune was based on trading pilchards) and as
a diplomat in the service of Elizabeth I, becoming part of her
courtly circle. Returning to Oxford in the 1590s he and an old
friend, Sir Henry Savile, set about the renewal of the university
library.[10]

In his autobiography, Sir Thomas Bodley set out his own personal
mission: 'I concluded at the last to set up my staff at the Library
door in Oxford,' he wrote, 'being thoroughly persuaded, that . . .
I could not busy myself to better purpose, than by reducing that
place (to which then in every part lay ruined and waste) to the
public use of students.'[11] He had already elaborated this idea in 1598
to the Vice Chancellor of Oxford, pointing out that 'Where there
had been heretofore a public library in Oxford: which you know
is apparent by the room itself remaining, and by your statute records
I will take the charge and cost upon myself to reduce it again to
its former use: and to make it fit, and handsome with seats, and
shelves, and desks and . . . to help to furnish it with books': Bodley
was himself willing to make a huge financial commitment to the
project.[12]

That the books came thick and fast to the new institution, from
1598 onwards, was a sign of how desperately the new library was
needed. Sir Thomas donated over a hundred and fifty manuscripts
from his personal collection, among them arguably the most sump-
tuous illuminated manuscript the Bodleian owns: a copy of Alexander
of Paris's version of the *Romance of Alexander*, written and illuminated
in Flanders, 1338–44, with which is also bound a manuscript version of
the same tale in Middle English, and a Middle English translation
of Marco Polo's *Li livres du Graunt Caam*. In this part of the volume
is one of the most famous paintings of Venice, executed in England
around 1400, which has for many years been reproduced in almost

every history of that city. The *Romance of Alexander* was undoubtedly commissioned by a very wealthy patron – very possibly a powerful noble or even royal family – as the finest scribes and artists combined forces to make this book truly magnificent. It is large for a medieval manuscript of this period, and every page has been richly decorated with floral designs and wonderfully evocative and imaginative marginal illustrations depicting scenes from everyday life. Even after seventeen years at the Bodleian, this volume still sends a shiver of delight down my spine – the sensory pleasures of the glimmering gold leaf, and the rich pigments brightening the page in combination with the beauty of the script, and the heavy sound that the large sheets of parchment make as you turn the pages. It is one of the world's great cultural treasures.

On 27 April 1857 a young undergraduate at Exeter College obtained special permission to see the *Romance of Alexander*. The undergraduate was William Morris, who was to become one of the most influential artists, designers, writers and political thinkers of the nineteenth century. Shortly after seeing the manuscript, Morris, Edward Burne-Jones and their fellow Pre-Raphaelites decorated the walls of the Oxford Union Library with Arthurian themes, influenced by the miniatures in the manuscript showing knights fighting battles, chivalric deeds and courtly rituals. For both Morris and Burne-Jones consulting such richly illuminated books was a profoundly influential experience, helping to forge the medieval aesthetic firmly in their minds.[13] Morris continued to draw inspiration from medieval aesthetics and ways of making things for the rest of his life. Central to this was the creation of his own books in the same style, for which he even set up his own printing press, the Kelmscott Press in London.

Thomas Bodley's network of friends and associates came forward with gifts of manuscripts, archives, printed books, coins, maps and other materials, and money to purchase new books. The materials included many manuscripts from the dissolved monasteries, but also state papers relating to national affairs of the previous century. They recognised that this new institution offered a range of attributes quite unlike any other library at the time. Some of these early donors were antiquaries like William Camden (the great historian), Sir Robert Cotton, Thomas Allen (the owner of St Dunstan's

Classbook) and Sir Walter Cope. Others were members of Bodley's own family, like his brother Lawrence, a canon of Exeter Cathedral, who persuaded the Dean and Chapter there to donate eighty-one manuscripts from the library in 1602. But Bodley was keen to do more than preserve the past. He wanted the library to remain relevant into the future too. In 1610 he entered into an agreement with the Stationers' Company of London which meant that a copy of every book published by its members, and registered at Stationers' Hall, would be deposited in the new library.[14]

One of the dreams of Western civilisation has been the accumulation of all knowledge documented in one library. It begins with the myth of the Library of Alexandria and returned strongly after the Renaissance with the growing sense that libraries could help their communities master all the questions of mankind, or at the very least offer them the opportunity to look up all the references in an important scholarly work. The Reformation devastated many of the libraries of Europe, and especially the libraries in the British Isles. The losses are unquantifiable in precise terms but we know from various different pieces of evidence that between 70 and 80 per cent of the contents of the pre-Reformation libraries of the British Isles were lost, and a slightly smaller proportion of the books on the shelves of the European monastic libraries.

The Reformation was damaging to books in other ways – especially the backlash against Hebrew books that was triggered by the Counter-Reformation. Looking at the few books to survive these various onslaughts, it is undeniable that we have lost a huge amount of knowledge from the Catholic Middle Ages – not just texts of authors that have not survived, but evidence of well-known authors being read in different religious communities or by different individuals. We have lost documentary evidence of everyday behaviour through the damage done to the medieval monastic archives, which as we know through the example of Magna Carta sometimes held unexpected but hugely important documents for safekeeping.

In the founding statutes of the library Sir Thomas Bodley laid down many detailed stipulations regarding the security, preservation and careful management of the institution, in part a direct response to the destruction of knowledge that had taken place earlier. By ensuring preservation, Sir Thomas could also ensure access to those materials not just by members of the university but by what Sir Thomas called 'the whole republic of the learned'. His ideas were novel in the provision of knowledge. No other library in Europe was so dedicated to the preservation of its collection, to the aggressive expansion of its holdings, and at the same time to broadening access to the community beyond its immediate constituency. The Bodleian's own archive documents the use made of the collection in the years following its formal opening in 1602, which included scholars from Danzig, Montpellier and Hamburg, as well as from other parts of the country.[15]

Another innovation that Sir Thomas made was to publish the library's catalogue of its holdings. The first substantial library catalogue to be published was that of Leiden University Library, in 1595, which also marked the opening of their new library building. A famous engraving of the library made in 1610 shows that the collections were arranged under seven categories: theology, law, medicine, mathematics, philosophy, literature, history.[16]

'There is nothing more to the credit of a library than that every man finds in it what he seeks,' wrote the influential writer on libraries, Gabriel Naudé, in 1627, criticising the Ambrosian Library in Milan (one of the few in Europe that was open to the public) for its lack of subject classification and its books 'stowed pell-mell by volume'.[17] In contrast the Bodleian was highly organised. It had been the first library in England to have its catalogue printed and circulated in 1605 (three years after the library opened to readers). The catalogue divided knowledge into just four groups: arts, theology, law and medicine, but also provided a general index of authors, and special indexes on the commentators on Aristotle and the Bible. The catalogue was the work of Thomas James, the first librarian. Much of the correspondence between him and Bodley survives, and a surprising amount of it is concerned with catalogues.

The first catalogues were lists (referred to as 'Tables') that were put up in wooden frames at the end of each bay of shelves in the newly restored space that today we call Duke Humfrey's Library: 'You must by no meanes omit, to take good notice of their orders, in placing and disposing their library-books: whether they do it, by the Alphabet, or according to the faculties.'[18] In the end, with the first catalogues placed on the shelves, it was the listing by faculty that formed the first catalogue. The catalogue is physically a small book, the size used to be called 'quarto', which refers to the format of the book; although it is only about 22 cm high, with over four hundred pages of text, over two hundred pages of appendix and sixty-four pages of index, it amounts to a substantial publication. The catalogue was widely circulated, sold at the Frankfurt Book Fair (still today the key annual gathering of publishers, and where new books are promoted) and began to be used by other collectors and libraries. Copies of the 1605 catalogue were owned by the great French collector, Jacques-Auguste de Thou, in Paris, for example, and by the Scottish poet William Drummond of Hawthornden in Edinburgh. In 1620 the Bodleian would innovate by producing a new edition of its catalogue arranged alphabetically by author – a practice that was to become standard in centuries to follow, but then a landmark in intellectual history.[19]

How the Bodleian differed from the other libraries of early modern Europe was in its approach to making this preserved knowledge accessible. Today the Bodleian catalogue is searchable from anywhere in the world, with over 14 million searches being made in the academic year 2018–19; more than three hundred thousand readers come to use the Bodleian's reading rooms from outside the university, millions more download our digital collections from every country in the world (with the exception of North Korea). This combination of preservation and access would mean that the Bodleian in the seventeenth and early eighteenth centuries would become the de facto national library.

Changes were also made to the keeping of documents in archives. At Oxford during the medieval period, the complex nature of the university, with its many colleges, halls and inns, meant that there was a plethora of documentary and administrative information that needed to be maintained. As soon as the university obtained powers of administration, and the right of conferring degrees and other rights over its members, the need for maintaining records also began. The earliest records are the books of statutes and ordinances relating to the studies and discipline of students. The oldest surviving letter written to the university – perhaps the earliest sign that the university was a notable institution – came from the papal legate (the

Pope's representative), Cardinal Guala, in 1217 or 1218.[20] As the university gradually became larger and more ordered, the early officials of the university (some of these roles still exist today – such as the proctors) began to keep Registers of Matriculations (matriculation is the formal admission of a student onto a course of study) and Registers of Congregation (the lists of the masters and other academic staff of the university). The modern equivalent of these lists are still consulted today as the 'master files' of who is (or was) entitled to degrees and other forms and privileges of membership of the university.

The same approach extended beyond the sphere of universities. The process of gathering knowledge for the purposes of government was established in the medieval period, but took a dramatic step forward in England during the sixteenth century, prompted by the change in religion brought about by Henry VIII and his ministers, Cardinal Wolsey and Thomas Cromwell. Wolsey's surveys of the 1520s, the *Valor Ecclesiasticus* (a great catalogue of returns from a survey of the revenues of the Church undertaken by Henry VIII's Royal Commissioners in 1535), and the Chantry Commissions of the 1540s, were all concerned with knowing the state of church finances with accuracy, so that the king could take control. Cromwell's introduction in 1538 of the requirement by law that all parishes should maintain registers of christenings, marriages and burials, and the introduction of registration of land conveyances, amounted to an unprecedented period of information gathering by the state, which would herald the start of governmental monitoring of data, held eventually in the state archives.[21]

Until this point the process of keeping knowledge had used a term now rarely used, but which sums up the value of preservation: muniment. Muniments are records kept to preserve evidence of rights and privileges. The practice of keeping these documents progressed to the level of a highly organised activity. The first centralised state archive was formed in 1542 in Simancas by Emperor Charles V for the records of Spain. In England in 1610 James I appointed Levinus Monk and Thomas Wilson to be 'keepers and registrars of papers and records'.[22] Individuals like Scipio le Squyer, Deputy Chamberlain in the Court of Exchequer, were employed not only to maintain the records in their care but also to make complex lists of them.[23] In 1610 the Vatican Archives in their modern form also came into being.

The process of ordering information was integral to the development of regulation and the growth of state finances, but it also began to be seen as having a beneficial public purpose. Part of the role of government was, after all, to ensure that citizens were well governed. In the seventeenth century, in circles around the Royal Society and Gresham College in London, prominent intellectuals promoted the gathering of social statistics as a means to make government 'more certain and regular' and to ensure 'the happiness and greatness' of the people.[24]

The idea that information must be diffused and made available to the public if government was to be open to correction also began to be understood. A key proponent was John Graunt who, in his *Natural and Political Observations . . . Made Upon the Bills of Mortality* (1662), was in two minds about whether the data collated in the bills of mortality (documents listing the numbers of deaths and analysing their causes in London) should be considered useful just for the government of the country, or for wider society: was it 'necessary to many'?[25] The bills were published to provide 'clear knowledge' aimed at encouraging a more complete understanding of the state of society in London, and to encourage individual citizens to behave better or, as Graunt phrased it, to secure 'the Bars, which keep some men within bounds' and away from 'extravagancies'.[26] The original data which the bills were produced from could be consulted in the archive of the Worshipful Company of Parish Clerks, who had the responsibility for collecting it, and as the diaries of Samuel Pepys later show, ordinary citizens did rely on the reports to manage their own behaviour. On 29 June 1665 Pepys recorded that: 'This end of the town every day grows very bad of the plague. The Mortality bill is come to 267 which is about 90 more than the last: and of these but 4 in the city – which is a great blessing to us.'[27]

The scientific theorist Samuel Hartlib proposed an 'Office of Address', which aimed at providing a great exchange of economic, geographical, demographic and scientific information open to the public: 'all that which is good and desirable in a whole Kingdome may be by this means communicated unto any one that stands in need thereof.' Hartlib's plan had strong support from a number of influential and prominent reformers, especially at Oxford, and when John Rous (the second librarian) fell ill, Hartlib was seriously proposed to succeed him, as it was felt at the time that his plan to develop a major communications agency would be best located in a great library, as he wanted a 'Center and Meeting-place of Advices, of Proposalls, of Treaties and of all Manner of Intellectual Rarities'. There were opponents to this scheme, however, and eventually Thomas Barlow, a Royalist sympathiser – who was, in historian Charles Webster's words 'academically orthodox' – was appointed.[28]

Many important documents were preserved by the Bodleian. The Magna Carta is the one that has had the most profound impact over time: we still adhere to its vital 39th clause which states that no free man should be imprisoned or dispossessed 'save by the lawful judgement of his peers or by the law of the land', and its 40th clause which makes illegal the selling, denying or delaying of justice. These clauses remain enshrined in English law to this day and can be found across the world, including in the American constitution, and were a key source for the UN Charter on Human Rights.[29]

One of the greatest legal thinkers of the Enlightenment, William Blackstone, brought a broader awareness of Magna Carta's legal and political significance to bear on the broader debates of the eighteenth century. His book *The Great Charter and the Charter of the Forest* (1759) drew on his close study of the engrossments of Magna Carta, which had been bequeathed to the Bodleian in 1754.[30] This book, and his magnum opus the *Commentaries on the Laws of England* (1765–9), were hugely influential on the fathers of the American Revolution (copies could be found in the personal library of Thomas Jefferson, for example), and on the intellectuals in revolutionary France. If the power of the actual documentary remains of the thirteenth-century Magna Carta is doubted, one of the seventeen surviving copies was sent to America in 1941 by Winston Churchill as a totem for ensuring American engagement in the Allied cause in the Second World War.

The destruction of libraries and archives during the Reformation prompted a generation of antiquaries to rescue records of the past and to collect as much of this material as they could. Things had changed since Leland had proudly assumed the role of 'antiquarius' for Henry VIII a century before. Antiquaries now seemed so strange to their contemporaries that they were often lampooned in plays and poems and cartoons. The *New Dictionary of the Terms, Ancient and Modern of the Canting Crew* in 1698 even defined an antiquary as 'a curious critic in old Coins, Stones and Inscriptions, in Worm-eaten Records and ancient Manuscripts, also one that affects and blindly dotes, on Relics, Ruins, old Customs, Phrases and Fashions'. But the 'Worm-eaten Records and ancient Manuscripts' these individuals saved were to become the foundational holdings of great institutional libraries in the late sixteenth and seventeenth centuries.[31] The antiquaries' obsession with the past preserved it for the future.

Bodley was part of a movement of individuals determined that the destruction of knowledge should not be repeated. Another was Duke Augustus the Younger of Brunswick-Lüneberg, an obsessive collector. By the time the duke died in 1666, he had 130,000 printed books and 3,000 manuscripts in his library – much larger than the Bodleian at the time.[32] After a youth spent in Germany surrounded by the religious upheaval and violence that eventually turned into the Thirty Years' War, the duke's motivation was to preserve knowledge. Like Bodley, he used agents to help build his collections (from as far afield as Vienna and Paris), and he even visited the Bodleian in 1603, just a few months after its official opening. Bodley's library inspired the duke to new heights of collecting and his books became the foundation of what is now a great independent research library (funded by the federal and state governments) at Wolfenbüttel, known as the Herzog August Bibliothek.

Bodley was meticulous in his preparations for the future. Statutes were drafted, funds were donated, old buildings were rebuilt and new ones planned and begun. The new role of librarian Bodley wanted to be carried out by 'some one that is noted and known for a diligent student, and in all his conversation to be trusty, active, and discreet, a graduate also and a linguist, not encumbered with marriage, nor with a benefice of Cure' (i.e. not a parish priest). When Thomas James, an eminent scholar who had worked on the King James Bible, was appointed, the founder and benefactor looked over his shoulder constantly. Their surviving correspondence paints a fascinating picture of the sheer minutiae involved in setting up a great library. The role is still called Bodley's Librarian to this day. (I am the twenty-fifth.)

The ark had to be watertight. In 1609 Sir Thomas compiled the deed establishing an endowment, as 'by good observation' he had 'found it apparent, that the principal occasion of the utter subversion and ruin of some of the famous libraries in Christendom has been the want of due provision of some certainty in revenue for their continual preservation'.[33] And then Bodley put his money where his mouth was and disinherited his own family.

Rear Admiral Sir George Cockburn at the burning of Washington, painted by John James Halls, engraved by C. Turner, 1819.

5

Spoil of the Conqueror

The sky was brilliantly illumined by the different conflagrations; and a dark red light was thrown upon the road, sufficient to permit each man to view distinctly his comrade's face . . . I do not recollect to have witnessed, at any period of my life, a scene more striking or more sublime.[1]

GEORGE GLEIG, A young Scotsman serving in the British army, watched Washington burn in 1814 with mixed feelings. He had travelled across the Atlantic as part of an expeditionary force led by Admiral Cockburn and General Ross to wage war against the United States and took part in the most devastating attack the city had ever seen. Gleig was a highly intelligent observer and although he was undoubtedly a biased witness of the British expedition to America of 1812–14 he was also troubled by what he saw.

When the British attacked Washington they set fire to the White House (known then as the Presidential Mansion) and the Capitol, in which the Library of Congress was situated. The Capitol had stood proudly on the hill, 'tastefully worked and highly polished' with 'numerous windows', a 'handsome spiral hanging staircase' and apartments, 'furnished as a public library, the two larger being well stocked with valuable books, principally in modern languages, and the others filled with archives, national statutes, acts of legislature &c. and used as the private rooms of the librarians'. A detectable note of discomfort is evident in Gleig's description: 'a noble library, several printing offices, and all the national archives were likewise committed to the flames, which though no doubt the property of government, might better have been spared.'[2]

The burning of Washington was indeed a heavy blow for the United States. The impact would be felt for generations to come.

The British were so reviled for their act of barbarity that it would become a useful myth to help bind the American nation together through succeeding generations – proof that their ability to overcome adversity and to rebuild their capital city and its government showed resilience, resourcefulness and determination to succeed.

In 1814 the Library of Congress was still new. Having beaten the British in the War of Independence, the new government was based around a Congress of two houses, the Senate and the House of Representatives. The first Congress (1789–91) considered where to locate their capital city and their government, and it was three of the founding fathers of the United States, Thomas Jefferson, Alexander Hamilton and James Madison, who agreed on a site along the Potomac river favoured by George Washington himself. The original location of what is now Washington, DC was a mixture of forest and farmland, remote from the great American cities like Boston, Philadelphia and New York. Siting government at a distance from the major urban centres provided symbolic intent to limit government's influence on the emerging nation, a political trope that continues to retain its place at the heart of American politics today.

As the government began to develop and grow, so too did its need for access to information and knowledge. The politicians and government officials were mostly well-educated men, but as early as 1783 proposals were made in Congress to import books from Europe. James Madison, today regarded as the 'Father of the American Constitution', chaired a congressional committee that recommended the purchase of works by 'such authors on the law of nations, treaties, negotiations, &c, as would render the proceedings conformable to propriety', as well as 'every book & tract which related to American antiquities and the affairs of the United States'.[3] This was not for pure historical interest – the motivation was to provide evidence to help defend against the anticipated claims of European powers over American territorial possessions.[4]

In 1800, a bill was passed that allowed congressional funds to be used for the purchasing of books. Madison's committee's list of over three hundred titles included the great Enlightenment 'bible', Charles-Joseph Panckoucke's edition of Diderot and d'Alembert's

Encyclopédie Méthodologique (1782–1832) in 192 volumes, and works by legal theorists such as Hugo Grotius and Edward Coke, but especially those of the English jurist William Blackstone, such as his *Commentaries on the Laws of England* published in four volumes (1765–9) and *The Great Charter* (1759). Political theorists such as John Locke and Montesquieu were represented, as was the economist Adam Smith's massively influential treatise *An Inquiry into the Nature and Causes of the Wealth of Nations* (1776). Its roll call of eighteenth-century thinkers also included Edward Gibbon and David Hume, but there were also more practical purchases listed such as maps.[5]

Despite such a compelling list of titles, Congress did not at first grant the committee the funds to buy the books. This was the earliest occurrence of what would become a familiar problem: the library depended on Congress for funds but Congress did not always see the library as a priority.

Following the War of Independence, the United States placed great importance on education, and it grew as a nation with a thriving trade in books, much of which was linked to Britain and other European printing centres. Early America possessed a large number of commercial circulating libraries, and non-commercial social and community libraries serving the desire for news and knowledge for those who could not afford to buy books.[6] Private libraries remained the preserve of the middle and upper classes, but the rise of circulating libraries, subscription libraries and libraries in places such as coffee houses was making knowledge more accessible to a wider audience, a process that would expand greatly through the nineteenth century on both sides of the Atlantic. The early congressmen were mostly from affluent backgrounds, many well educated, and most had their own private libraries, perhaps a reason why, initially, they did not see the need for a central congressional library.

In 1794 funds were allocated to Congress for the purchase of William Blackstone's *Commentaries* and Emerich de Vattel's *Law of Nature and Nations* for use by the Senate, but these were notable exceptions – it wasn't until 1800, when Congress was relocated to Washington and Madison's bill passed, that funds were allocated to the library. Even then, the bill that President John Adams signed in that year, 'Making further provision for the removal and accommodation of the Government of the United States', concerned itself more with issues of street paving and the housing of the president than it did with the library. What funds it did allow for the library were for:

> the purchase of such books as may be necessary for the use of Congress at the said city of Washington, and for fitting up a suitable apartment for containing them, and for placing them therein the sum of five thousand dollars shall be, and hereby is appropriated . . . the said purchase shall be made . . . pursuant to . . . such catalogue as shall be furnished, by a joint committee of both Houses of Congress to be appointed for that purpose; and that the said books shall be placed in one suitable apartment in the capitol in the said city, for the use of both Houses of Congress and the Members thereof, according to such regulations as the Committee aforesaid shall devise and establish.[7]

The priorities indicated here are important, as the first instinct of Congress was that their information needs would be limited to immediate functional purposes – essentially to cover legal and governmental issues. Making provision for their own operational effectiveness was particularly important because unlike New York and Philadelphia there was no other library in Washington.

The library's collections were not vast but grew rapidly. The first printed catalogue was issued in 1802 with 243 books on the list, and it needed a supplement the following year. This first library had basic legal and governmental works, mostly in English, including the British *Statutes at Large, Journal of the House of Commons* and the fourteen-volume set of *State Trials*.[8] Further purchases were made from London booksellers and publishers.[9] The first Librarian of Congress, Patrick Magruder, even placed advertisements in newspapers suggesting authors and publishers should gift books, as their presence in the library would advertise them to the most prominent men in the land. One notice in the *National Intelligencer* boasted: 'We observe with pleasure that authors and editors of books, maps, and charts begin to find that, by placing a copy of their works on the shelves of this institution they do more to diffuse a knowledge of them than is generally accomplished by catalogues and advertisements.'[10]

By 1812 the catalogue listed over three thousand volumes of books and maps, needing 101 pages to describe them all.[11] In these early years of independence the Library of Congress – and its rapidly growing collection of volumes covering a wide range of subject matter – symbolised a nation forging its identity. Knowledge, as the old adage goes, is power, and although the library's collections were still very small they were growing in tandem with the national government they were designed to serve.

It is therefore unsurprising that the Library of Congress should have been one of the British army's key targets when they reached Washington. The war had already brought great destruction. This was not even the first library destroyed. In the American army's attack on the British city of York (modern Toronto) in April 1813, one of the first encounters between the two armies, they had burned the library in the legislative buildings.[12]

In 1813, Patrick Magruder fell ill and was forced to take a prolonged period of absence from the library. His brother George was appointed acting clerk. On 19 August, the British arrived. As news of their advance became known, arrangements began to be made for evacuation.[13] George Magruder ordered that the library should not be evacuated until the clerks of the War Department were seen to pack up their administrative records. He didn't realise that most of the government departments had already begun to pack up and had sequestered wagons to help them take key items to the safety of the countryside.

Although many men serving in the government were also volunteers in the militia defending the city, a handful remained behind, including Samuel Burch, one of the assistant clerks in the library, and J. T. Frost, the assistant librarian, who had stayed behind for the purposes of opening and airing the books (important in the very humid atmosphere of Washington in the summer). On the afternoon of the 21st, Burch was allowed to leave his post in the militia and return to the library. On the 22nd he and Frost were finally informed that the clerks of the War Department had begun to move out of Washington.

At last the decision was made – but it was too late. The other departments had commandeered all the remaining wagons in the city and it took Burch hours to find one in a village outside

Washington. He came back with a cart and six oxen and he and Frost loaded some books and documents onto it during what remained of the 22nd, and on the morning of the 23rd they took it to a place of safety, some nine miles out of the city. Other small gestures were also made – for example, Elias Caldwell, the clerk of the Supreme Court, moved some of the court volumes to his home.[14]

British forces entered Washington on 24 August. Things rapidly went downhill from there. General Ross initially sent in a flag of truce with terms but then he was fired on and his horse killed. George Gleig wrote a vivid description of what happened next. It is worth noting however that the accusation of firing while under truce is a commonly used excuse in other episodes of library destruction:

> All thoughts of accommodation were instantly laid aside; the troops advanced forthwith into the town, and having first put to sword all who were found in the house from which the shots were fired, and reduced it to ashes, they proceeded, without a moment's delay to burn and destroy everything in the most distant degree connected with government. In this general devastation were included the Senate-house, the President's palace, and extensive dock-yard and arsenal, barracks for two or three thousand men, several large store-houses filled with naval and military stores, some hundreds of cannon of different descriptions, and nearly twenty thousand stand of small arms.[15]

The official historian of the Library of Congress Jane Aikin tells us that British troops piled books and other flammable materials that could be found inside the building and set fire to it. Although we don't know the exact details of what happened, the legend was taking shape. An account of the fire in *Harpers New Monthly Magazine*, much later in the nineteenth century, firmly attributed the start of the fire to British soldiers using books from the library.[16]

The devastation hampered the effective operation of the American government for a considerable time (although not for long enough to stop their army from winning a decisive victory at Baltimore in the battle for Fort McHenry). While the library was not targeted alone, its location within the central building of the US government, made it ideal as a target and as a source of combustible material to continue the fire. And yet, it seems at least one member of the British forces recognised the symbolic power of the library's destruction. Amid the destruction of the centre of Washington, which Gleig reports as nothing but 'heaps of smoking ruins', a book was taken as a memento by the leader of the conquering army.[17] A copy of *An Account of the Receipts and Expenditures of the U.S. for the Year 1810* (Washington: A & G Way, Printers, 1812), with a leather title label on the front cover and tooled with the inscription 'President of the U. States', was presented to the Library of Congress by the legendary book dealer A. S. W. Rosenbach on 6 January 1940. The book had been given by Rear Admiral George Cockburn to his brother, and was clearly a souvenir. Whether Cockburn himself picked it up, or whether a British soldier found the book, is not known; of all the mementos to bring back the book spoke volumes. 'By all the customs of war', wrote George Gleig, 'whatever public property may chance to be in a captured town, becomes, confessedly, the just spoil of the conqueror.'[18]

In the days following the fire it became clear that the devastation was complete – the stone edifice survived but inside all was gone. The British had struck a blow to the fledgling government, right at its heart. The members of Congress were unharmed, but with their building burned, and the information they relied on to function destroyed, their political status needed to be rebuilt fast.

Out of the ashes of the first Library of Congress, a new and better library was to emerge. The chief agent for this renewal had been one of the intellectual architects of the American Revolution and the foundation of the United States, Thomas Jefferson. By 1814 the former president was living in semi-retirement in Monticello, Virginia, a hundred miles to the south-west of Washington. Jefferson's personal book collection, arguably the most sophisticated and extensive private library in America at the time, had been built up over a lifetime of serious reading. Jefferson knew what it was like to lose a library to a fire: his first library of legal books had been burned in 1770, and he had to rebuild his collection again. A few weeks after the burning of Washington, Jefferson wrote a carefully crafted letter to Samuel Harrison Smith, the editor of the leading Republican newspaper based in the city, the *National Intelligencer.*

> *Dear Sir,*
>
> *I learn from the newspapers that the vandalism of our enemy has triumphed at Washington over science as well as the arts, by the destruction of the public library . . . Of this transaction . . . the world will entertain but one sentiment. They will see a nation suddenly withdrawn from a great war, full armed and full handed, taking advantage of another whom they had recently forced into it, unarmed and unprepared, to indulge themselves in acts of barbarism which do not belong to a civilised age . . .*
>
> *I presume it will be among the early objects of Congress to recommence their collection. This will be difficult while the war continues and intercourse with Europe is attended with so much risk. You know my collection, its condition and extent. I have been fifty years making it, and have spared no pains, opportunity or expense to make it what it is . . . so that the collection, which I suppose is of between nine and ten thousand volumes, while it includes what is chiefly valuable in science and literature generally, extends more particularly to whatever belongs to the American statesman. In the parliamentary and diplomatic branches it is particularly full. It is long since I have been sensible it ought not to continue private property, and had provided that at my death, Congress should have the refusal of it at their own price. The loss they have now incurred, makes the present the proper moment for their accommodation, without regard to the small remnant of time and the barren use of my enjoying it. I ask of your friendship, therefore, to make for me the tender of it to the Library Committee of Congress . . .*[19]

A lengthy period of discussion and argument over the value of Jefferson's offer ensued, with intense debate on the relative merits of spending large sums of money on replacing the lost library, at a time when national resources were scarce and funds could be better spent for military purposes. The tenor of these arguments would be repeated many times in the library's history in succeeding centuries.

Jefferson's offer to supply 'the American statesman' with all that he needed (and these politicians were of course all male at the time) was fortuitous as it would have taken a long time and careful curation to either rebuild the original 3,000-volume collection or emulate Jefferson's 6,000 to 7,000-volume personal library. Jefferson was therefore offering a shortcut to a major library collection, one that had the added value of having been collected by one of the people that had built the governmental edifice of the new nation, using some of the very books now on offer as intellectual fuel for the project.

Jefferson's offer was not entirely altruistic, as he had considerable debts that he needed to clear. He also made it plain that he was supporting his countrymen in their hour of need while at the same time making sure his collection was sold en bloc, avoiding the 'cherry-picking' that many book collectors fear will happen when their collections are sold. 'I do not know that it contains any branch of science which Congress would wish to exclude from their collection; there is in fact no subject to which a member of Congress may not have occasion to refer,' he wrote to Smith, making it quite clear that it was an all or nothing deal.[20]

In October 1814 Congress began to consider in earnest the business of replacing their library and established a joint committee who sought an independent valuation to help them make an informed decision on Jefferson's proposal. They, and in November the Senate, proposed a bill 'to authorise the purchase of the library of Thomas Jefferson, late President of the United States', and in December this bill was passed.[21]

The House of Representatives, however, postponed their deliberations until January and the debates were lengthy and rancorous. The federalists were concerned that the collection betrayed Jefferson's atheistic and immoral tendencies. One of their politicians felt that the acquisition would 'bankrupt the Treasury, beggar the people, and disgrace the nation'. Other opposition related to the works of Enlightenment thinkers like John Locke and Voltaire, whose presence revealed Jefferson's objectionable 'atheism, immorality, effete intellectualism and infatuation with France'.[22] American newspapers covering these debates joined in on both sides, with the *American Register* predicting that 'the next generation will . . . blush at the objections made in Congress to the purchase of Mr Jefferson's library.'[23]

Those in favour of the acquisition saw it as an opportunity to begin a 'great national library'. They did not, perhaps, use this language in the sense that we might today understand the meaning of the term, but Jefferson's collection had the breadth and depth to begin that process even if, in the end, not all of his library was acquired. Madison signed the bill authorising the purchase on 30 January 1815, the House having passed it with a majority of just ten. The deal struck with Jefferson and passed in Washington involved the purchase of 6,487 books for the sum of $23,950.[24] At a stroke the Library of Congress became one of the largest and most sophisticated institutional libraries in North America, with the exception of Harvard College Library, which had between 30,000 and 40,000 volumes by 1829.[25] The Library of Congress more than doubled the size that it was before the fire and dramatically increased the range of subjects covered, acquiring the output of Enlightenment publishers from across Europe that were barely present in the 1812 catalogue.

Despite this wonderful injection of books, the Library of Congress remained small by comparison to other great libraries. The Library of Trinity College Dublin held over 50,000 books by 1802. Cambridge University Library held over 47,000 volumes following the accession of Bishop Moore's Library in 1715, and by 1814 it was considerably larger, perhaps approaching 90,000. Meanwhile, the catalogue of printed books in the British Museum (now the national library in all but name) was published in seven volumes between 1813 and 1819, listing about 110,000 volumes, in addition to manuscripts, maps and other materials, making it more than fifteen times the size of the Library of Congress.[26]

With the Jeffersonian library secured, the next challenge for Congress was to find a suitable home for the collection. At first, Congress, and the library, were housed in Blodget's Hotel while the original Capitol building was repaired and renovated. The books arrived from Monticello in May 1815; two months later they were unpacked and arranged according to a pared-down version of Jefferson's own classification scheme, based on systems for organising knowledge developed by the English Renaissance philosopher Francis Bacon and the French Enlightenment thinker d'Alembert.[27]

In March 1815, Madison appointed George Watterston as the first true Librarian of Congress. George Watterston was a writer, published poet, newspaper editor and trained lawyer. The idea of the collection being the nucleus of a 'national library' was one that really seems to have fired Watterston's imagination and he sent a notice to the *National Intelligencer* asking writers, artists and engravers to deposit their works. The paper thought that 'the Congressional or National Library of the United States [should] become the great repository of the literature of the world', and that it was the government's responsibility to provide 'a great reservoir of instruction . . . for the use of the public as well as its own members'. Other contemporary articles at the time echoed these sentiments. Although they don't compare America with other nations, the implication is clear, that America needed a national library to gather all the world's useful knowledge. The shadow of Alexandria was to be felt again in nineteenth-century America.

The first catalogue was published in the autumn of 1815, describing itself as the *Catalogue of the Library of the United States*. The joint committee increased the salary of the librarian and extended those able to use the library to the staff of the Attorney General and the diplomatic corps.[28] In 1817 there was the first of a series of attempts to provide the library with the copies deposited for copyright with the Secretary of State, and in the same year calls began to be made for a separate building to be constructed to house the library. These calls, however, were to remain unheeded for some time.

The process of deciding whether to acquire Jefferson's library raised the point that the congressional library was de facto the core of a national library, and made the link that the library of government should be the hub of a broader collection of more than purely utilitarian value for politicians and the bureaucrats that surrounded them. That said, the impetus that the fire provided for the idea of the national library of the United States was tediously slow to build and would in fact require another fire, this time accidental, to really gather momentum.

On Christmas Eve 1851 a fire took hold in a chimney of the library and more than half of the library's 55,000 books were destroyed, including most of the Jeffersonian library. The rebuilding of the library had to wait until the end of the American Civil War, and for the appointment of Ainsworth Rand Spofford as the sixth librarian of Congress by President Lincoln. Spofford saw clearly the trajectory for the library to become the national library, and was able to articulate his vision, increasing congressional funds for acquisitions, organising the transfer of the Library of the Smithsonian Institution, and most importantly finally securing the library as the place for the legal deposit of US publications in the Copyright Act of 1870.[29]

The destruction of the library by the British in 1814 was the act of one state against another. It was a deliberate political act designed to weaken the centre of politics and government. In that sense the episode has echoes of some of the attacks on knowledge in the ancient world. The response to the destruction of the Library of Congress proved as transformational to its history as the destruction of Oxford's library had been in the 1550s. The new Library of Congress would not just be larger than the one that had been destroyed, it would be a resource that better suited a country forged on modern ideas of what it meant to be a democratic, enlightened nation. It would take time to become established, but when it did it became a global leader in the preservation of knowledge, and helped to fuel with information and ideas the most powerful nation on earth.

Franz Kafka, Prague, 1906.

6

How to Disobey Kafka

K EY TO THE fate of knowledge is the idea of curation. The term has sacred beginnings. It means 'to look after' and as a noun it commonly refers to a priest who 'looks after' parishioners. Priests are said to have the 'cure of souls' or the spiritual care of their flock. Across many Christian denominations an assistant priest is still called a 'curate'. Curators in libraries or museums have the responsibility to look after the objects in their care. In the case of librarians this responsibility extends to the notion of knowledge itself: the intellectual material contained within the object. The act of curating can involve decisions about what to collect in the first place, and also how to collect; what to keep and what to discard (or destroy); what to make instantly available and what to keep closed for a period of time.

The decision of whether to destroy or preserve a personal archive may be crucial. Thomas Cromwell, in the 1530s, maintained a large archive of personal documents, mostly in the form of correspondence, which enabled him to exercise his duties for Henry VIII, a period where the administration of the country went through a massive process of modernisation. Cromwell's own archive was naturally well organised and extensive, but we know this only through the part of it that survives (now split between the National Archives and the British Library). Personal archives will naturally contain the incoming correspondence, but in the early modern period secretaries in households would also make copies of all of the outgoing correspondence as well, in order to maintain control over both sides of the flow of information; 'so meticulous a mind as Cromwell's would have made sure his letters were there, ready for reference in case of need.' The fact that only the incoming correspondence survives leads to the inevitable conclusion that 'such a vast loss of the out-tray can only be the result of deliberate destruction'.[1]

At the time of Cromwell's fall from grace in the eyes of Henry VIII, and his arrest in June 1540, his staff began to destroy the copies of their master's outgoing letters, in case they might incriminate him. Holbein's famous portrait of Cromwell shows him looking off to the left, almost in profile. There is a weight of seriousness and a severity about him. He is dressed in a black fur-lined coat and a black hat. His plain clothes offer no clue to his personality. Rather than wealth or privilege this picture displays his grasp of knowledge: he is literally clutching a legal document tightly in his left hand, and on the table in front of him is a book. It is not the room or Cromwell's clothes that display wealth and power, but this volume, with its gold-tooling on the leather covers: the book is even kept tight by two gilded clasps. The painter is showing us what Cromwell felt was truly important.

Cromwell's archive of outgoing correspondence was destroyed in a domestic setting – the office in his private home. The domestic environment still witnesses the destruction of knowledge on a daily basis. My wife and I have had to clear the home of a family member, uncovering letters, photographs and diaries. We had to make decisions about which of these should be destroyed, and there were a number of very valid and legitimate reasons for doing this, which countless other families have had to encounter. The content may be too inconsequential, or take up too much space to keep, or it may refer to episodes which bring back unhappy memories for surviving family members, or reveal new knowledge that descendants, discovering for the first time, may wish to hide for ever.

Such personal decisions are made every day, but occasionally the decisions made about the fate of documents may have profound consequences for society and culture, especially when the deceased is well known in public life. Those left behind after the death of a loved one sometimes have to make decisions about the fate of personal archival material – letters and diaries especially – that have subsequently had a major impact on literary history. These decisions have often been made to save the reputation of the deceased but also to save the reputation of those who remain. It is in this sense that I argue that these acts are actually 'political': that is, concerned with the exercise of power – power over the public reputation, and over what becomes public and what remains private.

Private diaries and journals are now, in the digital age, kept less often, but they were a great cultural phenomenon of the nineteenth and twentieth centuries. Correspondence is still a major feature of personal communication but this happens now predominantly through email and digital messaging: private correspondence can often be as revealing as the private journal or diary. The writer may also keep the early sketches, drafts and versions of their literary production, and these are equally valued by the scholars and critics attempting to understand the process of literary creation. Personal archives of this kind can also include other materials: financial records (such as account books, which shed light on the success or failure of various literary enterprises), photograph albums (which can show aspects of personal relationships which letters do not reveal), and ephemera of various kinds (theatre programmes or magazine subscriptions can be illuminating to literary scholars). The shelves of the Bodleian's special collections stacks are full of boxes of such fascinating material, and include some of our most popular collections – the papers of such figures as Mary and Percy Shelley, J. R. R. Tolkien, C. S. Lewis, W. H. Auden, Bruce Chatwin, Joanna Trollope and Philip Larkin, among many others.

The deliberate destruction of literary papers by the author is a kind of extreme self-editing. It is done with an eye to posterity. So too are the acts of defiance of those wishes. This notion that the future will take a critical view of the past is one that underpins much of the motivation for attacks on libraries and archives throughout history.

Writers have been tempted to destroy their own writings since the dawn of time. In antiquity, the Roman poet Virgil, so the account of his biographer Donatus goes, wanted to consign the manuscript of his great (but at this point unpublished) epic the *Aeneid* to the flames. As he lay dying in Brindisi, according to this account,

> he had proposed . . . that Varius [Virgil's great friend and poet] should burn the *Aeneid* if anything should happen to him, but Varius

said he would not do it. Thus in the last stages of his illness he constantly called for his book-boxes, meaning to burn it himself, but when no one brought them to him he took no specific measures about it.[2]

Later writers and scholars have interpreted this account in different ways. Some have viewed it as a supreme act of humility: Virgil saw no merit in his work and wanted to see it destroyed. Others have said that the decision was the darkly neurotic act of a man in torment, an act of supreme self-curation. A third interpretation views the event as part of the forming of a literary reputation by passing the decision into the hands of another, who takes on the role of 'curator'. In this case the patronage of Augustus is key to Virgil, as it was the Emperor of Rome himself who saved this great classic for the future, and with it Virgil's reputation.

These different interpretations can be applied to the decisions made about the manuscripts – and reputations – of much later writers. Lord George Gordon Byron, for example, was arguably the most famous writer of the early nineteenth century. 'Notorious' might be a better description of his reputation. As a young man he travelled extensively in the Mediterranean, falling in love especially with Greece, which he felt should be freed from Turkish dominion. He came to the attention of the literati with his *English Bards and Scotch Reviewers* (1809), which was a powerful work of satirical literary criticism in response to the hostile reviews of his juvenile volume of verse *Hours of Idleness* (1807). He continued to write poetry as he got older, the first serious volume of which was *Childe Harold's Pilgrimage*, a kind of literary journey in verse. The book was published in parts as Byron completed writing each canto. The first two cantos were published in 1812; he famously remarked following its publication, 'I awoke . . . and found myself famous.' He published more poetry including *The Bride of Abydos* (1813) and *The Corsair* (1814), but his masterpiece was *Don Juan* (the first two cantos of which were published in 1819). Byron's ill-fated marriage, in 1815, to Annabella Milbanke produced a daughter, the pioneering mathematician Ada, Countess of Lovelace (1815–52). (The Bodleian's archives include the correspondence between mother and daughter.) Byron's other daughter, Allegra, with Claire Clairmont, stepsister of Mary Shelley, died aged five of typhus or malaria.

Byron's lifestyle brought him celebrity status and invitations to elite circles in London, but his fame grew with his tempestuous affair with Lady Caroline Lamb and his alleged affair with his half-sister Augusta Leigh (with whom he was widely reputed to have fathered another child, Medora). In 1816, at the height of his notoriety, Byron left England for Europe, at first for Geneva (entertaining Percy and Mary Shelley in his villa at Cologny, on the shores of Lake Geneva, and where Mary created the Frankenstein story in a party game). After this sojourn at Cologny, one of the great literary sleepovers in history, Byron continued to travel around Italy with the Shelleys, and wrote and published poetry throughout. His friendship with Percy Shelley was a constant feature of this period, ending tragically when Shelley drowned on the way home from a visit to friends, after his beloved sailing boat, which he had begrudgingly named *Don Juan*, for Byron, got into difficulties during a storm off the coast of Viareggio.

All aspects of Byron's life became the subject of gossip and comment: even his pets – he accumulated a menagerie while in Italy: 'ten horses, eight enormous dogs, three monkeys, five cats, an eagle, a crow, and a falcon; and all these, except the horses, walk about the house, which every now and then resounds with their unarbitrated quarrels, as if they were the masters of it', according to Shelley.[3] Byron moved on to his beloved Greece in 1824, where he died later that year of fever. Such a creative, productive but sensational life made Byron immensely famous all over the world. His death was a source of grief among the writers and poets. Tennyson recalled later in life that 'I was fourteen when I heard of his death. It seemed an awful calamity; I remember I rushed out of doors, sat down by myself, shouted aloud, and wrote on the sandstone: BYRON IS DEAD!'[4]

His poetry was widely read in Germany, France and America, as well as in Britain, and despite his notoriety, and the scandal that surrounded him, his friends and literary admirers maintained a passionate loyalty, amounting almost to a cult. It was this cult status that was to have an effect on the treatment of his private papers.

All through Byron's career as an author, it was the London

publishing house of John Murray that brought his work to the public. Founded in 1768 by the first John Murray, there would be seven men of that name who would successively run the house until 2002 when it ceased to be a private publishing enterprise and became part of the Hachette group. Until the sale of the firm, the house was based in handsome premises at 50 Albemarle Street, just off London's Piccadilly. The building is still used for literary gatherings, and one can still climb the elegant but creaky staircase to the drawing room on the first floor, still panelled and lined with bookshelves. Above the fireplace is a portrait of Byron. When standing in this room, it feels as if the conversations between publisher and author have only just finished.[5]

John Murray II was a brilliant publisher, making good decisions about which authors to publish, and how to reflect and shape the mood of the times with the authors the firm established in the early nineteenth century. This list included James Hogg, Samuel Taylor Coleridge and Jane Austen. Murray's relationship with Byron was especially close, although subject to ups and downs, as the impecunious writer relied on the publisher for advice, support and funding. In 1819, in the midst of public controversy surrounding Byron's *Don Juan*, the writer gave a manuscript of his private memoirs to his friend Thomas Moore, an Irish writer then living in England, encouraging him to circulate it among any friends whom Moore considered 'worthy of it'. Those who read the memoirs at some point included Percy and Mary Shelley, the Irish poet Henry Luttrell, and novelist Washington Irving, as well as his friends such as Douglas Kinnaird and Lady Caroline Lamb. Knowing that Moore was seriously in debt, Byron later suggested that he sell the manuscript, to be published after Byron's death. In 1821 John Murray agreed to pay Moore an advance on the understanding that Moore would edit the memoirs for publication. Crucially, Murray took possession of the manuscript of the memoir itself.[6]

After Byron's death in Greece became known in London in May 1824, the memoirs began to take on a different status. The intimate circle of Byron's friends who had read them did not include members of his immediate family. Battle lines were soon drawn between those who thought the memoirs ought to be published and those (such as John Cam Hobhouse, one of Byron's friends, and John Murray) who thought that it would stir up such moral disgust in public opinion that Byron's reputation, and those of his surviving relatives, would be irreparably damaged. William Gifford, the editor of the influential *Quarterly Review*, thought them 'fit only for a brothel and would damn Lord Byron to certain infamy if published'.[7]

Those who did not object to publishing the memoirs may have been swayed by the financial gain that could be achieved. Moore attempted to renege on the arrangement with Murray, as he thought he could make more money by taking the manuscript to another publisher. John Cam Hobhouse knew that Moore was trying to publish it for maximum personal gain but felt that Byron's family should be the ones to decide whether to publish or not. Hobhouse was not alone. He wrote in his diary on 14 May 1824: 'I called on Kinnaird, [who] very generously wrote a letter to Moore offering him £2,000 at once in order to secure the MSS in whose hands it was, for the family of Lord Byron – that is to say, in order to destroy the same MSS.'[8] Douglas Kinnaird was another close friend of Byron, who had been given power of attorney by the poet, looking after his financial affairs after he left England for the last time in 1816. This letter put Moore in a difficult position and he began to waver from his position of seeking to publish the memoirs for his personal gain, suggesting that a 'chosen number of persons' would decide the fate of the manuscript. Murray also wanted the memoirs destroyed and Hobhouse urged him to go through his own correspondence with Byron and destroy any compromising letters. Fortunately for us, Murray resisted this urge.

The matter came to a head on Monday 17 May 1824. Moore and his friend Henry Luttrell attempted to appeal directly to the men managing the affairs of Byron's sister and his widow, Robert Wilmot-Horton and Colonel Frank Doyle. They had agreed to meet at 50 Albemarle Street, the residence of John Murray, at 11 a.m. The men gathered in the front drawing room and it wasn't long before personal insults were flying, with accusations of the honour of gentlemen being insulted, alongside the core issue regarding the fate of the manuscript. Eventually the document was brought into the room by Murray along with a copy that had been made by Moore. What exactly happened next is unclear but the manuscript was ultimately torn up and burned in the fire in the drawing room.

The burning must have taken some time, as it was at least 288 pages long (we know this because the binding of the copy survives, still with blank pages, which begin at page 289). The destruction, from the various accounts of the participants, was finally acceded to by Wilmot-Horton and Doyle, acting on behalf of Augusta and Annabella – although it seems not with their express permission. Although Murray was the legal owner of the manuscript, he made the destruction possible, and could have resisted it on his own (with or without Moore's own pleading).

Both Murray's and Hobhouse's motivations were probably mixed. Hobhouse, recently elected an MP, may well have been anxious to protect his own reputation from association with Byron. Both may have been jealous that the poet had entrusted Moore with the memoirs and not them. For Murray, there was also a heightened sense of his own status in society – by siding with Byron's family he may have been trying to portray himself as a gentleman rather than a tradesman. The weight of moral feeling would have been an equally forceful influence on Murray, but he had to weigh up the short-term commercial gain of publishing the memoirs against the potential damage that association with a morally dubious publication would bring. The publishing house of John Murray was still in its infancy. It would survive thanks to a mixture of prudence and taking risks. On this occasion, risk lost the day.[9] It says something about the power of his friends' concern for the future, and their need to control history, that no copy of Byron's memoirs has come to light since the original was burned in the grate of 50 Albemarle Street.

If Byron's friends took the ultimate curatorial decision to save his reputation by destroying his memoirs, such decisions can take a different turn, and the close friends of a writer can sometimes disobey the wishes of their friend. The writer Franz Kafka left very similar orders to those of Virgil to his executor Max Brod who, like Varius, decided to disobey his friend. Kafka is now regarded as one of the greatest and most influential writers of all time.

Franz Kafka had embarked on a career as a writer but had published relatively little by the time of his death in 1924. In the last year of his life, Kafka, plagued by tuberculosis, embarked on a serious relationship with a young woman, Dora Diamant, whom he had met in the German seaside resort of Graal-Müritz, where they had both attended a Jewish summer camp. Diamant fell in love with Kafka the person, and not Kafka the writer, and was apparently unaware that he had written *The Trial* (written originally in German as *Der Prozess*) until it was published posthumously in 1925. After a brief return to his home town of Prague, in September 1923, Kafka went to live for a time in Berlin, and was joined there by Diamant, where they set up home together in the suburb of Steglitz, to the dismay of their respective families, as they were unmarried. This period was a relatively contented one for Kafka, who was able to live an independent life away from his family and, despite his continued ill health, and the financial constraints of living in Berlin during a period of rampant inflation (he had only a modest pension, on which he was drawing early because of his illness), Kafka and Dora were, for a time, happy.

Kafka had only published a few pieces during his lifetime, including a collection of short stories, *The Country Doctor*, and these were not financially successful, bringing him only a very small income in the form of royalties from his publisher, Kurt Wolff. Given his relative obscurity as a writer, many people have found it puzzling to realise that Kafka was unhappy at the thought of his unpublished work surviving him and being seen by others. In 1921 and 1922 he had made a decision that all of his works should be destroyed, which he mentioned to his close friend and executor Max Brod in conversation but also in writing. Later in life, Brod recounted his reply: 'If you seriously think me capable of such a thing, let me tell you here and now that I shall not carry out your wishes.'[10]

Berlin, during the autumn of 1923, was cold and difficult to live in. With little money to live on, and with his fragile health declining, Kafka (and Diamant) had actually burned some of his notebooks together. At least this was the story that Diamant told Brod at the time of Kafka's death, referring mainly to the notebooks that were with them during their time together in Berlin. Kafka had a habit of taking a notebook with him when walking around the city, and of buying new ones when he forgot to take one. Diamant destroyed around twenty notebooks at his behest – so she told Brod. But these notebooks were actually safe in Diamant's bureau. She regarded them as her most important private possessions.[11] Tragically, in March 1933, the Gestapo seized all the papers in her possession. Despite repeated attempts to find them, these notebooks, some thirty-five letters from Kafka to Diamant and the only copy of the text of a fourth novel, have never been found and were probably destroyed.[12]

However, despite this instance of destruction, a great deal of his literary work survived, the bulk of it still in his parents' apartment in Prague, although Brod also found the covers of notebooks, their contents lost – presumably materials which were successfully destroyed by Kafka.

After his death, Brod pulled together Kafka's papers from the hospital near Vienna where he had died, and from the room in his parents' apartment in Prague where the writer had a desk. That process unearthed two notes from Kafka to Brod, which he published soon after Kafka's death. The first gave very clear and unambiguous instructions:

Dearest Max

My final request: Everything I leave behind . . . in the way of diaries, manuscripts, letters (from others and my own), sketches and so forth to be burned . . . unread as well as all writings and sketches you or others may have . . . If people choose not to give you letters, they should at least pledge to burn them themselves.

Yours, Franz Kafka[13]

Brod's gathering process also produced a second note, but this one complicated the clear and simple instruction found in the first:

Dear Max,

This time I really may not get up again, the onset of pneumonia is certainly likely after the month of pulmonary fever, and not even writing it down will keep it at bay, although the writing has a certain power.

In this case, then, my last will regarding all my writings:

Out of everything I have written, the only ones that count are these books: Judgement, Stoker, Metamorphosis, Penal Colony, Country Doctor, and the story Hunger Artist . . . When I say that those five books and the story count, I don't mean that I have any wish for them to be reprinted and passed on to the future; on the contrary, if they should disappear completely, it would be in accordance with my real wish. But since they're there, I'm not preventing anyone from keeping them if he wants to.

However, everything else of mine in writing . . . is without exception, insofar as it can be obtained or recovered from the recipients (you know most of the recipients, the main ones being Frau Felice M, Frau Julie née Wohryzek, and Frau Milena Pollak: and in particular don't forget the few notebooks that Frau Pollak has) – all this is without exception and preferably unread (I won't stop you from looking at it, I'd prefer if you didn't, but in any case nobody else must see it) – all this is without exception to be burned, and I ask you to do so as soon as possible.

Franz[14]

Although these instructions are clear, they presented Brod with a serious dilemma, one that challenged the principles of friendship. Their friendship was long-standing. They had met in 1902 as students in the Charles University in Prague. Their intellectual powers were unequal, but they developed a personal relationship, which was marked by Brod's devotion. He had an accomplished way of operating in the world which, combined with his admiration for his friend's literary brilliance, enabled him to become a kind of 'agent' as Kafka tried to develop a literary career. Kafka's poor health, his natural reticence and deep self-criticism would make this self-imposed task incredibly difficult. Despite these challenges, Brod would remain a constant friend, not only providing him with the encouragement necessary to see his literary work develop and appear in print, but also practical help in dealing with publishers.[15]

Brod's dilemma was therefore clear: should he follow the final wishes of his friend, or should he allow his literary work to survive and seek a wider audience, something that he knew would have pleased Kafka? In the end, Brod chose to disobey his friend. In his defence he argued that Kafka would have known that Brod could not have gone through with the decision – if he had been really serious, he would have asked someone else to destroy the papers.

Brod was determined to provide Kafka with the place in literary culture that he felt he deserved, but which he had never realised in his lifetime. Brod was also aware of what Larkin would later refer to as the 'magical' quality of the manuscripts, and would use them to help forge this literary reputation. One story (perhaps the word 'legend' is the better term to use with Kafka) from Georg Langer recalls the visit of a writer to Brod in Tel Aviv in the 1940s. The writer had come to see the manuscripts of Kafka but was thwarted by a power cut. Even though the power was eventually reinstated, Brod refused to repeat the opportunity for the writer to see the manuscripts. Brod's close guardianship of the archive, his efforts to get Kafka's works published, and the biography of Kafka that he brought out in 1937, had all helped to create an amazing literary aura around Kafka (at least, initially, in German-speaking literary circles).[16]

Brod edited and arranged for the Berlin publisher Die Schmiede to publish *The Trial* in 1925, and he edited an unfinished work which Kafka's original publisher Kurt Wolff would issue as *The Castle* (in German *Der Schloss*) in 1926. The novel *America* (*Amerika*) would also appear in 1927 having been 'completed' by Brod from Kafka's working papers. Other works would follow that required more substantial editorial selection and compilation, from Kafka's diaries and letters, all of which was only possible because Brod had the physical objects in his possession. They did not take up much space, but they provided an entire career to be created in posthumous form, establishing Kafka's reputation as one of the greatest writers of modern times, but also providing Brod with an income and fame of his own.

English translations began to appear from 1930, the work of the Scottish literary couple Edwin and Willa Muir. Among the early readers in English were Aldous Huxley and W. H. Auden, both enthusiastic proponents of Kafka's writing. They followed a list of European writers, especially Walter Benjamin and Berthold Brecht, who helped to build Kafka's reputation in the interwar years. Had Brod not disobeyed his friend and destroyed the Kafka archive the world would have been deprived of one of the most original and influential literary voices of the twentieth century.

The Kafka archive has survived numerous dangers since Brod's act of preservation in 1924. In 1938, with the Nazis poised to enter the city and impose their reign of anti-Semitism, Brod was on one of the last trains to leave the city, with suitcases full of papers. In the 1960s, with the Arab–Israeli conflict bringing the risk of bombing to the city where Kafka's papers were being stored, Brod decided to move them to a bank vault in Switzerland. They rest now, largely, in three locations – the bulk of them in the Bodleian Library in Oxford, with other substantial portions in the Deutsches Literatur Archiv in Marbach, Germany, and others in the National Library of Israel in Jerusalem. All three institutions are working together, dedicated to the preservation and sharing of Kafka's extraordinary literary legacy.

The ethics of making decisions about the 'curation' of great literary works are complex and difficult. The deliberate destruction of Thomas Cromwell's outgoing letters was a planned act of political expedience to protect him and his staff. But as a result, our understanding of a key historical figure has been dramatically reduced (until Hilary Mantel filled the gap with a mixture of imagination and research in her trilogy of novels). The burning of Byron's memoirs may well have saved his devoted readership from shock and disgust at the time, but over the centuries the mystique of that lost work may well have added to his reputation as a writer ahead of his time, one whose life was as important as his work. The saving of Kafka's archive has taken much longer to serve as an aid to his reputation. Only in relatively recent years has Brod's curatorial decision been celebrated as a major contribution to the preservation of world culture. Imagine our culture without *The Trial* or *Metamorphosis*? We sometimes need the bravery and foresight of 'private' curators like Max Brod to help ensure the world has continued access to the great works of civilisation.

Louvain University Library before the burning in 1914.

7

The Twice-Burned Library

E XACTLY A CENTURY after the burning of Washington another invading army encountered a library, and saw it as a perfect way to strike a blow at the heart of their enemy. This time the action would have a global impact, as the means of spreading news had been transformed in the century since the burning of the Library of Congress troubled the young George Gleig. The burning of the library of Louvain University (known then as the Université catholique de Louvain) in 1914 by the invading German army would be the focus of profound political outrage; unlike the Washington incident, the fate of the library would figure as an international cause célèbre. Young Louvain Jesuit Eugène Dupiéreux wrote in his journal in 1914:

> Until today I had refused to believe what the newspapers said about the atrocities committed by the Germans; but in Leuven I have seen what their *Kultur* is like. More savage than the Arabs of Caliph Omar, who burnt down the Alexandrian library, we see them set fire, in the twentieth century, to the famous University Library.[1]

Louvain University was the earliest university to be established in the country that is today known as Belgium. Founded in 1425, the university had educated a number of great minds, including the theologian Saint Robert Bellarmine, the philosopher Justus Lipsius and the cartographer Gerard Mercator. The university was comprised of separate colleges (by the end of the sixteenth century there were forty-six of them), each of which had built up book collections during the Middle Ages, with the result that no central library existed until the foundation of the central university library in 1636. This library grew over the succeeding century and a half, its collections increasing in size through purchase and donation. Louvain was a comparatively rich university and its riches helped the development of the library. In the late seventeenth century a new approach to shelving, recently established in France, was adopted with bookcases fitted against the walls of the library, with windows above, as opposed to the old medieval and Renaissance fashion of bookcases projecting out from the walls into the library room. Between 1723 and 1733 a new library building was constructed, and as the eighteenth century progressed the wealth of the university meant that it could acquire collections beyond those needed for the immediate use of the scholars. This development was given a strong boost by the allocation to the library of the national privilege of legal deposit in 1759 by Charles Alexander of Lorraine, the governor general of the Low Countries (who also allocated the privilege to the Bibliothèque Royale in Brussels).[2] A few years later the library was the beneficiary of the forced closure of a neighbouring library – the suppression of the Jesuit order in 1773 allowed the library to purchase books from the library of the Jesuit house in the city (the books from the Louvain Jesuits are now dispersed across the world and continue to appear in the antiquarian book trade).[3]

The university suffered during the late eighteenth and early nineteenth centuries as the French Revolutionary Wars spread into Europe. Louvain's faculties were forcibly relocated to Brussels in 1788–90, and the university was formally suppressed in 1797, and then refounded in 1816. Almost 10 per cent of the books in the library – more than 800 volumes of incunabula (books printed before 1501), illustrated editions, and Greek and Hebrew books – were forcibly removed to Paris in 1794–5 by officials of the Bibliothèque Mazarine (a fate that befell other libraries in the region, including the Bibliothèque Royale). Other books were cherry-picked by the librarian of the École Centrale in Brussels.

The university and its library were temporarily closed again by the revolution of 1830, which created the Belgian nation. The university reopened in 1835 as the Catholic University and the library became a symbol of national renewal, an engine for intellectual and social power and a crucial element in cementing the university's new role in the Belgian national consciousness. It was also made a public library, one of three (with Liège and Ghent) in Belgium, but regarded as the greatest.[4]

By 1914 the library at Louvain had over three hundred thousand volumes in its collection, and a group of special collections of international quality. The importance of the library could be seen in its glorious baroque buildings. Its holdings reflected Belgian cultural identity, documenting the intellectual contribution of the greatest minds of the region, and preserving the university's strongly Catholic cultural flavour. It was also a national resource, as a library of legal deposit and open to the general public. There were almost a thousand volumes of manuscripts, mostly classical authors and theological texts, including the Church Fathers, and medieval philosophy and theology. It also held a sizeable collection of incunabula and uncatalogued collections of oriental books, and manuscripts in Hebrew, Chaldaic and Armenian. The university librarian before the First World War, Paul Delannoy, embarked on modernisation from the time of his appointment in 1912, as by that point the library had become organisationally behind the trend in academic librarianship, and the reading rooms were quiet. He began to sort out backlogs of cataloguing and to acquire new research collections, taking a more contemporary grip on the organisation of the institution, a process that was dramatically halted on the night of 25 August 1914. Just as at the Library of Congress the destruction that followed would be catastrophic, but would also eventually allow a great leap forward to take place.

German troops arrived in Louvain on 19 August 1914, having violated Belgian neutrality in marching through the country en route for France, and for about a week the town functioned as the headquarters of the German First Army. The Belgian civilian authorities had confiscated any weapons held by ordinary Belgian citizens in advance, warning them that only the Belgian army was authorised to take any action against German forces. Modern scholars of the First World War have failed to find any evidence of popular insurrection against the Germans. On 25 August there was a series of atrocities in Louvain, possibly triggered by a group of German troops who, in a state of panic, fired on some of their own troops. That night the reprisals began. Belgian civilians were forcibly removed from their homes and summarily executed – including the mayor and the rector of the university. Around midnight German troops entered the university library and set it on fire using petrol.

The entire building and almost all of its collections – modern printed books and journals as well as the great collections of manuscripts and rare books – were destroyed. Although Germany had been a signatory to the Hague Convention of 1907, which stated in Article 27 that 'in sieges and bombardments all necessary steps must be taken to spare, as far as possible, buildings dedicated to religion, art, science, or charitable purposes', the German generals remained hostile to its spirit, especially to the sense that war could be codified.

The Hague Convention would eventually incorporate much stronger sanctions for acts of violence against cultural property, but its power in the First World War was still relatively weak. The burning of Louvain University Library, and the response to it from the international community, would help change this, not least by the inclusion of a separate clause in the Treaty of Versailles dealing with the reconstruction of the library.

On 31 August the *Daily Mail* reported 'A crime against the world', stating that Germany could not be forgiven 'so long as the world retains a shred of sentiment'.[5] The leading British intellectual Arnold Toynbee felt that the Germans had deliberately targeted the intellectual heart of the university, without which it could not carry on its work. The French Catholic newspaper *La Croix* felt that the Barbarians had burned Louvain.[6] The German view, echoing the excuses given by the British army in Washington in 1814, was that there was civilian resistance in the city, with sniper fire on German troops, which triggered the atrocities.

In the immediate aftermath, Kaiser Wilhelm II of Germany sent a telegram to the American President – no doubt fearful that the incident might encourage the Americans to join the Allies – arguing that the German army had merely responded to attacks from the civilian population of the city. On 4 October 1914, following accusations of war crimes, a group of ninety-three prominent German artists, writers, scientists and intellectuals published a manifesto concerning the events in Louvain. It was entitled 'An appeal to the world of culture' and was signed by some of Germany's most prominent cultural leaders including Fritz Haber, Max Liebermann and Max Planck. They wrote: 'It is not true that our troops treated Louvain brutally. Furious inhabitants having treacherously fallen upon them in their quarters, our troops were obliged, their hearts aching, to fire a part of the town as a punishment.'[7] The controversy over the cause of the library's destruction has continued for over a century. In 2017, the German art historian Ulrich Keller laid the blame for the devastation once again at the feet of the Belgian resistance.

Romain Rolland, the French writer and intellectual who was a great admirer of German culture, wrote in puzzled indignation to the *Frankfurter Zeitung* in September 1914, addressing his words to his fellow writer Gerhard Hauptmann, calling on him and other German intellectuals to reconsider their position: 'how do you wish to be referred to from now on if you reject the title "Barbarian"? Are you Goethe's or Attila's descendant?' Hauptmann's response was unequivocal: better to live as Attila's descendants than have 'Goethe's descendants' written on their tomb.[8]

Not all Germans felt this way. Adolf von Harnack, director of the Royal Prussian Library in Berlin (now the Staatsbibliothek zu Berlin), a great biblical scholar in his own right, and one of the signatories of the 'manifesto of the 93', wrote to the Prussian minister of culture to suggest appointing a German official in occupied Belgium to ensure that libraries would not be damaged in the rest of the war. The proposal was accepted and in late March 1915 Fritz Milkau, director of the University Library in Breslau (now Wrocław in Poland), was sent to Brussels to take on this role. Milkau brought with him such people as a young reservist soldier who was librarian of the University of Bonn, called Richard Oehler, and they visited 110 libraries in Belgium discussing conservation and protection.[9]

The fourth anniversary of the destruction of Louvain University Library was marked by a commemoration held in the French port of Le Havre, the seat of the exiled Belgian government. The government officials were joined by representatives of the Allies who made up a diverse group including an envoy of the King of Spain and a delegate from Yale University. Public messages of support were sent from across the world as the mood of sympathy for Belgium shifted emphasis from outrage to support for rebuilding.

In the UK the John Rylands Library in Manchester was one of the most visible and generous of the libraries that felt deep empathy with the losses of Louvain. In December 1914 the governors of the library decided to donate some of their duplicates to Louvain in order to 'give some practical expression to the deep feelings of sympathy with the authorities of the University of Louvain in the irreparable loss which they have suffered through the barbarous destruction of the University buildings and the famous library'. They earmarked 200 books, which they felt would be the 'nucleus of the new library'. The John Rylands offered not only their own books but also to collect books donated for Louvain from private and public collections in the UK.

Henry Guppy, director of the John Rylands, was the driving force behind British support for Louvain. He issued a pamphlet in 1915 reporting an 'encouraging' response to the public appeal for donations of books coming from as far afield as the Auckland Public Library in New Zealand. In fact, Guppy's efforts were remarkable. In July 1925 the final shipment of books to Louvain was made, bringing the total to 55,782, which took twelve shipments to transfer and represented around 15 per cent of the books that were lost in the destruction of August 1914. The authorities in Manchester were enormously proud of their efforts, demonstrating that the plight of Louvain University Library touched ordinary members of the public far removed from Belgium.

As the war ended the international effort to rebuild the library moved up several gears. This process was aided by the special inclusion of the library in Article 247 of the Treaty of Versailles (28 June 1919): 'Germany undertakes to furnish the University of Louvain . . . manuscripts, incunabula, printed books, maps, and objects of collection corresponding in number and value to those destroyed in the burning by Germany of the Library of Louvain.'[10]

America too saw an opportunity to support the international effort to help Louvain rebuild its library, not just to show cultural and intellectual solidarity but as an opportunity to convey 'soft power'. Nicholas Murray Butler, the president of Columbia University, was very active in leading the American initiatives, and the University of Michigan at Ann Arbor sent books. In October 1919 Cardinal Mercier, the Archbishop of Mechelen and Primate of Belgium who had led the Belgian people in resistance to German occupation, visited Ann Arbor to receive an honorary doctorate of laws. His bravery during the war was cited in the presentation, which was made in a hall packed with over five thousand members of the university, and in response the Belgian cardinal was at pains to thank the 'boys' of America who had fought for the freedom of his country. After the Belgian National Anthem and the 'Battle Hymn of the Republic' were sung a book was presented to Cardinal Mercier. The book was full of symbolism. It was an edition of the Boethius text *De consolatione philosophiae* (The consolation of philosophy), which had been printed in Louvain in 1484 by a German printer, Johannes de Westfalia, who had come from Paderborn and Cologne to establish the first printing house in the Low Countries.

The irony of this particular vignette from history was not lost on the academic community at Ann Arbor. A Latin inscription was inserted into the book, which read: 'I was printed in the University of Louvain by a certain German who there received most kindly hospitality. After many years I travelled across the Atlantic Ocean, to another land, where I happily escaped the destiny which was so mercilessly visited on my companions by the Germans'. This particular edition was one of the 300 incunabula, which was part of the Louvain collection before the destruction of the library, and was therefore chosen to replace a particularly precious lost item.[11]

The architecture of the new library, which the Americans took it on themselves to raise the funds for, was to look to the past and not the future. The style of the new building chimed closely with the traditional vernacular of the Low Countries, particularly of the Flemish 'renaissance' of the seventeenth century. But the library was to be big: enough space for 2 million books and influenced by the latest thinking in design for research libraries, especially those in American Ivy League universities such as Columbia, Harvard and Yale. The cultural politics at play over the renewal of the library were to be expressed in the decoration of the structure. Over the main entrance was to be a statue of the Virgin Mary, acknowledging the Catholicism of the city, while two coats of arms would bear the heraldry of Belgium and the United States.[12]

The laying of the foundation stone in 1921 was similarly symbolic of this new Belgo-American relationship. Although the ceremony was attended by representatives of twenty-one countries and presided over by the King and Queen of Belgium, various cardinals and Marshal Pétain, the American involvement would take centre stage.

The president of Columbia University and the American Ambassador to Brussels read a message of goodwill from President Harding. Henry Guppy's view was that 'This was America's Day.'[13] Eight years later, on 4 July 1928 – the American Day of Independence – the official ceremony of inauguration of the newly rebuilt Louvain University Library was held. The American flag was prominent on stage and speeches were made by the American Ambassador, the chairman of the American committee to restore the library, representatives of the French committee and Cardinal Mercier. As if the American presence wasn't already overshadowing the Belgian, a statue of President Herbert Hoover was unveiled during the ceremony, to honour his support of the project. The rebuilding of the library would become a major source of diplomatic tension between America and Belgium, and helped to generate the isolationism in foreign policy that would dominate American politics in the 1930s.

Despite these grand celebrations the completion of the renovation had become a pressure point for America throughout the 1920s, as the project became symbolic of American prestige in Europe. By 1924 the problems of funding were becoming visible in the media, the New York Times describing the rebuilding of the library as 'A promise unfulfilled' in an editorial in November that year. The following month Nicholas Murray Butler dissolved his Louvain committee and passed the task on to Herbert Hoover, then US Secretary of State for Commerce. With other commentators in the United States bemoaning the failure to complete the library as a national disgrace, John D. Rockefeller Jr reluctantly pledged $100,000 towards it, seeing it as a patriotic duty rather than sharing any enthusiasm for the project. By December 1925 the funds had finally been found and the reconstruction of the half-finished library could recommence.[14]

A further issue then rose to the surface. The epigraphy planned for the building by its American architect, Whitney Warren – 'Furore Teutonico Diruta, Dono Americano Restituta' (the Latin is straightforward to understand: 'Destroyed by German fury, rebuilt by American donations') – had been conceived before the shift in political fault lines in Europe at the end of the 1920s. The sentiment of this inscription no longer seemed appropriate. Nicholas Murray Butler in particular began to have reservations about the wisdom of the inscription; he took up a new role that year as president of the Carnegie Endowment for International Peace, a philanthropic organisation much concerned with the role of libraries in post-war reconciliation in Europe. A battle in the pages of American newspapers now ensued between Warren and Butler, and this soon spread to Europe. It became a diplomatic and public relations issue, which exacerbated strong anti-American feelings in Europe following the 1927 execution of Sacco and Vanzetti, two Italian anarchists who were seen to be victims of unfair anti-European immigrant views prevalent in America. The battle over the inscription continued to the days immediately preceding the ceremony (on 4 July 1928) to mark the completion of the building. Warren, supported by Belgian nationalists, refused to change the inscription. The university authorities, backed by US government officials, refused to allow it to go up, and instead placed a blank space on the walls of the library. Lawsuits were filed by Warren in the following two years and the issue remained in the news on both sides of the Atlantic, with the blank facade defaced by Belgian nationalists on two occasions. In the end in 1936 the original inscription was placed on a war memorial in Dinant, and the issue over the library finally stopped being news, and both the Americans and the university authorities in Louvain breathed a sigh of relief.[15]

This peace would sadly be short-lived. Not only would the lesson of Louvain not be learned in the aftermath of the First World War, it would have to be taught again in the second. On the night of 16 May 1940, almost twenty-six years after the first destruction of the library, the reconstructed building was again mostly destroyed, and again it was the German armed forces that targeted and bombed it.

In *The Times* on 31 October 1940, in an article headed 'Louvain Again', the paper's Belgian correspondent reported that 'The Germans declare that it was the British who set fire to it this time, but nobody in Belgium has any doubt about the German guilt.' A German investigation committee conducted by Professor Kellemann of Aix-la-Chapelle (Aachen), which had discovered tins in the basement originating from the Far East, alleged that they had been packed with gasoline by the British who then set them off by detonating three grenades. It was reported in the *New York Times* on 27 June 1940 from Berlin as providing 'conclusive proof' that the destruction of the library was a British plot.[16]

The president of Columbia University, Nicholas Murray Butler, who had been so involved with the reconstruction, received a harrowing letter from the university librarian at Louvain:

> I am indeed grieved having to tell you that the library was nearly completely gutted by fire; that the fine stack rooms at the back, housing our precious collections, are no more and that only terribly twisted and molten girders remain of it. It is painful to behold . . . gone also the collection of incunabula, manuscripts, medals, precious china, silk flags, and catalogues. Practically, we have to start again at the bottom.[17]

The *Daily Mail* blamed the Germans as 'guilty of the crime of destroying the ancient library of Louvain' in an article by Emrys Jones in December 1940, following incendiary air attacks on London, and for them it was one of the acts by 'The Great Arsonists' of world history, alongside the destruction of the Cloth Hall at Ypres and the Cathedral of Rheims. It is as hard to prove the attack was deliberately aimed at the library in 1940 as it had been in 1914. The American-designed building, which had been claimed to be fireproof, did not protect the library's collections. Only 20,000 books are known to have survived the bombing, and another restoration effort was established to rebuild the library, which was reopened in 1950.[18]

The case of the double destruction of the library in the twentieth century is one that invoked, on both occasions, the sense of cultural loss epitomised by the destruction of the Library of Alexandria. The loss of the collection was more than the loss of great treasures – and the intellectual value of the destroyed treasures has been played down by some scholars who instead emphasise the national and civic pride embodied in the library – it was for many Belgians their 'bibliothèque de famille'.[19]

Like the Library of Congress, which was also destroyed twice within a few decades, the acts of reconstruction at Louvain were more than symbolic. Both libraries put huge efforts into remaking buildings, rebuilding collections of books and manuscripts that would be used and reused over successive generations, and perhaps more importantly allowing ways of working to be reconceived. The German army may have seen attacking the library as an opportunity to inflict psychological damage on their enemy, and in the short-term they were successful. The long-term result had the opposite effect. The library is very different today from the institution that was rebuilt in the 1920s and again in the 1940s and 1950s. Although the university was divided into two during the 1970s, with one speaking French, the other Flemish, the library of the KU Leuven (as it is known today) is an important hub for learning and educa-tion in one of Europe's leading universities, helping Belgium stay at the forefront of the knowledge economy of Europe.

The shock of the loss of the library was the focus of the world in 1914, and to a lesser extent in 1940, but its story has slipped from public consciousness over the subsequent decades. The Holocaust would set a new standard for public disgust and outrage; the burning of individual libraries pales in comparison with the murder of millions. In both Belgium and Germany, however, public opinion is still preoccupied with the events in Louvain in 1914 and 1940; one community still feels a sense of guilt and responsibility, another continues to try to understand the motivations for what happened.

YIVO materials being unpacked in New York, 1947.

8

The Paper Brigade

THE PERSECUTION OF the Jews of Europe under the Nazi regime fell with terrifying force not just on the People of the Book (as Jews have self-identified for thousands of years) but also on their books. It has been estimated that over 100 million books were destroyed during the Holocaust, in the twelve years from the period of Nazi dominance in Germany in 1933 up to the end of the Second World War.[1]

Books have always been central to Jewish religion and culture. At the heart of Jewish life is a particular book, the Torah (normally a scroll form), the most important in Jewish life, so much so that when Jerusalem fell to the Romans in CE 70, one of the Torah scrolls kept in the Temple of Jerusalem was paraded by the victorious Emperor Titus through the streets of Rome as a symbol of their victory. A myriad other books have immense significance in the life of Jews and, traditionally in Jewish culture, true wealth was measured in books – it was charity to loan them – and many special laws grew up around the treatment of books, ranging from the way parchment must be treated to make Torah scrolls, to the specifics of handling sacred books: for example, they must never be held upside down, or left open unless being read. Jews have had the preservation of knowledge written into their laws for millennia. The best-known expression of this compulsion to preserve is the *genizah*, which exists in synagogues all over the Jewish world. Derived from the Persian term *ganj* meaning 'hoard' or 'hidden treasure', genizahs are storerooms for the holding of scraps of texts which contain the written word of God; these words are treated in Jewish law as if they are living and when they become worn out they must be honoured appropriately. Normally genizahs take the form of small cupboards but, occasionally, as in the genizah

of the Ben Ezra synagogue in Fustat, in Cairo, they were maintained over centuries as vast stores. When the Cairo genizah was
dispersed at the end of the nineteenth century and the beginning
of the twentieth, it was found to contain hundreds of thousands
of scraps of books and documents dating back to the seventh and
eighth centuries, an astonishing archive of Jewish culture now
preserved in libraries around the world (including the Bodleian).[2]

Jewish books were not only publicly destroyed on many occasions,
but the subject of deliberate acts of theft and confiscation, as an
attempt to chart and understand the culture that the Nazi state
sought to eradicate. Along with this mass destruction of books there
were acts of preservation by communities and individuals who risked
(and sometimes lost) their lives to save the most important physical
form of their culture: the book.

The book-burning events of May 1933 took some time to escalate,
partly because of the negative international reaction to the book-
burnings. Writers were in the vanguard of those speaking out against
the burnings and signalling them as a warning sign. The deaf-blind
writer Helen Keller published a 'Letter to the Student Body of
Germany': 'You can burn my books and the books of the best
minds in Europe, but the ideas in them have seeped through a
million channels and will continue to quicken other minds.'[3] The
writer H. G. Wells (whose books had also been burned) spoke out
against 'the Clumsy Lout's revolution against thought, against sanity,
and against books' in September 1933, wondering 'where it would
take Germany'.[4]

In fact two new libraries were formed as a counterblast. A year
later, on 10 May 1934, the Deutsche Freiheitsbibliothek (German
Freedom Library, also known as the German Library of Burnt
Books) was opened in Paris. The German Freedom Library was
founded by German-Jewish writer Alfred Kantorowicz, with support
from other writers and intellectuals such as André Gide, Bertrand
Russell and Heinrich Mann (the brother of the German writer
Thomas Mann), and rapidly collected over 20,000 volumes, not just
the books which had been targeted for burning in Germany but
also copies of key Nazi texts, in order to help understand the
emerging regime. H. G. Wells was happy to have his name associated with the new library. The library became a focus for German

émigré intellectuals and organised readings, lectures and exhibitions, much to the disgust of German newspapers. Following the fall of Paris to the Germans in 1940 the library was broken up, with many of the volumes joining the collections of the Bibliothèque Nationale de France.[5] The Brooklyn Jewish Center in New York established an American Library of Nazi-Banned Books in December 1934, with noted intellectuals on its advisory board, including Albert Einstein and Upton Sinclair. The library was proclaimed as a means of preserving and promoting Jewish culture at a time of renewed oppression.[6]

The 10 May 1933 book-burning was merely the forerunner of arguably the most concerted and well-resourced eradication of books in history.[7] Although the quantity of books destroyed in this early phase was not huge (and may have been overestimated), the psychological impact was devastating, and following these events many Jews left Germany altogether.[8] The steady increase in anti-Semitic attacks continued as first Austria, and then the Sudetenland in Czechoslovakia were annexed by Germany. Attacks on books were an essential element of this campaign. As the burnings continued, various Nazi groups began to compile lists of undesirable authors (which included communists and homosexuals as well as Jews). The library sector was not immune to the appeal of Nazism, and one leading German librarian, Wolfgang Herrmann, compiled a list of banned authors that became influential throughout Germany, as did Alfred Rosenberg (who would become Reich Minister for the Occupied Eastern Territories), whose views on culture and ideas were important to Hitler and other leading Nazis. Such lists, enforced by the police and the Sturmabteilung (the Nazi Party's paramilitary wing), were used by the Propaganda Ministry under Joseph Goebbels to stir up anti-Jewish hatred, resulting in bookshops, libraries and private dwellings being purged of undesirable books. The banned booklists were seeds that landed on fertile soil in the aftermath of the First World War and the economic collapse of the 1920s. The rise of Nazism was supported by all sectors of society, and student groups were encouraged by Herrmann in particular to purge both their local lending libraries and their university libraries of the titles on these lists. Whipping up the hatred, Herrmann described the German lending libraries as 'literary bordellos'. At a conference of

German librarians in 1933 one speaker actively spoke in favour of the book-burnings and seizure of works by Jewish and left-wing writers.[9]

German society became intoxicated with Nazism, with the world of books, ideas and knowledge fully complicit in this phenomenon. As anti-Jewish laws continued to be passed, attacks on synagogues increased and many Jewish religious libraries were destroyed. The destruction became an integral part of the Holocaust, the most extreme example of organised cultural annihilation. On 10 November 1938, Reinhard Heydrich, the architect of the 'Final Solution', pointedly referred to the confiscation of Jewish archives in a telegram issued to the Nazi Party on the eve of Kristallnacht called 'Massnahmen gegen Juden in der heutigen Nacht' ('Measures against Jews tonight'). A process of targeting archives of knowledge for destruction then intensified: 'existing archive material must be confiscated by the police in all synagogues and business premises of the Jewish religious communities so that it is not destroyed in the course of the demonstrations . . . The archive material must be handed over to the responsible departments of the Sicherheitsdienst [Security Service]'.[10]

In 1939, at the outbreak of the Second World War, the Gestapo began a systematic programme of confiscation, but the motivations for seizing Jewish archival collections were split between confiscation and destruction. The Gestapo's work was superseded by a quasi-academic body, given official status, staff and funding, called the Institut zur Erforschung der Judenfrage (Institute for Study of the Jewish Question). Based in Frankfurt am Main, this body, which officially opened in 1941, was led by Alfred Rosenberg, the leading strategist for anti-Semitism.[11] The institute was intended to investigate the details of Judaism and its history as a religion, and its impact on European political affairs. At the heart of the institute's work was the accumulation of a massive collection of books and manuscripts in Hebrew or other Semitic languages and of books about Judaism.[12]

The institute worked alongside an organisation that operated in the field, the Einsatzstab Reichsleiter Rosenberg.[13] The Einsatzstab (a German term meaning 'operational group') had two principal tasks: the collection of material for the institute and the destruction of 'excess' material. Much of the leadership of this organisation was left to Dr Johannes Pohl, who had studied biblical archaeology in Jerusalem (1932–4), and who had been a Catholic priest for a time before becoming a member of the National Socialist Party. Pohl left the priesthood, married, and became the curator of Hebraica and Judaica in the Staatsbibliothek zu Berlin (the Berlin State Library), a position made possible by the forced expulsion of the previous curator, Arthur Spanier who was Jewish. Pohl's motivations are unclear but after he left the priesthood his views became violently anti-Semitic. He began to publish anti-Semitic articles in German newspapers and magazines, using his expertise in the Hebrew language and Jewish studies, for example, to expatiate on the dangers of the Talmud (the central text of Jewish law). In 1941 Pohl moved to Frankfurt to head the Jewish section of Rosenberg's institute.[14] By April 1943, Rosenberg's institute held over 550,000 volumes seized from the renowned Jewish collection of Frankfurt's City Library, and from libraries in France, the Netherlands, Poland, Lithuania and Greece. This process was well documented thanks to the institute's attention to detail and the regime's desire for orderly, well-documented bureaucracy.[15]

During the second half of 1941, with the launch of the Eastern Front, the Nazi regime shifted from persecution of the Jews to their destruction. As the German war machine rolled over Poland, Russia and the Baltic states the Jews became major targets for genocide. Various organisations devoted to enforcing extreme anti-Jewish policies moved behind the Blitzkrieg.[16]

In many ways the mass murder of the Jews by the Nazis was not a new phenomenon. For centuries, the Jewish peoples of Europe had suffered oppression, largely at the hands of the Christian communities they lived among. Waves of persecution had forced Jews to move from country to country: they had been expelled from England in the twelfth century and from Spain in the fifteenth. In other parts of Europe the levels of acceptance of Jews waxed and waned. In 1516 the Venetian authorities forced the Jews of their city to live in a constrained area, known as the Ghetto, from where we derive the term.

Censorship of Jewish books grew during the period 1500–1700:

for example, copies of the Talmud were ordered to be burned by papal edict in 1553.[17] The following year the first Catholic *Index Librorum Prohibitorum* ('Index of Prohibited Books') was printed in Venice in 1554. This list included more than a thousand condemnations of authors and their works, including the complete works of 290 mostly Protestant authors, ten of the works of Erasmus as well as the compilation of Jewish laws known as the Talmud.[18] In recent years scholars have begun to discover leaves from medieval Hebrew manuscripts that had been used by Christian bookbinders as waste material to cover registers of medieval documents in cities such as Cremona, Pavia and Bologna, the original Hebrew manuscript books having been confiscated.[19] Central and eastern European countries also persecuted the Jews, and periodically imposed censorship, triggered by the Reformation debates in the early sixteenth century. The Jews of Frankfurt, for example, had their books seized in 1509 and 1510, thanks to the efforts of Johannes Pfefferkorn (1468/9–1521), a religious controversialist, who had been raised a Jew but converted to Catholicism, then dedicated himself to the suppression of Jewish publications in the Catholic German states.[20] Further east, pogroms (organised massacres) became a familiar part of the suffering of the Jews (known as Ashkenazi Jews) living in the Pale of Settlement, the circumscribed area of the western parts of the Russian Empire (including what is today Ukraine, Belorussia, the Baltic states, parts of Poland, as well as western Russia), where the Jews were allowed to settle from 1791–1917.[21]

Despite their persecution, communities of Jews, whether in ghettos or living more freely, were able to thrive. Within eastern and central European culture, Hebrew and Yiddish were the languages of the Jews. Hebrew was used for religious services and rituals and Yiddish (originally a dialect of High German) served for everyday communication. As Hebrew was also the preferred language for intellectual culture, Yiddish was not even regarded as a 'proper' language by many Jews throughout the world, and the same went for the culture that coexisted alongside the Yiddish language. Yiddish had, however, by the early twentieth century become the native language of approximately 11 million people – roughly three-quarters of the world's Jewish population – and was already a language with centuries of historical development and tradition.[22] As the vernacular language of the majority of eastern European Jewry, Yiddish was more than a language, it was an entire culture and a way of life.

At the end of the nineteenth century a broad movement began that recognised the importance of Jewish culture in eastern Europe but also its fragility. Emerging from this movement were people who dedicated their lives to preserving Yiddish culture such as Simon Dubnow. Dubnow was a Russian Jewish scholar who, in 1891, published an essay in the journal *Voskhod* in which he argued that east European Jews did not sufficiently appreciate their own culture. He urged the public to begin collecting material that documented the culture of Ashkenazi Jews.[23] The essay inspired many people to send him material and also gave rise to the setting up of several historical societies. The movement continued to gather pace, and by the 1920s there were several similar ideas in the air in the cities of Berlin, Vilna (now known as Vilnius, the capital of Lithuania) and New York for advancing Yiddish scholarship. Dubnow was also aware that the culture of the Jews of eastern Europe was under threat from pogroms, migration and assimilation with Christian communities, processes that had not vanished with the end of the nineteenth century: the pogroms of 1918–20, for instance, killed hundreds of thousands of Jews.

In Vilna in Lithuania, Max Weinreich and Zalman Reisen – who in 1923 had proposed a 'Union of Yiddish philologists' – began to meet and they enthusiastically rounded up local activists to consider how best to preserve Jewish culture. Weinreich had studied at St Petersburg University, and completed his education with a doctorate at Marburg in Germany. Two educational organisations in Vilna held a meeting on 24 March 1925 which endorsed proposals to establish a Yiddish Academic Institute, and encouraged colleagues in Poland to do the same, writing that 'the Yiddish academic institute must and will without fail be created'.[24] Vilna was fertile ground for such an initiative. The city had a large Jewish population: in 1939 the Jews comprised just under a third of the city's demographic. Through the eighteenth and nineteenth centuries it was known as a powerful centre of Jewish culture and learning, and was the birthplace of prominent religious leaders in the eighteenth century (such as the celebrated Elijah ben Solomon Zalman, the 'Vilna Gaon', a brilliant rabbinical scholar), becoming referred to as 'Jerusalem in Lithuania'.[25] Weinreich and Reisen's new institute, which became known as YIVO (*Yidisher Visnshaftlekher Institut*), soon established itself as the focus of a 'movement' to collect Jewish history and culture in eastern Europe, and a tremendous energy began to surround the group there.[26]

Vilna was also a city with a strong culture of libraries, including the university library and other secular collections, but it could also boast one of Europe's richest collections of Jewish books in the Strashun Library, a community library, arguably the first Jewish public library in the world, which developed as an intellectual centre for the Jewish community in Vilna.[27] The library had been established by businessman and bibliophile Matityahu Strashun who, at his death in 1892, bequeathed his large collection of early and rare books to the Jewish community of the city. So a structure to house the collection was built adjacent to the Great Synagogue, with a board established to oversee the institution. The board allowed the library to be open seven days a week, including the Sabbath, such was the demand to access the knowledge in the library.[28] Another major collection was the Mefitse Haskala (the Association to Spread Enlightenment), which had been established in 1911 and was owned by the Jewish community, holding over 45,000 volumes in Yiddish, Russian, Polish and Hebrew.[29]

Once established in Vilna, YIVO grew rapidly through the 1920s and 1930s, becoming 'the national academy of a stateless people'.[30] The priority for Weinreich and Reisen was to survey the available primary documents and through research to identify gaps so that scholars could go out and collect primary data. This process of gathering material, mostly through the work of volunteers, was known in Yiddish as *zamlen*. The *zamlers* collected material from living people – both documents and oral testimonies – sending the materials they collected to the institute in Vilna for the scholars there to analyse. The idea at the heart of YIVO was more than just the process of collecting; at the forefront of its work was archiving, preservation and sharing of the knowledge collected by the *zamlers*. A bibliographic commission was a key part of these activities and during YIVO's first six weeks they collected 500 citations and within a year 10,000. By 1929 it had registered 100,000 citations and regularly received 300 newspapers of which 260 were in Yiddish. In 1926 they began to register all new books produced in Yiddish as well as all the most important articles in the Yiddish press and about Yiddish in other languages. By September 1926 over two hundred *zamlers* had donated a total of 10,000 items to the collections at YIVO.[31]

YIVO was not only to be a centre for Jewish studies, and a major library and archive for Jewish material, it began to be the spearhead of a mass movement. In late 1939 YIVO's founding director, Max Weinreich, was in Denmark giving a lecture on the work of YIVO and found that he could not get back to Vilna because Soviet forces had invaded eastern Poland and had moved into Vilna. As a result Weinreich looked to the only other place where YIVO was established that could be considered safe. From New York, where he had set up an office, presciently, in 1929–30, Weinreich was able to correspond with the YIVO headquarters in Vilna. In New York he continued the core YIVO mission of collecting; in 1940–1 he sent out a call for material and placed adverts in the Yiddish press in the United States and in YIVO's own newspaper published in New York. Although Weinreich did not realise it in 1939, YIVO, and the cultural, religious, social and intellectual life that it documented, would only survive because of the office in New York.[32]

In the hot summer of 1941 Hitler tore up the Molotov–Ribbentrop Pact and launched 'Operation Barbarossa' on an unsuspecting Russia. The Nazi Blitzkrieg was overwhelming, pushing the Russian army back rapidly. As part of this lightning attack, the German army captured Vilna on 24 June 1941. A team of the Einsatzstab Reichsleiter Rosenberg, led by Dr Herbert Gotthardt (who had been a librarian in Berlin before the war), arrived in the city just a few days later. At first they just visited synagogues and libraries, but soon they were arranging for the Gestapo to arrest Jewish scholars.[33] As in other cities with sizeable Jewish populations, a ghetto was established, into which the Jewish population were corralled and controlled. Dr Johannes Pohl, from Rosenberg's institute in Frankfurt, visited the city in February 1942 with three specialists and, having surveyed the city and the work that had been done since the seizure of Vilna, realised that a larger organisation would be required to deal with the various Jewish collections of books and documents. More to the point, Pohl realised that only Jewish specialists could undertake the task of identifying key materials. He therefore ordered the ghetto to provide him with twelve workers, to sort, pack and ship materials, and appointed a team of three Jewish intellectuals to oversee the work: Herman Kruk, Zelig Kalmanovitch and Chaikl Lunski. The Jewish guards of the ghetto called the group the 'Paper Brigade'.[34]

The Einsatzstab team, with their forced labourers from the ghetto in the Paper Brigade, were given space in Vilna University Library. The entire collection of the Strashun Library, all 40,000 volumes, was moved there for *selektsia*: a sorting between survival and destruction for the books, which mirrored the fate of human beings in the death camps beginning to be used all across eastern Europe.[35] Some of the books were to be sent to the Frankfurt Institute, others to nearby paper mills for recycling. The Jewish intellectuals in charge of this process were an extraordinary group of courageous scholars and librarians. They were led by Herman Kruk, who had been director of the Grosser Library, a library specialising in Yiddish and socialist literature in Warsaw, and who had fled to Vilna with other Jewish refugees after the Nazi invasion in 1939. He established a remarkable library in the Vilna Ghetto – technically a revival of the Hevrah Mefitse Haskala Library – and was assisted there by Moshe Abramowicz, who had worked in the library before the Nazi occupation, and a young woman, Dina, whom Abramowicz married in the ghetto. Zelig Kalmanovitch, who acted as Kruk's deputy, was one of the pre-war directors of YIVO, and Chaikl Lunski, the head of the Strashun Library, now worked as a bibliographic consultant, cataloguing books to be sent to Frankfurt. 'Kalmanovich and I don't know whether we are gravediggers or saviors,' wrote Kruk in his diary.[36]

A second worksite was soon opened up by Nazis in the YIVO building, and other Jews from the ghetto were needed to join the team making the selections, as the volume of material to be gone through was so great. By this point the Paper Brigade also included other women, such as Rachel Pupko-Krinsky, a former Gymnasium (high school) teacher of history who was skilled in medieval Latin, and creatives such as Abraham Sutzkever, a renowned Yiddish poet.

The Nazi rage against Jewish books in Vilna was not confined to institutional libraries; as the Gestapo raided houses looking for Jews, the Einsatzstab squad came afterwards looking for their books to ensure the eradication of their way of life. The hunt for Jewish books became increasingly aggressive; at one point the floor of the reading room of Vilna University Library was ripped up to look for Jewish books which may have been hidden there. By April 1943 the work of the Einsatzstab in Riga, Kaunas, Vilna, Minsk and Kiev had taken control of 280,000 volumes, and 50,000 in Vilna alone awaited shipment to Frankfurt.[37]

The destruction of Jewish books was recorded in meticulous detail by Pohl's team, with biweekly lists being kept of books sent to Germany, numbers sent to paper mills, with breakdowns by language and date of publication. A quota of 70 per cent was set for the proportion to be destroyed. Sometimes Nazis who could not tell the difference sent books to Frankfurt based solely on the attractiveness of their bindings.

In June 1942 Kruk recorded in his diary: 'The Jewish porters occupied with the task are literally in tears; it is heartbreaking to see this happening.' They knew exactly what fate awaited the books and documents that were not being sent to Frankfurt, and what it would mean for the organisation they were so dedicated to before the war: 'YIVO is dying,' wrote Kruk, 'its mass grave is the paper mill.'[38] For a time there was a disagreement about the right way to deal with the books. Some, like Kalmanovitch, argued that it was best for the books to be sent to Frankfurt – at least they would survive there. Others felt that there must be a better way.

As a response to the dreadful destruction being wreaked on the libraries of Vilna, members of the Paper Brigade worked out strategies to save books. Firstly, they realised that one simple response was to drag out the work for as long as possible. They would read the books to each other when the Germans were not in the room. This could be dangerous as the Germans overseeing the process would not look kindly on being duped, but the second strategy was even more dangerous. At the end of the working day they would hide books and documents in their clothes, and take them to the ghetto. Kruk had a pass that allowed him passage in and out of the ghetto without a body search, but if Nazis found books on other workers they risked being immediately stripped and beaten, and they would then be sent to the ghetto prison, or even to the Lukishki prison in Vilna, and then to the execution site for the Jews created by the Nazis at Ponar, outside Vilna. From this destination there was no return.

Between March 1942 and September 1943 thousands of printed books, and tens of thousands of manuscript documents, made their way back to the Vilna Ghetto thanks to the astonishing, risky and dangerous biblio-smuggling of the Paper Brigade.

One of the forced labourers in the Paper Brigade's sorting teams, the Yiddish poet Abraham Sutzkever, obtained a permit from the Gestapo to bring paper into the ghetto as fuel for the ovens, but instead he brought rare Hebrew and Yiddish printed books, manuscript letters by Tolstoy, Maxim Gorky and Mayim Bialik, one of the diaries of the founder of the Zionist movement, Theodor Herzl, and drawings by Marc Chagall, all of which were immediately and carefully hidden. Many of these documents survive today in the YIVO collections in New York. The Paper Brigade even created a ruse to bring unused office furniture from the YIVO headquarters into the ghetto. The Germans gave them permission, but the Brigade hid hundreds of books and documents inside the furniture. Once in the ghetto, the books and documents were extracted and then secreted in an elaborate and sophisticated system of hiding places. One of the residents of the Vilna Ghetto, Gershon Abramovitsh, who had been a construction engineer before the war, built a bunker sixty feet underground, which had its own ventilation system, an electricity supply, and even a tunnel leading to a well which was physically outside the ghetto.[39] The bunker had originally been conceived as a hiding place for the weapons of the ghetto underground – and for Abramovitsh's mother, but she was happy to share it with the rescued books and documents. Some of the textbooks and children's books smuggled in were delivered to clandestine schools. Others were of great practical use to the partisan groups forming within the ghetto: one was a book which showed how to make Molotov cocktails.

Despite the personal risks that the Paper Brigade were taking, and their heroic efforts to smuggle books and documents to the ghetto, the majority of the material was still going to the paper mills outside Vilna. Members of the Brigade sensed that their time was almost up. Kalmanovitch wrote in his diary on 23 August: 'Our work is reaching its conclusion. Thousands of books are being dumped as trash, and the Jewish books will be liquidated. Whatever part we can rescue will be saved, with God's help. We will find it when we return as free human beings.'[40]

On the 23 September 1943, after several weeks of occupation spent rounding up the terrified inhabitants, the brutal liquidation of the Vilna Ghetto began. The ghetto's own extraordinary library was closed and the books destroyed.[41] The members of the Paper Brigade received no special treatment; along with their fellow inhabitants of the ghetto most of them were murdered by the Nazis at Ponar, or were sent to forced labour camps in Estonia, most never to return.[42]

Unknown to the Paper Brigade, a parallel effort to save records of east European Jewish life from destruction was undertaken 300 miles to the south-west of Vilna, in the Warsaw Ghetto. Here a clandestine group called the Oyneg Shabes documented daily life in the ghetto over its three years of existence, creating more than 30,000 pages of essays, poems, letters and photographs. They recorded folk humour, jokes, messianic hopes, stories, poems, but also rants about other Jews working for the Nazis in the ghetto and even details of the behaviour of the Jewish police that controlled the ghetto in concert with the Nazis. Even ephemera such as decorated paper sweet wrappers were preserved.

The material was, as in Vilna, buried in the ghetto (in ten boxes and three metal milk churns), but these materials were not pre-existing books and documents, rescued from the rich book culture of the city: the Warsaw collections were there to document the life of the ghetto itself, and of its inhabitants. As in Vilna these acts of preservation were intended to allow the future to remember the past. Emanuel Ringelblum, the leader of Oyneg Shabes, was discovered hiding with his family and thirty-four other Jews and murdered in March 1944, just a few days after the annihilation of the Warsaw Ghetto.[43]

The Oyneg Shabes archive was recovered in two parts. The first was in September 1946, the result of a systematic search in the ruins of the ghetto. Two milk churns containing the second part were uncovered on 1 December 1950. The third portion is still missing. Some 1,693 items comprising 35,000 pages were recovered from the Ringelblum part of the archive alone, and they contain minutes, memoranda, diaries, memoirs, last letters, essays, poems, songs, jokes, novels, stories, plays, classroom compositions, diplomas, proclamations, posters, photographs, drawings and paintings. The collection is now in the Jewish Historical Institute in Warsaw and is digitally available in the archives of the United States Holocaust Memorial Museum in Washington, which also displays one of the original milk churns.[44]

In Vilna, a few members of the Paper Brigade, with other Jews from the ghetto, managed to escape and join the partisans in the forests. One of these was the poet Abraham Sutzkever who joined the Jewish partisan brigade Nekome-nemer ('The Avengers'). On hearing the news of the liberation of Vilna, Sutzkever and Justas Paleckis, the president-in-exile of Lithuania, raced to the city passing the wreckage of the routed German army on the roads, the corpses of German soldiers issuing a stench of putrefaction that was 'more pleasant to me than any perfume', so Sutzkever recorded in his diary.[45]

When he returned to Vilna after the Germans had been forced out by the Soviet advance, Sutzkever discovered that the YIVO building had been hit by artillery shells, and the documents secretly hidden there had all been destroyed. Most of the members of the Paper Brigade had been moved to forced labour camps or murdered in the final phases of the Nazi genocide. A handful – Sutzkever; fellow poet Schmerke Kaczerginski; librarian Dina Abramowicz; Ruzhka Korczak, a student activist of the socialist Zionist 'Young Guard'; Noime Markeles, another student and communist who worked in the brigade with his father; Akiva Gershater, a photographer and expert in Esperanto; and Leon Bernstein, a mathematician – were the only members of the Paper Brigade to survive.[46] They gathered in the ruins of Vilna and began to look for the hiding places inside the ghetto, some of which had been discovered by the Nazis and their contents burned. Miraculously, the underground store developed by Gershon Abramovitsh was intact and the materials were brought to the surface, their survival a symbol of hope for the few remaining Jews of the city. Two other hiding places in the ghetto were also intact. The surviving members of the Paper Brigade who had escaped from Vilna, led by Sutzkever and Shmerke Kaczerginski, were joined by Abba Kovner, former commander of the ghetto underground. They now established a Jewish Museum of Culture and Art as a kind of successor to YIVO with formal approval of the Soviet authorities who were now the official government, under the auspices of the People's Commissariat for Education. They took this step as they realised that under Soviet control, no private institutes such as YIVO would be tolerated. In the new museum, housed in the former ghetto library, they began to secure the recovered collections. Twenty tons of YIVO materials were found at a paper mill, and thirty more tons of paper materials were found in the courtyard of the Refuse Administration of Vilna. Potato sacks full of books and documents began to arrive at the museum.[47]

As summer turned to autumn, life turned sour for the Jews returning to Vilna. The Soviet authorities began to assert control and Jewish cultural activities became a target for political suppression. When Sutzkever and his colleagues discovered that the Soviets had sent the thirty tons of books discovered in the Refuse Administration back to the paper mills again, the YIVO members in Vilna realised that the books and documents were going to have to be saved *again*.

The Soviet authorities were not only vehemently opposed to all forms of religion, but they were particularly anti-Jewish, and throughout the 1940s Jews began to be associated with America as so many Jews had moved there. Gradually, the three museum staff became involved in smuggling the books out again, sending some to the YIVO office in New York. The situation in Vilna had become so severe that Kaczerginski resigned in November 1945, and he and Sutzkever fled to Paris. In 1949 the YIVO collections were requisitioned from the museum by the KGB and placed in the basement of the Church of St George – appropriated as a storage facility by the Book Chamber of the Lithuanian Soviet Socialist Republic – located next to a former Carmelite monastery. The materials remained there undisturbed for forty years.

From this point onwards the survival of the YIVO and other Jewish materials in Vilna was due to the heroic efforts of a Lithuanian

librarian, Dr Antanas Ulpis.[48] Ulpis was director of the Book
Chamber, a proto-national library which preserved and documented
all books published in Lithuania. His bibliographical survey of
Lithuanian publications remains a standard work of reference to this
day. Located in the monastery next to the Church of St George,
the Book Chamber used the church as a storehouse for its collections. Ulpis was highly sympathetic to the Jews in Lithuania and
made the unusual step of appointing Jews to senior staff positions
during the 1950s and 1960s. He was allowed to travel through
Lithuania seeking material for the Book Chamber and managed to
preserve a number of important Jewish collections that had survived
the Nazis but were once again vulnerable to destruction under the
Soviets.

Ulpis also obtained material from other libraries in Vilna that
had inherited parts of the Paper Brigade's collection. As the government had by now declared all forms of Jewish culture anti-Soviet,
and ordered the removal of Yiddish items from circulation, libraries
were reluctant to hold on to it. Ulpis persuaded library directors
to contribute archival materials outside his collecting policy. He
knew that the Jewish materials would be destroyed if the communist authorities became aware of them, so he secreted them in the
church – even the organ pipes were used to hide Jewish documents.
(Many years later when his son was perplexed to be unable to play
the organ, only his father knew the real reason why it wouldn't
sound.) Ulpis hid other books in 'plain sight', putting them beneath
or within groups of more conventional books. He gambled on the
communist authorities not probing too deeply into the hundreds
of thousands of books stored there. Ulpis spent many years ensuring
that his collection remained a secret, inspired by the hope that one
day the political climate would allow him to reveal its presence.
Antanas Ulpis died in 1981 before he saw his dream of the return
of the Jewish books and documents to the community that had
created them. He kept his secret well.

During the 1980s, the policy of glasnost (a Russian term made
popular by Mikhail Gorbachev, meaning 'openness and transparency'), and the general thawing of the Cold War, allowed an opening
up of political and intellectual life in the communist countries of
eastern Europe. It was now possible for Jewish organisations to meet

openly and for Jews to have a public life of their own again. I witnessed glasnost at first hand when visiting Poland in 1987. The Library of the Jagiellonian University in Krakow became one of the sources of change in that city, thanks to a library of English language materials managed by the British Council. All across the Soviet bloc, libraries were an essential part of these massive changes, and the Book Chamber in Vilna was no exception.

In 1988 an article in a Soviet Yiddish magazine claimed there were over 20,000 Yiddish and Hebrew books in the collection. These began to be examined in greater detail, and the director of the Book Chamber opened up discussions with Samuel Norich, then director of YIVO in New York. Norich visited Vilna and discovered that in addition to the printed books there were tens of thousands of documents, many of them the materials collected by the YIVO *zamlers*, secretly preserved by the Paper Brigade. At this point the collections, which had been saved multiple times by people risking their lives, became embroiled in cultural politics once again. Norich was anxious to have the documents returned to YIVO. With the rebirth of the Lithuanian nation, however, the collections were seen in a different light – a symbol of Lithuanian national culture before the Soviet era. On 30 May 1989 the National Library of Lithuania was created anew out of its previous iterations – national, Nazi-occupied, Soviet and national again – it had begun in 1919 with the founding of the Central Library of Lithuania. In 1990 Lithuania declared independence from the Soviet Union. There was a period of great political volatility – military intervention was narrowly avoided, the Soviet regime finally collapsed and Lithuania returned to democracy. In 1994 it was finally agreed that the documents could be moved to YIVO's headquarters in New York for conservation, cataloguing and copying, before being returned to the National Library of Lithuania.

On 25 October 2017, the website of the Martynas Mažvydas National Library of Lithuania posted an announcement that a further 170,000 pages of Jewish documents had been identified in the Church of St George, in the Lithuanian National Archives and in the Wroblewski Library of the Lithuanian Academy of Sciences. The volume of material that Ulpis managed to hide away was astonishing. In 1991, 150,000 documents were discovered. The material concerned the Jewish communal bodies, the organisation of Jewish life in eastern Europe, the work of Dubnow and others in the early days of YIVO, of Yiddish theatre in the interwar period, and included such treasures as the record book of the Vilna Synagogue, which details the religious life of that institution during the time of Elijah ben Solomon Zalman, the celebrated 'Vilna Gaon'.[49]

The collections were once again to be catalogued, preserved and copied at the expense of YIVO, but the physical objects were to remain in Lithuania under the stewardship of the National Library. One of the major differences between this project and the previous initiative was that now digitisation could make the materials accessible via the internet. The director of the National Library, Professor Renaldas Gudauskas, was keen to promote his institution as having 'preserved one of the most significant collections of Jewish heritage documents in Lithuania and the world'. Ten documents were placed on public exhibition in New York as a symbol of the collaboration between the National Library and YIVO – they included a booklet of poems written in the Vilna Ghetto by Abraham Sutzkever. The survival of this fragile booklet through numerous attempts at destruction was a testament to the astonishing dedication of numerous individuals to preserving the knowledge of the Jewish communities of eastern Europe.[50]

The treasures that have reappeared in Lithuania after seventy-five years may not be the last pieces of knowledge to have survived the Nazis. After the Allies captured Frankfurt in 1945 the vast looted collections of Rosenberg's Institute for the Study of the Jewish Question were moved to a depository at Offenbach where they could be appraised, sorted and returned to their rightful owners.[51] One American visitor to Offenbach in 1947 described it as 'a mortuary of books'.[52] Various committees were established to deal with the return of these collections, including a 'Committee on Restoration of Continental Jewish Museums, Libraries, and Archives', which was chaired by the eminent British scholar Cecil Roth.

To keep Jewish archives in Germany, the country responsible for the Holocaust, was felt by many Jews in Israel to be unthinkable. The prominent Kabbalah scholar Gershom Scholem wrote to the great rabbi and scholar Leo Baeck that 'where the Jews have migrated is where their books belong'. There were, however, some cities where a small remnant of earlier Jewish citizenry remained, such as Worms, Augsburg and Hamburg, and where the transfer of archives was fiercely resisted, as it symbolised the failure of continuity of European Jewish settlement. A campaign was mounted in the city of Worms by the former municipal archivist Friedrich Illert, who had helped to save the Jewish records from the Nazis, and who, along with Isidor Kiefer, the former chair of the city's Jewish community who had settled in New York, hoped that the archives would help create 'a little Jerusalem' in Worms once again. The case was symbolic of those Jews in Germany who wanted to keep their communities alive, as the ultimate triumph over evil. In Worms and Hamburg court cases were fought over the fate of the Jewish archives, with German archivists and local Jewish leaders fighting to prevent the transfer of 'their' archives to institutions in Israel. They ultimately lost their cases, through political pressure from Konrad Adenauer, the first Chancellor of the Federal Republic of Germany, who was anxious to show cooperation between post-Nazi West Germany and the state of Israel.[53]

Some Jewish library collections have remained elusive long into the twentieth century. In the last ten years alone, 30,000 books have been returned to 600 owners, heirs and institutions, these efforts supported more recently by the facility to post lists of books awaiting restitution online (by organisations such as the Conference on Jewish Material Claims Against Germany, and the World Jewish Restitution Organisation). Since 2002, the Zentral- und Landesbibliothek Berlin (ZBB) has been systematically searching for Nazi looted materials among its collections and returning them, funded since 2010 by the Berlin Senate. The task is very slow and difficult: Berlin City Library searched 100,000 books; of the 29,000 books they identified as stolen, just 900 books have been returned to owners in more than twenty countries. Since 2009, 15,000 books from fifteen Austrian libraries have been returned to owners or their heirs.[54]

Alfred Rosenberg was tried at the International Military Tribunal at Nuremberg in 1945–6 for war crimes and crimes against humanity. The records of the trial of Rosenberg refer frequently to libraries and archives, the Soviet prosecutors focussing on his campaign to plunder Estonia, Latvia and Russia, and he struggled to defend himself against the evidence they presented. His only defence against the French prosecutor was to use the old excuse that he only acted because he had 'received a government order to confiscate archives'. Rosenberg's indictment stated that he was 'responsible for a system of organized plunder of both public and private property throughout the invaded countries of Europe. Acting under Hitler's orders of January 1940 . . . he directed the Einsatzstab Rosenberg which plundered museums and libraries'. He was also convicted of planning the Final Solution and was responsible for the segregation, shooting of Jews and forced labour of youths. He was sentenced to death by hanging on 1 October 1946.[55]

One of the most heavily used collections of Jewish materials in the Bodleian today is the Coppenhagen collection, formed by the family of that name in Amsterdam. Isaac Coppenhagen (1846–1905) was an important teacher and scribe; he, his son Haim (1874–1942) and grandson Jacob (1913–1997) built an important collection of Hebrew books in their home. With the invasion of Holland in 1940 the collection was moved to a Jewish school. As the Nazi persecution of Jews in Holland became more severe the collection was seen to be at risk, and with the aid of non-Jews the books were moved to a nearby Dutch school and hidden. Jacob too was given refuge by non-Jews, but the rest of his family were murdered in the Nazi death camps. Some of the books in the Coppenhagen collection were seized by the Nazis in Amsterdam and were removed by the Einsatzstab Reichsleiter Rosenberg: at least two books in the collection in Oxford today have the stamps of the Offenbach Archival Depot, evidence that the books had been plundered from a private library.

Despite the ferocity of the Nazis the impulse for preservation ultimately prevailed. As the smoke cleared from the wreckage, books and archives began, slowly, to resurface. Emanuel Ringelblum, Herman Kruk and countless others were murdered, but their sacrifice enabled the memory of their culture and faith to persist, even if it was only a small fragment of what had existed before. The work of Abraham Sutzkever, Dina Abramowicz, Antanas Ulpis and groups like the Paper Brigade and Oyneg Shabes enabled the documents that survived to have a meaning beyond the paper and parchment they were written on. YIVO in New York, the Bodleian in Oxford, the National Library of Lithuania in Vilnius (as the city became more commonly known) continue to preserve the cultural record of Jewish life. As I write, the new National Library of Israel is being constructed in Jerusalem, a 45,000-square metre building housing the largest collection of written Judaica ever amassed (including the archive of Abraham Sutzkever): a home of the book for the People of the Book.

Philip Larkin at All Souls, 1970. Possibly a self-portrait.

9

To Be Burned Unread

PHILIP LARKIN, WHO was one of the most important poets of the twentieth century, was also a librarian, active on various committees alongside his role as chief librarian at the University of Hull (from his appointment in 1954 to his death in 1985). He understood as an insider the different aspects of literary archives from both sides – a rare combination, although there have been others such as Jorge Luis Borges, who was both a great writer and the director of the National Library of Argentina. (Casanova, too, spent his last years working as a librarian.)

During the 1960s and 1970s many archives of British writers were being acquired by university libraries in North America: Evelyn Waugh's papers were sold to the University of Texas at Austin (in 1967) and Sir John Betjeman's to the University of Victoria, British Columbia (1971). Larkin became involved with an effort to raise awareness of the value of literary archives in Britain, as part of a national scheme to improve funding. He gave the notebook containing his earliest poems to the British Library in 1964 to start it off, even though he wrote self-deprecatingly to his lover Monica Jones that the manuscript was 'jammed with unpublished poems etc. I must say they are fearfully dull, stodgy humourless thin Yeats-and-catpiss'. But, he added, 'Still.' He knew the value of his own material.[1]

In his essay 'A Neglected Responsibility', written in 1979, Larkin wrote eloquently to encourage universities and writers to value literary collections:

All literary manuscripts have two kinds of value: what might be called the magical value and the meaningful value. The magical value is the older and more universal: this is the paper he wrote on, these are the words as he wrote them, emerging for the first time in this particular combination . . . The meaningful value is of much more recent origin, and is the degree to which a manuscript helps to enlarge our knowledge and understanding of a writer's life and work.[2]

These two values are why such collections are now so prized by university libraries, provoking competition between institutions and high prices demanded by dealers. They provide raw materials for students to work on, encourage academic productivity and enrich teaching opportunities. The 'magical' aspect of the documents emerges in seminars where students studying a text are allowed to get close to the original manuscript, or in exhibitions where a wider public can see the drafts of works they may be familiar with in other cultural contexts (such as films or TV productions).

Some writers have a real sense of the research value of their archives, having perhaps had interactions with scholars and sensing that people will wish to study them long into the future. There are of course writers with a purposeful sense of the archive ensuring their posthumous reputation, and they use their own papers as a way to 'curate' how they will be studied long after they have died. Other writers see their archives as a way of gaining extra income. Often it is a mixture of motivations. What is omitted from an archive can be just as meaningful as what is included.

Andrew Motion – one of Larkin's literary executors – described the librarianly order in which Larkin kept his own poetic archive, neatly storing it in boxes, alphabetising the correspondence and making it relatively easy for his executors to make sense of his papers.[3] His archive was placed, some time after his death, in the Brynmor Jones Library at the University of Hull where he had spent most of his working life, and a smaller but still significant part in the Bodleian in Oxford, where he had been an undergraduate and where he did research for his edition of the *Oxford Book of Twentieth Century English Verse*, published in 1973. In order to complete this research, he was awarded a Visiting Fellowship at All Souls College and given a precious key by the Bodleian: a key to the stacks of this great copyright library, access to which was only granted to readers on rare occasions. Naturally, Larkin enjoyed the privilege immensely.

Yet on his deathbed, Larkin urged his long-term lover Monica Jones to burn his diaries as he lacked the strength to do so himself. Not surprisingly, she felt unable to perform such a task alone – who would want to be responsible for destroying the writings of one of the country's most famous poets? The destruction of Larkin's diaries was instead delegated after his death to Betty Mackereth, Larkin's devoted secretary of twenty-seven years (latterly another of his lovers, as was his assistant librarian Maeve Brennan). Mackereth took more than thirty volumes of his diaries into his office in the Brynmor Jones Library a few days after his death on 2 December 1985, removed their covers, and shredded their contents. Just to make sure that nothing could survive, the shredded pages were then sent to the university boiler house and incinerated. The covers are still to be found among the Larkin papers at Hull covered in press cuttings stuck on them by the poet.[4]

There had been more volumes of diaries at an earlier stage in his life but some of these had been destroyed by Larkin himself. A publisher in 1976 had suggested bringing out a selection of them, and this had encouraged Larkin to go back through the diaries, a reflective act that had prompted him to destroy the earlier volumes. Presumably the idea that they should all be given the same fate was lodged at the same time. Mackereth herself was in no doubt that she did the right thing. Andrew Motion, in his biography of Larkin, quoted her:

> I'm not sure I was right to keep the covers, but they're interesting aren't they? About the diaries themselves I'm in no doubt. I must have done the right thing because it was what Philip wanted. He was quite clear about it; he wanted them destroyed. I didn't read them as I put them into the machine, but I couldn't help seeing little bits and pieces. They were very unhappy. Desperate really.[5]

Larkin made an interesting choice in destroying them completely, given his profession of librarian and championing the cause of literary manuscript acquisition and preservation. Jones and Mackereth were very clear in their view of Larkin's wishes. He had begun to think about his literary legacy as early as 11 March 1961 after a spell in hospital. He wrote to Jones that:

One thing that makes me ashamed is my refusal to let you use my flat. This has been a worry all through, & springs from the fact that I had left a few private papers & diaries lying around. Such things, which I suppose I keep partly for the record in the event of wanting to write an autobiography, & partly to relieve my feelings, will have to be burned unread in the event of my death, & I couldn't face anyone I thought had seen them, let alone being willing to expose you or anyone else to the embarrassment & no doubt even pain of reading what I had written.[6]

As a librarian and one interested in literary manuscripts, Larkin knew that there were alternatives to this shocking fate. In 1979 he wrote to his friend Judy Egerton after he had been to Devon to look at the papers of their old undergraduate friend Bruce Montgomery who had recently died: 'Was alarmed to find he had kept all my letters since 1943! Since Ann [Bruce's widow] is short of money . . . I feel she shd be free to sell them, & yet . . . She has quite cheerfully offered them back again, but I don't think I should take them. Problems!' The Bodleian eventually acquired the Montgomery letters but with the agreement that some of the papers could not be opened to the public until 2035: Larkin would have known very well that a long closure period (perhaps even an extremely long one) could have been applied to his own papers.[7]

However, an alternative to Larkin's diary does survive and was almost destroyed by accident. Throughout their relationship Larkin and Monica Jones exchanged thousands of letters and postcards. Her letters to him were bequeathed to the Bodleian by Larkin, but his letters to her were so frequently sent and so expansive in their personal revelation that they cumulatively bring us as close to a diary as can be recovered from his literary remains.

Larkin was a great writer of letters. He corresponded extensively with a number of friends and family including James Sutton, Bruce Montgomery, Kingsley Amis, Monica Jones, Judy Egerton, Robert Conquest, Anthony Thwaite, Maeve Brennan and Barbara Pym. The largest series of letters are the ones he sent home to his parents over the period 1936–77: over 4,000 letters and cards in all (a similar number sent back to him from his parents also survives).[8] Even so, perhaps the most personal and important of these major correspondences was that between Larkin and Monica Jones, with whom he had the longest romantic relationship of his life. He sent Jones more than 1,421 letters and 521 postcards, amounting in total to more than 7,500 surviving pages. Many of the letters were lengthy, regularly in excess of six pages, sometimes as long as fourteen pages, and they were often sent every three or four days. After her death the collection remained in her home in Leicester, where she had been an academic. Burglars broke into her flat, stealing cheap electrical goods, but trampling over the papers which they strewed around her home, not realising that the value of the archive was many times more than the TV they had stolen.

The letters were purchased from her estate by the Bodleian Library in 2004. They offer deep insight into Larkin's character; his motivations, his thoughts on all kinds of topics, from his colleagues to politics, are revealed in these letters, more so than in the other correspondences in the public domain owing to the closeness of their relationship.

Why was Larkin so unhappy at the thought of others reading his diaries? He was a shy person, sometimes known as the 'Hermit of Hull', and wrote of his own difficulty in revealing his personal thoughts in his own writing. His poetry is infused with melancholy and the reflections are mostly not direct. Occasionally the reverse is true and he searingly confronts his own feelings, opens up his inner thoughts in a shocking way, most famously in 'This Be the Verse'.

When he asked Motion to join Monica Jones and Anthony Thwaite as one of his literary executors, Larkin said that: 'There won't be anything difficult to do. When I see the Grim Reaper coming up the path to my front door I'm going to the bottom of the garden, like Thomas Hardy, and I'll have a bonfire of all the things I don't want anyone to see.' Motion sets this instruction against the fact that at his death the main group of diaries, together with his other papers, were intact. Monica Jones, he records, felt that Larkin was trying to deny his impending death and to have destroyed them would have been an admission of his own mortality. More convincing is the inherent dichotomy of Larkin's position. He simply couldn't make his mind up. On the one hand he was passionate about preserving literary manuscripts – even giving one of his own poetic notebooks to the British Library. On the other, he was highly uncomfortable about letting others, especially those close to him, see his innermost thoughts, as set down in the diaries. Even his will was so contradictory that the executors had to seek the advice of a Queen's Counsel before deciding that they were entitled under law not to destroy any more of the Larkin archive but to put the bulk of it in the Brynmor Jones Library at Hull.

The example of Larkin demonstrates the impact that one individual's self-censorship can have on their legacy. The loss of his diaries has created an enigma about the thoughts of this very private person, with efforts to reconstruct those thoughts through the letters, which may fill some of the gaps. Interest in Larkin's life and work has grown since his death, boosted to some extent by the enigma created by his final wishes to have his diaries destroyed.

The destruction of Byron's memoirs is one of the most notorious acts of literary damage limitation. Those who were close to him wanted to protect his posthumous reputation, an act that literary scholars have regretted ever since. A poet of similar popularity two hundred years later – Ted Hughes – would be at the centre of another act of literary destruction, of the last journals of his first wife, the equally great poet and writer Sylvia Plath. The relationship between Hughes and Plath has come under intense scrutiny, taking up many pages of discussion and criticism in print. One aspect of this relationship that remains unclear concerns the fate of some of the contents of Sylvia Plath's personal archive following her suicide in 1963. Her suicide and the circumstances of the relationship between the two poets leading up to this tragedy have been the focus of much debate – in particular whether Hughes's behaviour towards her was a major factor in Plath taking her own life. The precise details of Plath's state of mind are unknowable, not least because Hughes destroyed Plath's journals. Hughes claims the act was to protect Plath's reputation and to save their children from reading harrowing entries in the journals written in the days leading to her suicide. Many have speculated that the destruction could rather have been motivated to protect Hughes's own reputation.

Plath died in London and was at the time still married to Hughes although they were separated. Hughes was having an affair with Assia Wevill. He, as next of kin, and because Plath left no explicit will, became the executor of Plath's estate and kept many of her papers as part of his own, until 1981 when he chose to sell them through Sotheby's to Smith College, with the proceeds going to their children, Frieda and Nick Hughes.[9] Aurelia Plath, Sylvia's mother, decided to sell the letters she received from her daughter over the years to the Lilly Library at Indiana University in 1977. One of the complications is that Hughes, as executor to her will, also held control of the copyright in Plath's literary estate, and controlled the way Plath's own words could be circulated in print. Even though Plath's archive found its way to libraries, the circulation of Plath's thoughts as they were laid down in the letters to her mother and in her private journals could not be shared in print without Ted Hughes's express permission.[10]

As literary executor Hughes was able to carefully curate Plath's reputation as a poet. In his estimation the manuscripts he found on her desk after her death were particularly powerful and brilliant. In 1965 he published the first major posthumous collection of her poems, *Ariel*, and other poems were slowly released to literary magazines. *Ariel* became a literary sensation and has remained in print since its first publication, having reprints in hardback and paperback, and presumably earning a considerable income for Hughes. On the publication of Plath's *Collected Poems* it became clear that Hughes had altered the order of poems in *Ariel* from that found in Plath's manuscript, removing some and replacing them with other unpublished poems. Although Hughes explained that his motivations were to avoid causing offence to living individuals depicted in the poetry and to provide a wider perspective on Plath's work, his intervention was viewed by some as evidence of his desire to further control her legacy. It is certainly clear from his subsequent treatment of her archive, and the very detailed and careful management of the process of publication, that Hughes was as concerned with his own reputation as he was with that of his deceased first wife, and that he considered the two inseparable.[11]

In 1982 Hughes published *The Journals of Sylvia Plath*, a heavily edited and selected version of the eight volumes of manuscript journals, and additional gatherings of papers that he had just sold to Smith College. It was not published in the UK where Hughes and their children lived but only in the United States. In the preface he recounted the process of discovering and dealing with Plath's unpublished journals. He describes them as 'an assortment of notebooks and bunches of loose sheets', referring also to two 'maroon-backed' ledgers that were not included in the materials he sold to Smith College. These, he tells us in the preface, covered the period leading up to her death, during the most strained period of their marriage. One of these volumes he describes as having 'disappeared' and the other he confesses to having destroyed in order to protect his children from the intrusive and hurtful comments that would follow if the content of that journal were to become publicly known.[12] Not only did Hughes destroy (at least) one notebook, he also carefully edited his publication so that the contents of two notebooks that covered 1957–9 were not included, his intention being to keep them closed to researchers and to publication until fifty years after her death. In the end he relented on this and allowed all the surviving journals to be published, a decision he made just before his own death in 1998.[13] Writing in a different publication in the same year Hughes changed his story very slightly, even moving from the first to the third person to recount it: 'the second of these two books her husband destroyed, because he did not want her children to have read it . . . The earlier one disappeared more recently (and may, presumably, still turn up).'[14]

The critic Erica Wagner has suggested that the missing journal may be in a trunk in the Hughes Archive at Emory University in Atlanta, which is not to be opened until 2022 or until the death of Ted Hughes's second wife, Carol.[15] The dealer in rare books and manuscripts who managed the sale of the archive to Emory, the late Roy Davids, felt that Hughes had a deep sense of archival integrity, and that if he had found the volume he would have presented it to Smith College to join the other journals there.[16] Another interpretation, of course, is that Hughes destroyed both of the journals, although his most recent biographer, Jonathan Bate, feels that a further possibility is that the volume was destroyed in the fire at Lumb Bank, the house that Ted and Carol Hughes occupied in Heptonstall, Yorkshire, where a mysterious fire took place in 1971. At the time the local police felt that the fire may have been set deliberately.[17]

Hughes was not the only family member seeking to 'manage'

the dissemination of Sylvia Plath's personal writings after her death. The letters of Plath in the Lilly Library in Indiana University contain black marker pen redactions made by Aurelia Plath, and her edited selection of these papers, *Letters Home* (1975), was also strewn with cuts and omissions. These redactions had been made by Aurelia who edited the publication, although as Ted Hughes owned the copyright he also had a say in what could be published. Both Aurelia Plath and Ted Hughes made their editorial decisions to protect their own reputations, although the process uncovered problems between the two. Aurelia removed any negative representation of her by her daughter, and Hughes was similarly anxious to ensure that no negative criticism of him appeared in print. The two ended up in a dispute over his requests for material to be withdrawn from the draft of the book. He wrote to Aurelia in April 1975:

> It seemed to me, after I'd cut the letters, that though the book now lacks the sensational interest of all the inside dope on me, & though it lacks those early love letters which somehow Sylvia sent to you rather than me – I mean those early letters about me – nevertheless it does still give, very brilliantly & fully, her relationship with you. And I know that was what you wanted. All I've done really, Aurelia, is extract my private life, in an attempt to keep it private.[18]

The set of interrelated decisions relating to the management of knowledge in the case of Sylvia Plath must be considered to be political. The cycle of subsequent release of the material into the public domain – the sale of the archive, the first expurgated edition of the journals and the letters, the subsequent relinquishing of the bar on publication – were acts that had Hughes, rather than Plath, at the centre. He stood to gain the most from his actions – in terms of both reputation and finances – but, to add further complexity to the moral questions at stake here, he also had his own personal privacy to contend with. He too was emotionally affected by Plath's death and held profound concerns for their children.

But the task has been completed and it is possible now to use the surviving text of the journals to assess Plath's life and work alongside her published writings, the text of her letters and the other literary forms in which her work survives. These texts continue to provide rich material with which to appreciate Plath's contribution to literature. We cannot truly comprehend what has been lost, but it has become possible to understand aspects of her inner mental life when she was writing what Hughes and critics have since described as her most profound and significant work. To quote Tracy Brain: 'We know very little about the contents of the absent journals, yet so much of what critics do – and do not do – with Plath's writing is affected by them. Important pieces of Plath's body of work are missing: the very pieces, so the thinking goes, that might just make sense of it.'[19] The destroyed material discussed in this chapter might well have ended up in a university library or a national library if it had survived. Held in such an institution these collections would not only have been preserved but would have been made available for study and shown in exhibitions or digitised for the public to appreciate.

Writings containing the inner feelings of an author have the potential to transform our appreciation of his or her work. The Kafka material, since it came to the Bodleian, has been used by editors like Sir Malcolm Pasley to broaden the reputation of Kafka through scholarly editions; the manuscripts have been translated into many other languages and have been used for exhibitions, films and plays. It is hard to argue that the world is a poorer and less interesting place because Max Brod defied the wishes of Franz Kafka. But does this argument, which at its heart suggests that the public interest of posterity must trump the private interests of those who created the work, or who held the interests of the author close, suggest that those who destroyed Byron's or Plath's journals were wrong to do so?

When we look at the knowledge of the ancient world we have to piece together evidence that exists only in fragments. Sappho's work was so important that for centuries she was referred to as simply 'The Poetess', just as Homer was 'The Poet'. Homer's two epics have survived more or less intact, whereas Sappho's lyrics are known to us only through the works they influenced, such as those of Plato, Socrates and Catullus. Had the Library of Alexandria, which we know held a complete set of her lyrics, survived, how differently might we view the literature of the ancient world today?

None of the decisions taken in these case studies was easy or straightforward. In this particular domain of knowledge, the private and the public vie with each other for supremacy. The difficulty comes from the fact that writers make their living, and their reputations, by taking part in the public realm: their work is, after all, 'published', that is to say 'made public'. The public interest in the thoughts of great writers is clear but so is their right to privacy. Ted Hughes held the privacy of his children (and of himself) at the forefront of his mind when he destroyed parts of Sylvia Plath's journals.

Working in a library that measures time in centuries, one answer to these questions is, perhaps, to take a long view. The stacks of the Bodleian are full of manuscripts that are 'closed'. That is to say we have made a promise to some of those who have given or deposited papers with us, for the sake of preservation, that we will not make their contents available to the public until an agreed amount of time has elapsed. This might be after the death of the writer or owner of a collection, or even longer. In the case of Bruce Montgomery, Philip Larkin's Oxford friend, we agreed to keep the collection closed until thirty years after his death, with some of the material closed for a further twenty years. Byron's autobiography and the journals of Plath and Larkin could have been preserved, but remained closed for as long as their executors chose, being released to scholars only after the death of all those closely affected by their contents. The preservation of knowledge is ultimately (as Max Brod knew) about having faith in the future.

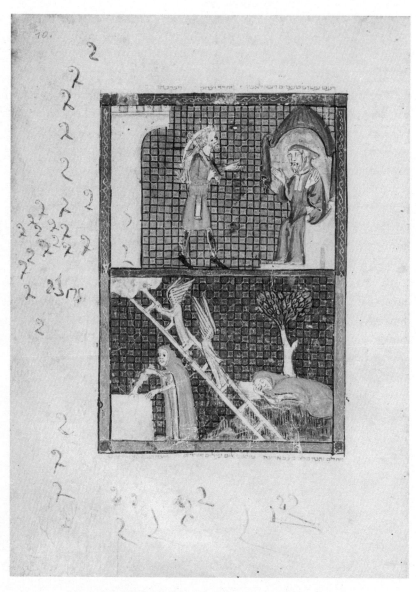

Esau coming back from the hunt, and Jacob's ladder.
From the Sarajevo Haggadah, c.1350.

10

Sarajevo Mon Amour

O N THE EVENING of 25 August 1992 shells began to rain down on a building in Bosnia's capital city of Sarajevo, the infamous site of the assassination that triggered the First World War. These were not ordinary shells and the building was not an ordinary structure. The shells were incendiaries, designed to raise fire rapidly on impact, especially when surrounded by combustible material. The building they hit was the National and University Library of Bosnia and Herzegovina and the shells were fired by the Serbian militia who had surrounded the city as part of the strategy of the Serbian president, Slobodan Milošević, to destroy Bosnia.

The Serbs then placed marksmen to pick off the firefighters and even used anti-aircraft guns turned not toward the skies but horizontally. The staff of the library formed a human chain to remove materials from the burning structure but the relentless shelling and sniper fire made it too dangerous for all but a few of the rare books to be saved. At around 2 p.m. that day one member of the library's staff, Aida Buturović, was shot by a sniper.[1] She had been a talented linguist working to support the collaborative network of libraries in the country. She was only thirty years old and joined a casualty list of 14 deaths and 126 wounded from that day in Sarajevo.[2]

The writer Ray Bradbury reminded us in 1953 of the temperature at which paper burns – Fahrenheit 451 – but an entire library takes a long time to be destroyed. The ash from the burnt volumes fell on the city over subsequent days like 'black birds', in the words of Bosnian poet and writer Valerijan Žujo.[3]

Although the motivations for destroying libraries and archives vary from case to case the erasure of a particular culture has featured prominently. The book ravages of the European Reformation had a strong religious flavour to them and there is a sense that Catholic communities were targeted by the destruction of their libraries, as the content of those libraries was regarded as heretical. The destruction of Louvain University Library had a cultural component too with its national status as a centre of knowledge. The attacks on libraries and archives during the Holocaust were a cultural assault in its broadest sense: it was not merely the religion of the Jews that the Nazi machine sought to eradicate but all aspects of Jewish existence: from living beings to the gravestones of their ancestors.

The National Library of Bosnia and Herzegovina was situated in a building known locally as *Vijećnica* (City Hall). It housed over 1.5 million books, manuscripts, maps, photographs and other materials. Together these provided the recorded memory not just of a nation but the culture of an entire region, one that had a significant Muslim population. The shells that struck the building did not do so by chance. The library was not accidentally caught in the crossfire of a regional war, it was deliberately targeted by Serbian forces that sought not only military domination but annihilation of the Muslim population. No other buildings nearby were hit – the library was the sole target.[4]

Just forty-five years after the end of the Second World War and the public exposure of the full horrors of the Holocaust, with the perpetual refrain of 'never again' ringing in the world's ears, cultural genocide once again returned to Europe. It emerged during the break-up of Yugoslavia into a series of separate states. The motivations for this cultural genocide were a complex knot of issues. Nationalism was mixed with racial and religious hatred, and was given political expression.[5]

During the summer of 1992 many student backpackers Interrailing around Europe had Yugoslavia on their itineraries. Shoved in their backpacks were the new guidebooks aimed at young people travelling on a tight budget. They might well have taken the latest edition of *Yugoslavia: The Rough Guide*, which gave them a few introductory pages on the history of the region. It had been dominated by the Turks for five hundred years, was bordered by many countries, had fought Nazi occupation during the Second World War, and had been brought together by General Tito. The country was currently suffering the effects of years of communist rule under Tito: economic depression, underinvestment in key infrastructure and hyperinflation. Following the death of Tito in 1980 the cohesion of the federation of republics began to break down:

> The fiercely defended individuality of the Republics persists. Only four percent of Yugoslavs describe themselves as such on their pass-ports. Strikes, demonstrations, and a resurgence of nationalism, especially in Serbia, have for the first time since the war threatened the future of the alliance.[6]

This political and social fragmentation was inevitable given the history of the region. The rise of the Ottoman Empire in the sixteenth and seventeenth centuries had been resisted by the European monarchies. Bosnia's Ottoman rule lasted for almost four hundred years. In 1878 Vienna replaced Istanbul as the imperial centre from which the region was governed. The Austro-Hungarian Empire was approaching its zenith as a political and cultural force at the time that it supplanted Ottoman rule and, invoking an inter-national mandate to occupy and 'civilise' the province, the new rulers brought their own administrative order to bear on the region.

The 1910 census for Bosnia recorded a majority Christian Orthodox population (43 per cent) followed by a Muslim one of 32 per cent and a Catholic one of 23 per cent. This religious complexity, where no one group dominated, also fostered a cultural amalgam, where architectural styles, music, food and literature all intermingled. There were political tensions within the ethnic groups and these tensions were influenced by the strength of the neigh-bouring republics of Serbia and Croatia, both of which had laid claims to the lands of Bosnia, citing the presence of people with Serbian or Croatian ethnicity as the justification. Serbia in particular looked hungrily at its neighbour. The Serbs had asserted their own nationalist aspirations early on. By 1878 they had managed to form an independent state and over the century that followed would continue to make claims over Bosnia, maintaining strong ties with the ethnic Serbs in the republic during the disaggregation of com-munist Yugoslavia, which had united the countries after the Second World War.

Although this background cast a looming shadow over Bosnia, many visitors in the twentieth century remarked on how peacefully the different ethnic groups coexisted. Nowhere was this coexistence more visible, or remarkable, than in its capital city of Sarajevo: 'Mosques, minarets and fezes – holding the gorgeous east in fee while the river cools the air, splashing through the town and the bridge on which whatsisname was assassinated', wrote Lawrence Durrell.[7] Sarajevo defied the historic tensions within the region, and this was reflected in the great library of the city, which served the whole republic.

The Balkans as a region had a strong book culture. In the Middle Ages, Catholic religious orders such as the Cistercians were present in Slovenia, fostering scriptoria and libraries, and further south Jewish, Orthodox and Ottoman communities had flourishing book-making centres. Sarajevo was one of the hubs of book culture. The city boasted one of the finest collections of Arabic, Turkish and Persian books and manuscripts in the Gazi Husrev-beg Library established by the second 'founder' of Sarajevo in the early sixteenth century; by the 1990s it was one of the oldest continuously functioning libraries in Europe. The Jewish community in Sarajevo also had its own library, in La Benevolencija. Other religions also maintained libraries. The Franciscan order had a convent and seminary in Sarajevo and built up a library to serve their religious mission.[8] In the late nineteenth century the Habsburg rulers, encouraging the modernisation of Bosnia, created a regional museum, the Zemaljski Muzej, which contained a research library. From its foundation in 1888, the museum library had grown to roughly a quarter of a million volumes and preserved one of the region's greatest artistic treasures, the Sarajevo Haggadah.

The Oriental Institute in Sarajevo, founded in 1950, also provided a major centre for the documentation of Bosnian culture, with a focus on Arabic, Persian and Hebrew books, manuscripts and documents, and – of particular regional significance – a collection of documents in Adžamijski, an Arabic script used for Bosnian Slavic texts, symbolic of the cultural crossroads that Sarajevo had become. It was the most important cultural and intellectual centre of its kind in south-eastern Europe.

The National and University Library of Bosnia and Herzegovina was founded in 1945. By 1992 it had 150,000 rare books, 500 medieval codices, hundreds of incunabula and major archives, as well as the country's main holdings of newspapers and journals from the region, and scholarly material from across the world necessary for a serious educational establishment. The library served not only as a cultural resource for the nation but also as the University of Sarajevo's research base. One of the special functions of a national library is to document the intellectual heritage of a country, and one of the defining collections in the National and University Library was their collection of 'Bosniaca', a 'collection of record' which brought together all publications ever printed in Bosnia and books about Bosnia wherever they were printed or published. The collection – and the staff – naturally reflected the multicultural nature of Bosnia.

The building that housed the National and University Library was originally constructed in the late nineteenth century at the height of Austro-Hungarian rule as the city's Town Hall; it was designed to reflect the cultural legacy of the city's Moorish history. Positioned at the end of a grand street, Vojvode Stepe, it was designed in a pseudo-Moorish style, which the Habsburg rulers clearly thought would fit in seamlessly with the Turkish buildings of the cobbled Baščaršija area of Sarajevo, the heart of the Ottoman city. The collections were the ultimate target for the shelling, but the significance of the building did not lie purely in its intellectual and cultural associations. From 1910–15 it had been the seat of the first Bosnian Parliament, a symbol of independent democracy that the Serbian aggressors would have known about and deplored.

It took three days (25–27 August) for the library to burn through, three days during which it might have been possible to rescue part of the collections. Smoke damage may have rendered the volumes of the library unusable and even hazardous to health, but if the flames had been quelled after the first shells were fired, some of the library could have been saved. But then the intensity of the heat exploded the slender marble columns of the main reading rooms, causing the roof to crash into the space below, making the rescue of the collection no longer a realistic option for the fire-fighters of Sarajevo. One of them reported: 'there have been mortars falling here for hours, this makes the job very difficult.'[9] Their desperate efforts were also hampered by low water pressure, due to damage to the water pumping system of the city caused by the warfare of the previous months. The firefighters worked flat out to suppress the fire but the repeated shelling meant that fires continued to engulf the building. The front pages of the world's newspapers didn't even carry the story.[10]

The National and University Library was perhaps the most conspicuous intellectual and cultural casualty of the conflict but it was not alone. Across Bosnia dozens of libraries and archives received the same treatment. Archive collections in Muslim areas were brutally treated and here the ethnic cleansing of individuals was matched by the destruction of documents in land registries – where the records of Muslims holding property were destroyed and even gravestones bulldozed to eradicate the suggestion that Muslims had been buried in Bosnian soil.

It has been estimated that more than half of the provincial archives of Bosnia were destroyed: more than 81 km of history.[11] These documents recorded in minute detail the citizenship of these communities: births, marriages and deaths were written down for centuries, and land ownership recorded in great detail (as Ottoman custom dictated). These documents help root a community in their environment, allowing those roots to be traced back in time and made personal through the evidence of families which had existed in those localities over succeeding generations. Future claims of residence, ownership and possession, the very right to exist, were wiped out, or so the nationalists attempted to do. The records of Muslim existence were 'cleansed' alongside the humans themselves, or as Noel Malcolm has put it: 'The people who organized such acts were attempting, in the most literal way, to erase history.'[12]

In the town of Doboj, after the Serb militias had destroyed the mosque and the Catholic church, special forces (the 'red berets') arrived from Belgrade seeking baptismal records in the Catholic rectory. Fortunately, according to the parish priest, 'good people, local Serbs' had hidden the registers at his request, as he knew that this would be a further step in the cultural genocide that was being inflicted on the town.[13] In Herzegovina, the country's south-western region, the historic city of Mostar was also a target for the Serbs. The archives of Herzegovina were repeatedly targeted, along with the library of the Catholic archbishopric and the University Library in the city. The destruction of the beautiful and historic medieval bridge at Mostar became *the* symbol of the damage done to the cultural life of Bosnia during the conflict, but millions of books and documents in hundreds of public libraries and archives were destroyed and received scant attention in the press.

Other libraries and archives in Sarajevo also suffered. The Oriental Institute was the first victim, with phosphorous shells being deliberately fired at the building on 17 May 1992, destroying the entire collection. The shelling, and the inferno that resulted, destroyed 5,000 manuscripts, 200,000 Ottoman documents, over 100 Ottoman-era cadastral registers (listing land ownership) and a reference collection of 10,000 printed books and journals. Not even the catalogue to the collection survived. Just as with the National and University Library no other surrounding building was hit.[14]

The libraries of ten of the sixteen faculties of the University of Sarajevo were also attacked and destroyed, mostly in the terrible year of 1992, with an estimated loss of 400,000 volumes. On 8 June 1992, the Franciscan convent in a suburb of the city was seized by Serb forces and the friars were ejected. With no protection for the convent library, its 50,000 books were plundered, either destroyed or looted, some of them emerging in the antiquarian book trade around Europe in subsequent years.[15]

In September 1992, when the Holiday Inn in Sarajevo was shelled, the BBC reporter Kate Adie furiously demanded to know from the Serbian battery commander why the hotel where all the foreign correspondents were staying was targeted. In an astonishing admission, he profusely apologised saying that the target was in fact the National Museum across the street – they had missed and the shells had fallen on the hotel by mistake.[16]

In all, it is estimated that 480,000 metres of archives and manuscripts held in institutional collections across Bosnia and around 2 million volumes of printed books were destroyed in the conflict.[17]

From the moment shells started exploding in the National and University Library, strenuous efforts were made to save the collections. Library staff and people of Sarajevo – Serbs, Croats, Jews and

Muslims – together formed a human chain to remove books but only managed to recover less than 10 per cent of its holdings. The services of the library were heroically maintained – over a hundred students managed to complete doctoral degrees during the siege, despite the horrific conditions. The Oriental Institute continued to hold seminars and symposia, the staff operating the services from their homes. Numerous groups offered help, from international library associations to individual libraries, such as the University of Michigan and Harvard University Library. UNESCO quickly endorsed the international community's pledge to support the rebuilding of the library.

The repair of the library building was undertaken in stages, starting in 1996–7 (financed by a donation from the region's former colonial ruler, Austria), at first with the aim of simply stabilising the structure. On 30 July 1998, the World Bank, UNESCO and the city of Mostar launched an appeal for the restoration of the famous bridge in the city, the Stari Most, bringing competition for international funding to the former Yugoslavia. The World Bank regarded the Mostar Bridge as 'the symbol of all Bosnia', and huge resources for reconstruction were thrown at the project by the international community to the exclusion of almost every other cultural heritage initiative in Bosnia.[18]

In the meantime the project to rebuild the library became increasingly mired in political difficulties. In 1999 the European Commission contributed a second tranche of funding, although the work did not begin until 2002 and stopped again in 2004. Ten years after the end of the war the library was still in ruins and even the ownership of the building was disputed – did it belong to the library or the city? The two bodies had differing views on what function the building should have after the reconstruction. But eventually, after further Spanish and EU funding, the building has been reconstructed, and is now a monument to the 15,000 lives lost during the siege of Sarajevo. The Balkan wars of the 1990s left hundreds of thousands dead and millions displaced or dispossessed. The ethnic cleansing that so shocked the world and which brought Milošević and others to The Hague to stand trial for their crimes overshadowed a parallel tragedy – the loss of the intellectual and cultural memory of the region through the deliberate savagery meted out to the libraries and archives.

The Serbian leaders who planned and executed the savage attacks across Bosnia were eventually brought to trial at the International Criminal Tribunal for the Former Yugoslavia, held at the International Criminal Court in The Hague. The leader of the Serb nationalists, Radovan Karadžić, denied that his forces were responsible for the attack on the National and University Library, blaming instead the Muslim population of Sarajevo as, he claimed, they didn't like the architecture of the building.[19] Fortunately the court had appointed an expert adviser with all the knowledge needed to expose these falsehoods: unsurprisingly it was a librarian who would highlight the place of libraries and archives in the cultural genocide in Bosnia.

András Riedlmayer, of the Fine Arts Library at Harvard University, completed a doctorate in Ottoman history and developed a thorough knowledge of the history and culture of the Balkans. He offered his services to help rebuild the libraries of Bosnia as soon as he heard of the devastation, making field trips to gather evidence across the former Yugoslavia.[20] His travels through the region sometimes put him in danger from uncleared mines or from rioting. Over the course of his work for the International Criminal Tribunal, Riedlmayer documented 534 individual sites, some of which were inspected at first hand, but for the others he relied on photographs, testimonies and other forms of documented evidence.[21]

Riedlmayer is one of the few librarians to have faced war criminals like Milošević, Ratko Mladić and Karadžić directly, eye-to-eye, in a courtroom. Thanks to his knowledge of the libraries and archives of the region, Riedlmayer was asked to give evidence in the trial of Milošević, countering with hard facts when Milošević denied the incidents that he was accused of.[22]

The International Criminal Tribunal broke new ground in successfully prosecuting war crimes against cultural heritage, especially against ethnic and religious buildings, as well as libraries and archives. Compared with the attacks and the damage caused, however, the number of prosecutions was tiny, but it did set a precedent and established a sense of redress. The fate of libraries and archives has tended to be lost amid the devastation of war. The 1954 Hague Convention for the Protection of Cultural Property in the Event of Armed Conflict did nothing to prevent the devastation of the National Library in Sarajevo or the many other libraries in Bosnia. However, the existence of the tribunal did result in efforts to hide the evidence of genocide and other war crimes – showing perhaps that the laws had some deterrent effect.[23]

Stanislav Galić, the Serbian general who directed the sniper and shelling campaign that hampered the efforts of library staff, fire-fighters and citizens to save the collections of the National Library, appeared before the court, and in 2006 was sentenced to life imprisonment. Galić's successor during the siege, Mladić, was also indicted in 1996 at The Hague with 'intentional and wanton destruction of religious and cultural buildings . . . including . . . libraries', and he too was sentenced to life imprisonment in 2017. He was joined in the dock by Karadžić and Milošević. Milošević was in poor health and died in 2006 before judgement could be reached. Despite the linkage in the tribunal between crimes against cultural heritage and crimes against humanity, the destruction of the National Library was deleted from the Schedule of Incidents in the prosecution's amended submissions for the trials of Karadžić and Mladić, and there were no convictions for its destruction.[24]

Thousands of historic buildings were destroyed in the war. The priceless books, manuscripts and documents that were also lost received much less press attention. Attempts to restore damaged collections and replace destroyed books have only dealt with a frac-tion of what was lost. The contents of the National Library included many unique items, an irreplaceable body of material. Destroying the library struck at the heart of Bosnia's culture and crippled the university's ability to educate the next generation. The chief of the Sarajevo fire brigade, Kenan Slinić, when asked what motivated him and his men as they risked their own lives to save the library, said: 'Because I was born here and they are burning a part of me.'[25]

One library in Sarajevo managed to escape the destruction. The staff of the research library of the National Museum evacuated most of their 200,000-volume collection, together with the artefacts of the museum, dodging the bullets of snipers and the artillery bombardment that rained down on the city at an average of 400 shells per day. The director of the museum, Dr Rizo Sijarić, was killed by a grenade blast in 1993 trying to arrange plastic sheeting to cover holes in the walls of the museum to protect the collections that remained inside.[26]

This heroic action enabled the Hebrew manuscript known as the Sarajevo Haggadah to be saved. It is an important illuminated manuscript with a long and complex history, created in Spain in the middle of the fourteenth century and taken by Jews who were expelled from the Iberian peninsula in 1497. The Sarajevo Haggadah has become a symbol of the multicultural strength and resilience of Sarajevo, and of Bosnia-Herzegovina, and is now the most famous book in the region. It passed through many hands and survived many conflicts before being purchased by the National Museum of Bosnia in 1894. During the Second World War the manuscript was hidden from the Nazis by the museum's chief librarian, Derviš Korkut, who smuggled the Haggadah out of Sarajevo. Korkut gave it to a Muslim cleric in the town of Zenica where it was hidden under the floorboards of either a mosque or a Muslim home. In 1992, the Haggadah manuscript survived a museum break-in and it was discovered on the floor with many other items the thieves believed were not valuable, and was later stored in an underground bank vault. To quell rumours that the government had sold the Haggadah in order to buy weapons the President of Bosnia presented the manuscript back to the National Museum at a community Seder in 1995 – and it remains accessible there to this day.[27] In November 2017 it was added to the Memory of the World Register, maintained by UNESCO for the preservation of the world's documentary heritage.

Bosnia is not alone in witnessing cultural genocide in recent times. A decade earlier it was the city of Jaffna. Jaffna is the capital of the northernmost province of Sri Lanka, a region where struggles between the Sinhalese and Tamil communities have been a stark feature of society since Sri Lanka gained independence from Britain in 1948. In the northern provinces of the island the Tamils, many of whom are Muslim, are a minority. In May 1981, amid unrest triggered by local government elections, two hundred policemen went on a rampage.

On the night of 1 June the Jaffna Public Library was burned down, destroying its entire collection of 100,000 books and 10,000 manuscripts built up since the foundation of the library. Although there had been a library in Sri Lanka since the early nineteenth century, the first truly public library did not arrive until the creation of the Jaffna Public Library in 1934 and although it moved to a new location and was rededicated in 1954–9, by 1981 it had become 'part of the Jaffna psyche and the desire of its people to attain higher levels of education'.[28]

The Tamil community had always placed great emphasis on the importance of education, and the burning of the library was a deliberate act, perpetrated by policemen and intended to intimidate the Tamils, but also to destroy their aspirations for the future. As journalist Francis Wheen wrote at the time, the destruction of the library, bookshop and newspaper headquarters 'were clearly a systematic onslaught on the Tamil culture'.[29] One Tamil political group asserted that the destruction of Tamil libraries by the Sri Lankan police were part of a policy of 'cultural genocide'.[30] The Sri Lankan government attributed the violence of May and June 1981 to rogue security forces, and following international pressure pledged 900,000 rupees in compensation. Despite this additional funding, the library had still not been rebuilt when twenty-three members of the Jaffna Municipal Council resigned in protest at this failure in 2003. It finally reopened the following year and continues to be used today.

In Yemen, another culture is facing threats of the same kind. The civil war in Yemen has claimed tens of thousands of lives and turned hundreds of thousands into refugees. Yemen's libraries have been seriously damaged. The libraries of the Zaydi community are a unique feature of Yemen's cultural life, as the intellectual heritage of their faith is fostered by its manuscripts, which have been in the country since the ninth century CE. Zaydism is a branch of Shi'a Islam (otherwise found only in the Caspian regions of northern Iran) and is strongest in the mountainous parts of Yemen. The Zaydi community embraces the Houthis – the rebel group opposed by Saudi Arabian-led (and, until December 2018, US-backed) coalition forces.

The Zaydi intellectual tradition is particularly rich, as reflected in the manuscripts in its libraries, due to the openness of the sect to non-Shi-ite ideas, and the location of Yemen, easily accessible to Muslim groups from the Arabian peninsula, North Africa and the Indian Ocean. Zaydis preserve the teachings of the Mu'tazilites, a medieval school of Islamic rationalist thought that promotes the use of human reason as a way to access holy wisdom.[31] The destruction of Zaydi libraries has been in part due to the general devastation wrought by the war, with libraries caught in the crossfire. Much of the destruction has, however, been deliberate, the result of sectarian hatred from Salafi militants, although there has been a long tradition of looting and destruction in the various conflicts that Yemen has witnessed.

Digital technologies are being deployed by librarians to help fight back against the permanent loss of knowledge. Before András Riedlmayer gave evidence at the International Criminal Tribunal at The Hague he had been valiantly trying to rebuild Bosnia's libraries through the 'Bosnian Manuscripts Ingathering Project'. Riedlmayer and librarians around the world tracked copies of manuscripts destroyed in Bosnian libraries (especially the rich holdings of the Oriental Institute Library in Sarajevo). Some of these copies (mostly on microfilm) were found in institutional libraries, some in the private working collections of scholars. Riedlmayer and his colleagues made digital scans of the copies. Only a small number of manuscripts were recovered in this way and copies are not as important as originals. But as a way of helping institutions recover, and for knowledge to serve the local communities in Bosnia, this project was a major step forward.[32]

Digitisation and copying is also playing its part in Yemen. A project undertaken jointly by the Institute of Advanced Study at Princeton and the Hill Museum & Manuscript Library at Saint John's University, Collegeville, Minnesota is digitising Zaydi manuscripts in Yemen and across the world where Zaydi manuscripts have been collected. Digitisation projects collaborating with the US initiative have been funded in European countries, including Italy, Germany, Austria, the Netherlands. To help protect the Zaydi manuscript culture, over 15,000 volumes in all will be captured digitally and made available to raise the profile of the community and highlight the importance of this rare branch of human knowledge.

Contained within the threatened Zaydi manuscripts is the cultural memory of a community that has endured since the tenth century. One library, founded in Ẓafār by the Imam al-Manṣūr bi-Llāh 'Abd Allāh b. Ḥamza (reigned 1187–1217), has had a more or less continued existence to this day, although it is now held in the Mosque of Ṣan'ā. In the face of a violent war being waged by forces with immense power, that unique culture is at risk of being erased. Despite these threats the preservation of knowledge goes on.[33]

One of the Bodleian's Ethiopian manuscripts with members of the British Ethiopian and Eritrean communities, August 2019.

11

Flames of Empire

I N THE MAZE of modern shelving in the climate-controlled stacks of the Bodleian's Weston Library, you can find a small run of shelves that contain one of the library's founding collections, given in 1599 just as Sir Thomas Bodley's idea was taking shape. This particular collection of books was given by his friend Robert Devereux, the energetic Earl of Essex, at the time one of England's most powerful men, a bookish courtier, who was for a time the Queen's favourite. Pull one of these from the shelves and you will find that it is bound in black leather with a coat of arms tooled in gold on the covers. The coat of arms is not that of Devereux, as you might expect, but that of the Bishop of Faro in what is now Portugal.

Faro is described in the travellers' guides as 'a prosperous, busy city'. The area around the cathedral is recommended as having a 'delightful uneven space', and the cathedral is mentioned as having Gothic 'bones'. Nearby the Bishop's palace looms over Faro's Old Town. The guidebooks also point out that 'Pillaged by the Earl of Essex, the bishop's library formed the nucleus of the Bodleian in Oxford.'

The theft of knowledge has a long history. The collections of libraries and archives can sometimes contain materials that have been the result of plunder in wars and territorial disputes. This appropriation deprives communities from access to knowledge just as decisively as burning down a library or archive. Winston Churchill may or may not have coined the phrase 'history is written by the victors' but history is written through access to knowledge. This chapter is concerned with the control of history and issues of cultural and political identity.

The fact that so many ancient books are now in Oxford poses

a set of interesting questions. When do bodies of knowledge, like the Bishop of Faro's library, become legitimate political targets? Does their removal from the communities that originally owned them count as an act of destruction? Similar issues surround objects in museums brought back to Europe from imperial ventures – acquisitions such as the Benin bronzes, found in museums all over Europe, which are the subject of discussion in the museum world today.[1]

The bishop's library came to the Bodleian through an unusual route – it was war booty during the intermittent conflict with Spain (1585–1604), which involved many factors. One was religion – Spain was a Catholic country and sought to impose its faith on England, which had relatively recently turned its back on Catholicism and religious leadership from Rome and had established the Church of England, a Protestant branch of Christianity with the monarch as its head and not the Pope. Elizabeth's Catholic predecessor had been married to the Spanish King Philip II. The marriage had been hugely unpopular in England and much of Elizabeth's foreign policy had been aimed at undermining Spanish power across the globe. The Spanish in turn never lost sight of England as a potential target for their own imperial objectives. Sir Francis Drake's series of attacks on the Spanish Navy in 1587 were famously known as 'singeing the King of Spain's beard'. These skirmishes finally turned to open war with Spain's unsuccessful invasion attempt in 1588. The war had become an imperial, Atlantic conflict, one that sought to establish control over the seas, and with it access to the colonial empires that would drive economic power. Spain had shown how this control could turn a country into a global empire bringing it extraordinary wealth. England saw opportunities, not just to defend its religious position but to go further. A decade after the defeat of the Armada, England was still using its navy to attack and to defend itself against Spain.

These ongoing skirmishes, in which religion, politics and trade were intertwined, involved a number of the leading figures of the English court. On the evening of 3 June 1596, an expedition led by Robert Devereux sailed from Plymouth bound for Spain, where he had intelligence that another invasion of England was being planned, a fear fuelled by a Spanish raid in Cornwall earlier in the year. The fleet reached the port of Cadiz on 21 June. Essex was the first to land with his troops, storming the city in a dramatic raid. A few days later, with smoke from the burning port of Cadiz still smelling on their clothes, the Essex raiding forces sailed west and staged a repeat performance on the neighbouring port of Faro on the Algarve. Soon after landing, Essex 'quartered himself on the bishop's house', as one contemporary account describes it. While in the palace, Essex and his raiding party discovered the library of Bishop Fernando Martins Mascarenhas and selected from it a chest full of printed books, all with the bishop's coat of arms embossed on the covers. They removed the books from the palace library and took them with all kinds of other plunder on board their ships.[2]

Once the expedition had returned to England, Essex gave the collection to Sir Thomas Bodley's new library. The books were arranged on the newly designed shelves and listed in the first printed catalogue of the library, published in 1605.[3] To Essex, Bodley and others in the country, these books would have been seen as a legitimate 'prize'. England was at war with the Spanish Empire, defending not just its religion, but its territory as well. Mascarenhas was also the infamous Grand Inquisitor of Spain, in charge of religious enforcement, and as such may have overseen the torture of English seamen. The bishop was also responsible for censorship in Spain and under his authority was compiled a list of authors who were condemned on religious grounds, the *Index Auctorum Damnatae Memoriae* issued in Lisbon in 1624, a variant focussing on authors on the list of prohibited books, the *Index Librorum Prohibitorum*, first compiled under the authority of the Spanish Inquisition in Louvain in 1546.

In a strange twist of fate the Spanish *Index* proved an inspiration for Thomas James, the Bodleian's first librarian. James had described the books as having come to his library 'by divine providence', noting that some of them had 'whole leaves pasted together, the sentences blotted, and the books tormented in a pittifull manner'. The mere sight of the books, he said, 'would grieve any mans heart to see them' – surely the words of a true bibliophile, and an ardently Protestant one as well. James was particularly interested in the books that the compilers of the Catholic *Index* wanted their readers *not* to be able to read. In fact it became a source of ideas for new accessions for the Bodleian, with the library publishing, in 1627, a list of all the books in the *Index* that were not in the Bodleian, and therefore some of the books that he *most* wanted to acquire.[4]

The books still rest on the shelves of the Bodleian and have moved only a few yards in the 419 years they have been there, well cared for and always accessible to researchers from all over the world. Thomas James, however, has his name listed by Mascarenhas in the 1632 edition of the Spanish index of prohibited books (the *Novus librorum prohibitorum et expurgatorum index*), and was therefore banned from being read in Spain. Mascarenhas never got his books back but he did get his revenge.

Whilst the seizure of the library of the Bishop of Faro was opportunistic, and not the primary goal of the expedition, the theft of the Bibliotheca Palatina (the library of the Prince Electors Palatine, maintained in the city of Heidelberg in Germany) most certainly was. The Bibliotheca Palatina was one of the most celebrated libraries in the sixteenth century and a focus of civic, regional and Protestant pride. At the Reformation the people of the city of Heidelberg came out in favour of the Protestant reformers. Calvinist refugees were welcomed into the city and the university, and in 1563 the Heidelberg Catechism was promulgated there, becoming the official statement of Protestant faith throughout the Palatinate. The library had been created through the plunder of the Reformation and it mirrored in some ways the transfer of books from monastic libraries to secular libraries, and housed many manuscripts formerly in the Abbey of Lorsch, just to the north of Heidelberg, which was dissolved in 1557. Among the treasures of Lorsch Abbey was the famous Codex Aureus or the Lorsch Gospels, a superbly illuminated manuscript from the late eighth century and a witness to the artistic power of Charlemagne's court.

When Heidelberg was captured by the Catholic League of Maximilian of Bavaria in 1622, Pope Gregory XV, who, as the first Jesuit-trained pope, knew the intellectual value of libraries, saw an opportunity to greatly enrich the papal library in Rome, the Bibliotheca Apostolica Vaticana. Pope Gregory arranged for the powerful position of Elector Palatine – one of the five electors of the Holy Roman Emperor – to pass to Maximilian. This was a triumph for Maximilian, and as a rather extravagant 'thank-you' present Maximilian presented the library to Pope Gregory within five days of the capture of the city, writing that the library was given 'as booty and in demonstration of my most obedient and due affection'.⁵ Eventually the books were transferred to Rome – the shelves of the library being chopped up to make packing cases. They transformed the Vatican Library, adding 3,500 manuscripts and 5,000 printed books, almost doubling the collections; not only were medieval manuscripts acquired but also contemporary Protestant literature – of practical use to help the papacy develop counter-arguments. The removal of the library was a symbol of the transfer of power: the arsenal of heresy was disarmed by its move to the epicentre of orthodox faith. Walking around the Vatican Library today you can still see the names of the added collections: 'Codices Palatini Latini' (which is the shelf mark given to the Lorsch Gospels, for example), and 'Codices Palatini Greci': the Latin and Greek manuscripts from the Bibliotheca Palatina.

As the fates of the Bishop of Faro's library and of the Bibliotheca Palatina show us, the forced removal of books and documents from one country to another has a long history. In more recent times the phenomenon has become known as 'displaced or migrated' archives. The fate of these records – some of them destroyed to hide evidence of maladministration and the abuse of power, some physically removed from the former colony and taken back to Europe – becomes a key question in who controls the histories of the former colonies: the newly independent nations or the former colonial powers?

The legacy of empire takes many forms for the European nations that spread their influence across the globe in the eighteenth and nineteenth centuries. Colonies were often run as departments of the civil service of the 'home' country, with many of the colonial administrators being people on tours of duty rather than citizens of the colonised territory. Archives were an essential part of the colonial enterprise. These records documented, often in striking detail, the behaviour of the colonial administration, and the rigour of record-keeping would often reflect the level of control. As such, the process of de-colonisation and independence of former colonies would make records critically important. Their documentation of often embarrassing behaviour by the colonial administration made them a target for destruction, but they were also valuable sources for the history and identity of a new nation and worthy of preservation.

Through the late nineteenth and twentieth centuries archival practice in the West has evolved with the notions of 'archival order' and 'archival integrity'. This thinking developed from the work of the British archivist Sir Hilary Jenkinson (1882–1961) whose approach remains central to modern practice today. The order of an archive should follow the development of the administrative structures whose records are being archived. According to established practice, archives of the colonies were thought of as part of the archives of the colonial power. Normal record-keeping practice would involve, when the department is closed down, using established processes – looking at retention and disposal schedules, and deciding which papers should return to the 'parent' archive, kept back in the 'mother country'. This has resulted, over the past seventy years or so, in a series of highly contentious issues that have pitted some of the newly independent nations against their former colonial overlords, with the legitimacy of historical narrative being central.

This matter continues to be an important one for Britain, as it had the largest empire of the European powers. The moving of archives from the colonies just prior to independence has led to the creation of a massive group of 'migrated' archives back in the UK, held by the parent organisation within government, the Foreign and Colonial Office record stores, known as FCO 141. For many years the existence of these records was either denied or, at best, subject to evasive comment by officials, but now this huge body of knowledge has been formally and publicly admitted, and the records transferred to the UK National Archives, catalogued and made available to scholars.[6] In addition to these 'migrated' archives there were also many instances of deliberate elimination, sometimes through administrators following accepted procedures for managing records, but also as a result of attempts to hide evidence of appalling behaviour by former colonial officials that would have serious political and diplomatic consequences if it came to light.

The process of appraising records involves selecting some of them for either destruction or return, and does not necessarily imply malicious intent to hide evidence. The destruction of records would not necessarily have been carried out to protect personal reputations or hide evidence of wrongdoing. Not all the records generated by a government department can be kept – to do so would be madness and unaffordable madness at that. Previous legislation designed to help manage public records has allowed for disposal of valueless records, especially in the Colonial Office, which, by the early twentieth century, was a vast bureaucracy generating a huge amount of documentation in order to run the empire effectively from London.[7] Typically the National Archives today will only keep 2–5 per cent of the records generated by a government department and this approach was the standard when applied to colonial records. Clerks working in the registries (departments which stored and tracked records that were needed by administrators) would routinely apply the guidance they had received on the retention of records, and would destroy records no longer necessary for current use in administration or that they did not feel had any long-term value for historians. Often these decisions were influenced by more pragmatic concerns – did they simply have enough space to keep unwanted files?

After the end of the Second World War many of the colonies of the European powers campaigned for independence. The process particularly affected Great Britain, Belgium, Holland and France. In deciding what to do with those records, the colonial administrators had to make decisions: should they destroy material as it was no longer necessary, should they pass it over to the newly independent governments or should they send it back to the parent country?

The first major experience of the process of independence of former colonies for the UK was India in 1947, closely followed by Ceylon the following year. In the period leading up to independence, whole runs of records were transferred back to the Foreign and Commonwealth Office in London, rather than being subject to appraisal on a file-by-file basis, which should have happened prior to the return of any files. The head of the Special Branch of the Ceylonese police was surprised, during the process of sending the records back to London, to discover his own file among the mass of material being sent back.[8]

Malaysia became independent from Britain in 1957. In Kuala Lumpur in 1954 the main registry of the colonial government of Malaysia became over-full and large numbers of records, many dating back to the nineteenth century, were destroyed as they were assumed to be duplicates.[9] Vital knowledge of Malaysia's early history was lost in the process. Thanks to the work of historian Edward Hampshire we know that some of these records were destroyed for more sinister reasons. He discovered a document that provided guidance given to the colonial administrators in Malaysia, highlighting those 'documents which it is undesirable should remain in Malayan hands', which were those that reflected 'the policy or point of view of the UK government which it is not desired to make known to the Federation government' and, what was worse, those that 'might give offence on account of their discussion of Malayan problems and personalities'.[10]

The destruction of archives was thus to hide the racist and prejudiced behaviour of the former colonial officials. Five lorryloads of papers were driven to Singapore (which was still a British colony at this time) and destroyed in the Royal Navy's incinerator there. Even this process was fraught with colonial anxiety: 'pains were taken to carry out the operation discreetly, to avoid exacerbating relationships between the British government and those Malayans who might not have been so understanding,' wrote the British high commissioner in Kuala Lumpur, in a classic piece of British understatement. Interestingly, a note has been discovered revealing that the Colonial Office wanted the new government of Malaysia to inherit records that were for the most part complete, specifically to ensure 'that as regards historical material the British could not lay themselves open to the charge of raiding archives for historical purposes and that the material should be left for Malayan historians to study'. The reason why this guidance was not followed, according to Hampshire, was due to the inherent conservatism of the officials on the ground.[11]

Migrated archives have become even more contentious over time as the former colonies seek to understand their historical past. In 1963, just before Kenya became independent, a clerk working at Government House in Nairobi burned many bundles of documents in a brazier on the lawn. Many of the records that documented the brutal suppression of the Mau Mau insurgency were destroyed there, in order to stop them coming into the hands of the new government. Some of this material found its way back to Britain to the famous FCO 141.[12] It took a high court case brought in 2011 by veterans of the Mau Mau rebellion, seeking compensation from the British government, for the existence of the records, transferred in four crates with 1,500 files in November 1963, to become public. Only in 2014 were the records appraised, catalogued and passed to the National Archives. The 'Kenyan Emergency', as the Mau Mau rebellion was euphemistically referred to by the British, forced an approach to records kept in Kenya involving a process of retention and disposal that was inherently racist: only officers that were 'British subjects of European descent' were allowed to decide whether to keep or destroy them. The implication is that it was not 'safe' to allow Africans to decide the fate of their own history.[13]

These experiences were not confined to Britain. Other European colonial powers went through a very similar process. In South East Asia, for example, as Dutch authorities waged a rearguard action against the impending tide of nationalism and independence, archives were one of the symbols of power that the Dutch held on to – creating their own version of FCO 141, known as the Pringgodigdo Archive, a collection of papers relating to the nation- alist cause seized by Dutch paratroopers in 1948 and analysed in detail by the Dutch military intelligence agency.[14] The collection was formed to support a political campaign to discredit the inde- pendence fighters, in order to develop support for the war against the insurgents. Ultimately it failed to generate the kind of stories hoped for. Eventually Indonesia gained its independence, and after a passage of time a rapprochement with the Dutch government took place. The Indonesian government began to look for economic and political support from Western nations, from the Dutch in particular, and as part of this process a cultural agreement was forged which allowed Indonesian archivists to be trained in the Netherlands, heralding a degree of increased cooperation. Eventually the Pringgodigdo Archive was rediscovered, although thought lost for many years, and returned to Indonesia in 1987.

★

In both the British and Dutch examples the former colonies had the upper hand. It was their administrators who made the decisions about which papers should be destroyed and which papers should be migrated back to the 'mother country'. Even then, knowledge of the existence of contentious files has been deliberately suppressed, and whole series of records kept out of the public domain, and even their existence officially denied.

The French developed an outpost of the Archives de France in Aix-en-Provence in the late 1950s, called the French Overseas Archive (AOM), with the express aim of uniting the archives of the now-defunct ministries with those transferred from the 'former colonies and Algeria' (Algeria was not formally regarded as a colony by the French but as an integral part of the French state).[15] The first director at Aix was Pierre Boyer, who had been the director of the Archives of Algiers and who took up his post in 1962, the year that Algeria became independent. The collections were large – 8.5 kilometres of archives came to stock the new facility, which was subsequently extended in 1986 and 1996. The original team of staff was small, just Boyer and three others, who were initially supported by a team of soldiers from the French Foreign Legion, the famous military unit that played a major role in French colonial expansion in the nineteenth century: the new archive facility could hardly have been more intertwined with the French colonial experience. Boyer had himself been complicit in the destruction of archives in Algiers, in the lead-up to independence, with a now-famous episode where he sailed into the Bay of Algiers in June 1962 and tried to sink thirty cartons of police records. When it became clear that they would not disappear below the waves, he doused them with petrol and set fire to them. Presumably the files were not treated this way because they were just taking up too much room. The contents must have been highly contentious and dangerous to the reputation of France if they had fallen into the hands of the nationalist Algerians.[16] A few days earlier the OAS (the clandestine terrorist organisation of French colonists who sought to prevent independence) set fire to the library of the University of Algiers.[17] These few cartons are the tip of an unknowable iceberg of documents destroyed in Algeria, but many tens of thousands of files were sent to France; the majority may have ended up in the new facility run by Boyer in Aix. But many more were spread among the *fonds* (organised groups of documents) of other ministries (such as the defence ministry), as a result of statements made at the highest level in France at the time – from the president, Valéry Giscard d'Estaing – that 'these archives are among the constitutive elements of our national patrimony, as well as of our national sovereignty'.[18] All of these have been claimed back by the government of independent Algeria at various points.[19]

The issue of archives became more intense in Algeria as the country celebrated the 50th anniversary of its independence in 2012 – a suitable moment for historical reflection and celebration of nation-building. The absence of the national archival material became increasingly evident, exposing differing historical narratives concerning the fight for independence. There is a hope in Algeria that the return of the archives might help avoid further social conflict.

Displaced and migrated archives continue to be a major issue between the former colonies and their former colonial overlords. Even today the relationships between colonial power and former colony remain complex. The archive of the Rhodesian army was removed from Rhodesia at the point when it became independent Zimbabwe, and for a time held in South Africa. It was for many years stored in a privately run museum in Bristol, the British Empire and Commonwealth Museum, but when that institution closed through lack of funds the collection became orphaned. The National Archives of Zimbabwe have claimed that it is part of their national patrimony and that it was removed illegally. An important historical source remains inaccessible both to the international community of scholars and to citizens of Zimbabwe. One of the chief concerns over this case is that the records reveal details of the behaviour of the army during the lead-up to independence that may not show the army in a good light.[20]

In the summer of 2019 the Bodleian held a display of manuscripts from its small but significant Ethiopian and Eritrean collections. The manuscripts on show revealed interesting information about the history, culture, language and religion of the region. Among the manuscripts are some which are part of what is known as the 'Magdala Treasure'.

The Magdala expedition into Ethiopia (1867–8) was notable on a number of counts. The British Indian Army (commanded by Sir Robert Napier) invaded Ethiopia in order to rescue British civil servants and missionaries held hostage by Emperor Tewodros II. Tewodros was angry at Queen Victoria's failure to reply to a letter he had sent. Hostages were freed, the Ethiopian army was annihilated and the fortress of Magdala stormed, falling to a final assault in April 1868, when the emperor committed suicide. The British Indian Army left soon after.

There was widespread looting of Ethiopian art treasures and cultural artefacts. According to one account, fifteen elephants and two hundred mules were required to carry away the booty. One contemporary witness, Gerhard Rohlfs, reported that

> . . . we came to the Kings own apartments and here the soldiers had torn everything apart and piles of objects of all kinds lay in confusion . . . It was a regular junk shop on a large scale . . . at the time we did not know that when an English Army takes a city all the goods that fall into the hands of the troops are their property and are sold for the common benefit.[21]

The objects looted at Magdala found their way into state and private collections. Most of the books and manuscripts went into the Library of the British Museum (now the British Library), the Bodleian, the John Rylands Library in Manchester (now part of the University Library there), the Cambridge University Library and some smaller British collections. The theft of Tewodros's library amounted to depriving Ethiopia of national cultural, artistic and religious treasures. There have been repeated calls for the 'Magdala Treasure' (as it is commonly known) to be returned to Ethiopia.

The displaced library collections could have a positive role to play in supporting cultural identity. The Bodleian's display in August 2019 was attended by thousands of people from the British Ethiopian and Eritrean communities (including the Ethiopian ambassador to Britain), but it did not refer to Magdala even though one of the manuscripts on show had been one of the looted treasures. The display had been curated not by the staff of the Bodleian but by members of the Ethiopian and Eritrean communities living in the UK.[22] The issue of Magdala and other examples of looting and imperialist behaviour were, of course, well known to the members of the curatorial team, but the captions did not refer to these histories. They concentrated on the personal responses to the manuscripts, often very sensory responses, evoking childhood memories and the experience of being in Africa, or of being of African descent but living in the UK and being British. The avoidance of the issues of looting was not deliberate, the focus was rather on the engagement between the communities and the manuscripts (an accompanying catalogue did explicitly deal with the provenance of the manuscripts).[23] The exposure that the exhibition has given to Ethiopian and Eritrean culture was hugely positive to the curatorial team, who did not want anything to overshadow the opportunity to celebrate the cultural importance of the manuscripts and the culture they represent.

The removal of knowledge from a community even if that knowledge is not destroyed can have very serious consequences. The narrative of the past can be controlled and manipulated, and cultural and political identity can be seriously undermined when communities do not have access to their own history. Many of the former colonies of the European powers have been independent countries for many decades, and some of them remain concerned that their history continues to be locked inside foreign record stores. It is vital that the communities from which these materials have been removed should be allowed to take control of the narrative of history once again.

Kanan Makiya and Hassan Mneimneh examining Ba'ath Party files in the Iraq Memory Foundation offices, Baghdad, November 2003.

12

An Obsession with Archives

O PPRESSIVE REGIMES ACROSS the globe throughout history have maintained their grip on populations they sought to control through documentation. In ancient Mesopotamia record-keeping for the purpose of raising taxation was perhaps the first example of comprehensive surveillance of people. After the Norman Conquest of Britain in 1066, the new regime surveyed the land to understand how it was arranged, who owned property of all kinds and where they were to be found. This was written down in a series of documents, the most famous being the Domesday Book. Eventually regimes would use secret surveillance to maintain control. During the French Revolution, and in Nazi Germany and Communist Russia citizens were closely monitored and documented in detail, and these documents would enable a fierce grip to be applied.

At the end of the Second World War the Russians held on to East Germany and half of Berlin. The German Democratic Republic (GDR) became the front line of the Cold War for the next forty-five years. On 8 February 1950 the communist regime created a state security organisation, the Stasi. The Stasi functioned as the GDR's secret police, intelligence agency and crime investigation service, with ultimately 270,000 people working for it including 180,000 informers or 'unofficial collaborators'. It spied on almost every aspect of East Germans' daily lives as well as carrying out international espionage. It kept files on about 5.6 million people and amassed an enormous archive, which holds 111 kilometres of files in total. As well as written documentation, the archive has audiovisual material such as photos, slides, film and sound record-ings. The Stasi even had an archive of sweat and body odour samples which its officers collected during interrogations.

After the Central Committee of the Socialist Unity Party stepped down on 3 December 1989, the Stasi became the last bastion of the dictatorship. Across East Germany political organisations, led by the Neue Forum, became concerned that the Stasi might try to burn their records and files, in order to cover up their activities. On the morning of 4 December, detecting smoke from the chimneys of the Stasi district headquarters in Erfurt, local political groups concluded that the Stasi must be destroying files. With the help of other citizens a women's group, 'Women for Change' (in German: *Frauen für Vertrauen*), occupied the building and the neighbouring Stasi remand prison, where the Stasi stored files for safekeeping.[1] This instigated the takeover of Stasi buildings all over East Germany. Citizens gained access to the Stasi headquarters in Berlin on 15 January 1990. The unified German state soon took responsibility for those records, and when the Stasi Records Act was passed in December 1991 it set out the rights of people to view them. By January 2015 over 7 million people had applied to view their own Stasi files.

The East German Stasi were to prove an inspiration for the use of surveillance and documentation for other oppressive regimes in central and eastern Europe and in the Middle East. The subsequent use of their archives would also be an example of how these records can be used to heal a broken society.

The issue of archives as central to the social order, the control of history, and the expression of national and cultural identity continues to be a pressing concern in the twenty-first century. At the time of writing, a significant proportion of the national archives of modern Iraq are located in the United States, the country still seen by many in Iraq as their enemy. These documents are essential to form a thorough understanding of the tumultuous events that have shaped the country, the entire region, and to some extent the whole world since the assumption of power of the Ba'ath Party in 1968, but they could also serve a beneficial social purpose in helping Iraq come to terms with decades of civil conflict.

The most important of these collections is that of the Ba'ath Party. The Hizb al-Ba'ath al-'Arabī al-Ištirākī (the Arab Ba'ath Socialist Party) was the sole and dominant force in Iraq's political and governmental affairs for thirty-five years. From his taking over the presidency in 1979 until his overthrow in April 2003 Saddam Hussein used the organisation and resources of the Ba'ath Party to assert an extraordinary degree of control over the country, due mainly to the state security organisations which sponsored surveillance of citizens, a culture of informants, and the forced suppression of any perceived dissent.[2]

During Saddam Hussein's period in command, training and guidance was provided at various times by the East German Stasi, although in a much more limited way than the Ba'athist Iraqis would have preferred.[3] The Iraqis reached out to the Stasi after the Ba'ath Party seized power in 1968. The Stasi trained Iraqi officers in covert surveillance (especially bugging), the use of secret ink and in decoding communications, as well as in the protection of high-ranking political officials.[4]

The Ba'ath Party collections have been moved to the United States because of a sustained interest in Iraq by the international community. But their removal there was also due to the influence of a handful of individuals, whose passion and determination would be critical to their preservation, often in the face of profound criticism, and even at the risk of their lives.

The first collection relates to Kuwait. Saddam Hussein's invasion of Kuwait in 1990 was executed with lightning speed: the whole country was overrun and occupied within twenty-four hours. Following the invasion came the formal annexation when Kuwait was declared an Iraqi province. The invasion was roundly condemned by the international community. In November 1990 the United Nations passed a resolution giving Iraq until 15 January 1991 to withdraw, and authorising the use of force if it did not comply. The allied attack began on 16 January 1991 and liberation from Iraqi domination followed on 28 February.[5] As the Iraqi forces pulled out of Kuwait in a hurry they left large caches of documents behind them. These were taken to the United States where they were digitised by the US Defense Agency; over time a portion of them have been declassified. Digital files of the Kuwait material eventually found their way to the Hoover Institution at Stanford University where they are known as the Kuwait Dataset.[6]

The Kurdish uprising of 1991, which followed in the wake of the disaster in Kuwait, was the result of decades of friction between the Ba'athist government of Iraq and Kurdish peoples in the north of the country. The ferocity of the Iraqi attacks from the mid-1970s, known as the 'Anfal', which the Kurdistan Democratic Party called 'a racist war of extermination',[7] turned it into an international incident. Kurdish villages were routinely shelled and bombed, the weapons used including napalm and poison gas. In response, Kurdish forces took advantage of the international pressure on Iraq following the first Gulf War to push the Iraqis out of their territory, overrunning a number of administrative centres, including regional command centres of the Ba'ath Party in northern Iraq, at Sulaymanïyah, Dahuk and Erbil. In the process the Kurds seized millions of administrative records, by some estimates weighing in at an impressive 18 tons. The Kurds knew the value of these documents and removed them to caves in remote parts of Kurdistan and other areas for safekeeping. The condition of the documents was poor – they were crammed into sacks and ammunition crates – and had lost all sense of 'archival order'; yet those documents were to have a profound impact on world affairs and the future of Iraq.

In November 1991 Kanan Makiya travelled to the Kurdish-held regions of northern Iraq. Makiya, an Iraqi expatriate, is a central figure in the story of the archives of Iraq, and through him the documentary record would move to the centre of international politics and determine Iraq's history over many decades. One of the extraordinary aspects of Makiya's actions is that he used archives as the heart of his campaign as evidence to expose injustice, the reign of terror and cruelty and to make the international community stand up and take action: he would develop what he calls an 'obsession' with archives.[8]

Makiya's parents had fled Iraq in the 1970s, his father having fallen foul of the totalitarian regime; they relocated their architectural practice to London. Makiya was a student at MIT studying architecture while his parents were fleeing Baghdad. In London he associated with dissident groups and even co-founded an Arabic bookshop which helped to disseminate publications about the Middle East – not just classical Arabic culture, but especially current affairs, as he felt that the West was, at the time, 'drowning in a sea of lies', unable to see the truth of what was happening in Saddam Hussein's Iraq.

In 1989, under the pseudonym Samir al-Khalil, Kanan Makiya published a book called *Republic of Fear*, which drew on the sources he found circulating among the dissident community, but also those he found in the British Library, the Library of Congress and in the Widener Library at Harvard, in order to expose the tyranny of Saddam's Iraq. Subsequent editions appeared under his own name and he instantly became a prominent opponent of the Iraqi regime. In 1991 it was reissued as a paperback, and was read again as the political situation in Kuwait following the Iraqi invasion in August 1990 made its contents intensely relevant and took the book on to the bestseller lists. From this point Makiya became a key intellectual figure in opposition to the Iraqi regime.[9]

Makiya was seen as an ally by the Kurds who showed him documents that he began to realise could be of invaluable use in raising awareness of the human rights violations perpetrated against the Kurds. As he put it, his earlier book had been 'like a physician judging a person's malady from external symptoms only. What the documents would do is allow the physician to look inside the patient's body.'[10]

The main groups of records were under the control of the allied Kurdish political organisations – the Patriotic Union of Kurdistan and the Kurdistan Democratic Party – united in their hatred of Saddam's Iraq. As the 1990s progressed they realised that handing them over to the United States could enhance the status of their organisations. They reached an agreement that allowed for the documents to be airlifted out of Kurdish-held northern Iraq via an airbase in Turkey and placed in the custody of the US National Archives.[11] The archivists then got to work, rehousing them in 1,842 archival boxes, allowing them to be safely handled by staff of the Defense Intelligence Agency and Middle East Watch under the direction of Joost Hiltermann whose team had digitised 5.5 million documents by the end of 1994. By this point the documents were being treated as one archive. In 1997, the Senate Foreign Relations Committee transferred the documents (and a copy of the digital files) into the custody of the University of Colorado at Boulder. The transfer was made strictly under terms that Kanan Makiya insisted on: the rightful ownership of the files lay with the Iraqi people, held in trust in the United States until a state existed in Iraq that was willing to preserve them in an archive similar to the one established in Germany, where the archive of the Stasi was made available to the public.[12]

In 1992, Kanan Makiya had established a small research group called Iraq Research and Documentation Project (IRDP), based at Harvard University's Center for Middle East Studies, and arranged for copies of the digitised files of the majority of the boxes (but not all of them) to be given to the IRDP. Over the course of the following year the digitised files were put into a database system and metadata was added to these files: names of individuals, originating departments, key event dates, and summaries of contents. The IRDP website in 1999 boasted that it was 'the single largest collection of Iraqi records ever to become public'. Makiya's intention was that it be studied and analysed for the good of Iraqi society. This broader social purpose, made all the more urgent due to the human rights violations happening every day in northern Iraq, was at the heart of what he was trying to do: provide evidence of injustice and to raise awareness of what was happening to the Kurdish people so that pressure could be brought to bear on the international community to intervene. The ethical dilemma soon became clear, however. Publishing original documents was putting the lives of Iraqis at risk, as putting these documents in searchable form online exposed the names and personal details of many individuals to those forces that might cause them harm. The decision was made to take any files that revealed personal details down from the public website.

Makiya's advocacy for regime change in Iraq, which he developed through the information he had gleaned from the archives captured by the Kurds, became very influential in American foreign policy circles as the 1990s turned into the twenty-first century. His was one of the voices listened to by the White House as the mood began to shift towards a second Gulf War and the forcible removal of Saddam and the Ba'ath Party from power. The Iraqi archives in the United States began to be searched for hints about weapons of mass destruction. Makiya's passionate view about the Iraqi regime began to make a difference to the hardening of attitudes in Washington.

A critical turning point for him was an appearance on a popular current affairs TV programme, *Now*, hosted by veteran American political commentator Bill Moyers, alongside the writer Walter Isaacson and historian Simon Schama, where he urged a second Gulf War, and made a profound moral case for a successful transition.

The show, which was broadcast on 17 March 2003, went straight to the hot topic of the day: the anticipated invasion of Iraq. 'The American army is not just going in there to destroy things. It's going there to build things,' Makiya said to Moyers. The presenter questioned him on the evidence for injustices in Iraq and he replied, referring to the archives, 'We've got evidence coming out of our ears. I have lists of disappeared people. I just said, a million and a half people killed, Iraqis killed, since 1980, violently at the hands of the regime.' Later in the programme Moyers put the million-dollar question to him: 'And you are convinced war is the right option?' Makiya replied: 'There's no alternative. There's a war already going on. And it's a war being waged on the Iraqi people.'[13] Such advocacy was highly influential in governmental circles. On the eve of the war Kanan Makiya was close to the US leadership, with George Bush personally informing him that there would be an invasion. Less than a month later US forces invaded Iraq and Makiya watched the invasion with the president in the Oval Office.[14] He was unprepared for the chaos that would ensue.

'Ancient archive lost in Baghdad library blaze', proclaimed the *Guardian* on 15 April 2003, reporting that: 'As flames engulfed Baghdad's National Library yesterday, destroying manuscripts many centuries old, the Pentagon admitted that it had been caught unprepared by the widespread looting of antiquities, despite months of warnings from American archaeologists.'[15] As the invasion continued, the focus of attention would move from libraries to museums; looted antiquities would dominate the agenda of the world's press in terms of cultural heritage: Mounir Bouchenaki, UNESCO's Assistant Director General for Culture, would describe the looting of artefacts as a 'catastrophe for the cultural heritage of Iraq'. Equally, if not more catastrophic for the country, was the destruction and sequestration of archives and libraries occurring across Iraq, which would continue almost invisibly to the international press for the following fifteen years.

As traditional forms of documentation came under attack new forms were emerging. The invasion of Iraq was the first conflict in modern history to be live-reported on social media. The 'Baghdad Blogger', Salam Abdulmunem, provided a vivid insight into life in Iraq's capital city, evoking the fear and trepidation of what was to come. 'Impossibly long lines in front of gas stations last night', he blogged on 17 March 2003, adding that there were 'rumors of defaced picturs [sic] of Saddam in Dorah and Thawra Districts'. Television was still accessible to Iraqis, and Salam wrote: 'The images we saw on TV last night . . . were terrible. The whole city looked as if it were on fire. The only thing I could think of was "why does this have to happen to Baghdad". As one of the buildings I really love went up in a huge explosion I was close to tears.' The invasion of this Second Gulf War (as it has since come to be known) came at a terrible cost in human life: between 4,000 and 7,000 Iraqi civilians and 7,000 to 12,000 members of the security forces lost their lives. Fewer than two hundred British and American troops were killed.[16]

The archives of the Ba'ath Party were being abandoned to their fate in a series of underground chambers beneath Baghdad as the American bombs fell on the city. The archive is known by various terms of description but most commonly as the Ba'ath Regional Command Collection (BRCC); it had for the most part resided in a network of rooms underneath the Ba'ath Party headquarters in Baghdad. In addition to this largely paper archive, there was a collection of audio recordings made at the behest of the Iraq Security Services. As the party held such a prominent and central position in the Iraqi state, its papers take the form essentially of governmental records (unlike the position of most countries which can more easily separate political party records from national archives).

Kanan Makiya had no notion of it as a collection, and even less did he sense that this would become such a key part of his life, and of the future of his country in the years to come. He had been invited to a meeting in the south of Iraq in June 2003 with around sixty other Iraqis who were gathered to 'think through the transition'. He was optimistic about the future of post-Saddam Iraq: 'Iraq is rich enough, developed enough, and has the human resources to become as great a force for democracy and economic reconstruction in the Arab and Muslim worlds as it has been a force for autocracy and destruction,' he wrote shortly after the invasion.[17]

Post-invasion Baghdad was a place of chaos, rumour and destruction. When a US Army captain asked Kanan Makiya for advice about a large quantity of documents in the basement of the central headquarters of the Ba'ath Party in Baghdad, Makiya was curious. He was taken down into a labyrinth of basements 'like Aladdin's cave'. The basements were knee-deep in water in parts, and there was no electricity, but the network of rooms contained shelf after shelf of documents, many of them on racks that had fallen over, splaying their contents over the floor. Makiya examined some of the documents and files and could see immediately that this was a major source of information. He knew instantly that it had to be saved.

Makiya's parents had built a large house in Baghdad before they fled the country in 1971 and this was fortunately situated in the Green Zone, an area protected by the US military. He found US officers based there and managed to use his influence with Paul Bremer, the most senior civilian administrator at the Coalition Provisional Authority, to move the documents out and transferred to his control. He could hardly believe his luck: his parents' old house was now the official headquarters of the organisation he established to deal with the Iraqi archives, the Iraq Memory Foundation (IMF). The material began to be moved from the basement to the house and the process of digitising it began.[18] Hewlett-Packard donated scanners, and the IMF staff, augmented by a team of Iraqi volunteers, were able to scan 80,000 pages a month (given that the archive today amounts to more than 6 million pages this was not nearly fast enough).[19] It was very dangerous work: attempts were made to destroy the archive, possibly by former Ba'ath Party officials, and members of the team received death threats. At one point a rocket landed on the roof of the house but miraculously did not explode. Given the descent into violent civil war within Iraq, a decision was made to remove the archive, which felt like a sensible precaution.

The Department of Defense funded its removal under supervision by Makiya's team, to a huge military hangar in Virginia. Here a large-scale processing facility was set up, with an assembly line who were able to scan 100,000 pages per day. Within nine months the job was done. Documents from that collection, and from the material captured by the Kurds, went on to form evidence heard by the tribunal accusing Saddam Hussein of crimes against humanity. He was found guilty and sentenced to death by hanging on 30 December 2006.

The Ba'ath Party archives are now in the Hoover Institution at Stanford University in California. The various accounts relating to the move of the archive all agree that it was originally set up as a short-term arrangement.[20] The archive would be secured and administered by a highly professional team of staff, but history was already being controlled by the victor of the Second Gulf War. Saad Eskander, director of the Iraq National Library and Archive, wrote:

> Within the space of three days, Iraq National Library and Archive lost a large portion of Iraq's historical memory. Hundreds of thousands of archival documents, and rare books were lost forever . . . As a direct result of the two fires and lootings, the National Archive lost about 60 percent of its archival materials. In one word: it was a national disaster on a large scale. These losses cannot be compensated. They formed modern Iraq's historical memory.[21]

The material found by the Kurds, and the Ba'ath Party archive, were not the only collections taken from Iraq. The Iraqi secret police files also found their way to the University of Colorado Boulder.[22] Collections of documents in numerous government and defence buildings were discovered and removed. These collections were much larger than the Ba'ath Party archives and were taken to Qatar where they were digitised to help in the search for weapons of mass destruction, the motivation being very different from the rendition of documents by the Kurds, which was to expose the abuse of human rights. This set of files is the largest of them all – estimated to be over 100 million pages. Selections were made and released online by the Conflict Records Research Center at the National Defense University, and the majority of these records were returned in May 2013, when 35,000 boxes on 634 pallets were loaded into transport planes and flown back to Iraq.[23] The Ba'ath Party records, however, remain.

Given the collapse of civil society in Iraq, and the role that archives played in the case for invasion, was the removal of the archives the right thing to do? Kanan Makiya now regrets his urging for the invasion in 2003 but not the removal of the archives. The Iraqi state had 'rotted during the 1990s . . . hollowed out by sanctions from the west',[24] and as a result the 2003 invasion was not a real war, as there was no opposition: 'the whole pack of cards came tumbling down'.

No one outside Iraq, including himself and the decision makers in the Bush administration, realised that the Iraqi state had become so corroded. Nor did he expect the social order to evaporate so quickly after the invasion: 'the snowballing of the catastrophe that is post-2003 Iraq transfixed me'.[25]

Archives played an important part in shaping the political arguments that led to the Second Gulf War and its aftermath. The impact of the two Gulf wars on the world has been profound, stimulating global terrorism on an unprecedented scale, with the social and economic catastrophe that has swept up Iraq and other countries in the region, and the deaths of hundreds of thousands across the globe arguably the result. Has the continued absence of the Iraqi archives delayed the healing of that society?

It is possible to contrast the effects of access to archives in Iraq with that of East Germany after the collapse of communism. The contrast between what happened in the former eastern bloc countries and Iraq is one that puzzled me for many months as I grappled with the ethical problems of the removal of the Iraqi archives. Without them, how could they face up to their difficult past?[26] In Germany an organisation called the Gauck Authority was set up after the fall of the Berlin Wall in 1989 to administer the process of opening up, in a very controlled manner, access to the Stasi archives. Could Iraq have achieved similar levels of social progress that the opening up of archives – albeit mediated by the Gauck Authority – had enabled in the former East Germany? Arguably the process in Germany was successful because the West German economy was strong enough to allow it to be well resourced. Joachim Gauck, the former East German priest who set up the Gauck Authority (and later became Germany's president), developed a sophisticated organisation that could carefully control the release of information to citizens, so as not to compromise the safety of others. By 1994 Gauck employed 3,000 staff, with a huge budget, and they were able to process millions of requests for access to, and information from, the files.[27] Without the funds to resource it properly the whole enterprise could have been disastrous. This could well have been the case in Iraq.

A further set of documents relating to Iraq's most recent history has appeared in several different, and unrelated, online presentations. The most high-profile and controversial of these has been the work of Rukmini Callimachi, a *New York Times* journalist embedded within the Iraqi army. She accessed buildings recently seized from ISIS control and came across 15,000 pages of documents and computer hard disks – information that has been central to her work on 'The ISIS Files', relating to the terrorist organisation calling itself Islamic State, which started as a splinter group of al-Qaeda and which attempted to take control of territory in Syria and Iraq. Callimachi was not granted – and did not seek – permission to remove the documents from Iraqi territory, she just took them. She has since been working with the George Washington University to digitise, translate and publish the documents online, alongside lengthy journalistic materials in the form of a podcast and pieces in the newspaper, only allowing others to access them after her own journalism has been published. This process raises the familiar issues surrounding the legal and moral authority to remove and publish documents from their country of origin.[28]

The documents have revealed a lot of important information about how the Caliphate, established in June 2014 by ISIS, operated. There is a good deal of detail on the workings of the administrative structures, and the way they affected the lives of ordinary people through, for example, setting prices (ranging from the cost of caesarean births to satsumas) or detailing the punishments for certain crimes (death for homosexuals, eighty lashes for those found drinking wine). These documents are very different to the earlier documents removed from Iraq, as ISIS was not an Iraqi organisation but a transnational body stretching across Iraq and Syria and not replacing the political structures of Iraq but asserting a new one. Key ethical questions remain concerning Callimachi's behaviour: were the documents removed illegally? Was it responsible to publish them, especially when living individuals are mentioned in the documents, potentially putting their lives at risk?

The amount of documents now being published by Callimachi is small in comparison to the vast caches removed by the US government but it shows the continued centrality of archives in understanding political and social events across the globe. During the last decade the position of the Iraqi archives, especially those of the Ba'ath Party, have been the subject of great critical debate, involving prominent individuals and organisations. The key questions remain: were they illegally taken? Should they be returned?

The Iraqi documents have a complex history. The first tranche, found by the Kurds, played a decisive role in prompting the Second Gulf War, but they also exposed the horrors of the regime of Saddam Hussein. The Kurds can hardly be blamed for using them to draw attention to the horrific acts perpetrated against them. The Ba'ath Party documents saved in Iraq by Kanan Makiya have shown the control exercised by the Ba'athist regime in shocking detail. The role of informers, the execution of dissenters, the war against the Kurds, all the details of these aspects of life in Iraq and more have since been made more widely known as a result. Had they remained in Baghdad, even the American military may have struggled to protect them. But the documents have not been in the hands of the Iraqi people, and it has not been possible for them to play a role in their country's social development such as the opening of the Stasi archives achieved in East Germany.

Inspired by the Holocaust museums in Europe and America and by the experience of South Africa, where the Truth and Reconciliation Commission had used archives and oral testimonies as part of their social healing, Kanan Makiya saw the possibility of creating a museum in Baghdad to house the material he had found. The atrocities of the past had to be 'remembered'.

Iraqis have had a decade of trying to forget the past forty years. A new generation deserves the opportunity to 'remember' or to understand what happened – but as Iraqis rather than as members of an imposed regime. Sadly, as I write in early 2020, the Iraqi archives held at the Hoover Institution have not been returned to the safekeeping of the Iraqi government. The geopolitical situation in the region has not made this possible. But without the ability to use those archives to face up to their past, the Iraqi people will struggle to move into the future.

Aerial photograph of Led by Donkeys' banner during the anti-Brexit march, London, April 2019.

13

The Digital Deluge

W E ARE AT a moment in history where knowledge is changing dramatically in the way we interact with it. The age we now live in is an era of 'digital abundance', where digital information saturates our lives.[1] The volume of information created daily, held in digital form and available online, is astonishing. In a typical minute in 2019, 18.1 million text messages were sent, 87,500 people tweeted, and over 390,000 apps were downloaded across the globe.[2] Not only must we be concerned about the narrative of those texts, or the images in those tweets, but the underlying data that underpin them is also now part of societies' knowledge.

Many libraries and archives are now 'hybrid' collections, dealing with both traditional and digital media together. In many institutions, digital collections will often fall into two categories: those that have been digitised from existing collections of books, manuscripts and records, and those materials that were 'born-digital', created in digital form from the start, such as email, word-processing files, spreadsheets, digital images and so on. Scholars don't just write articles in learned journals, they create research data from scientific instruments or other scholarly processes, often in huge quantities. The scale of the digital collections of many libraries and archives has been growing rapidly. In the Bodleian we have, for example, around 134 million digital image files, spread across multiple storage locations, which require preservation.[3] Such an abundance of information has become normal. We now take for granted the ease and convenience of being able to access information, and we regard the opportunities for research in all fields that it enables as routine.

As our everyday lives are increasingly played out in digital form, what does this mean for the preservation of knowledge? Since the digital shift has been driven by a relatively small number of powerful technology companies, who will be responsible for the control of history and for preserving society's memory? Is knowledge less vulnerable to attack when it is controlled by private organisations? Should libraries and archives still have a role to play in stewarding digital memory from one generation to the next as they have done since the ancient civilisations of Mesopotamia?

Libraries and archives have been very active in digitising their collections and putting them online so they can be shared. The phenomenon of Distributed Denial of Service (DDoS) is familiar for anyone publishing information online. DDoS attacks work through software that subjects a public website to a bombardment of queries, thousands or even tens of thousands of times a second, from a range of internet addresses, and often utilising a piece of automated software called a botnet. This normally overwhelms the servers hosting the website being attacked. These kinds of attacks can be regular and frequent, sometimes the work of idle hackers who are attracted to the challenge of 'taking down' the website of a large, famous, venerable or respected institution (such as the Bodleian, which has suffered such attacks from time to time), but there is growing evidence that states are also using DDoS against their rivals and enemies. The organisations on the receiving end of these attacks respond by building a stronger infrastructure, costing more and more. But this kind of attack is just the most 'straightforward' variety in the digital world. There are also more insidious forms.

A new existential challenge faces libraries and archives, one that affects the whole of society. Knowledge in digital form is increasingly created by a relatively small number of very large companies, which are so powerful that the future of cultural memory is under their control, almost unwittingly, with consequences and implications that we are only just waking up to. They are collecting knowledge created by us all and we now refer to it simply as 'data'. This data is gathered from the entire globe, and because it relates to our interaction with their platforms the companies often have exclusive access to it. They are using it to manipulate our behaviour in many different ways, mostly by trying to shape our purchasing habits, but this influence is also entering other areas of life – our voting behaviour and even our health. They are doing this in secretive ways, which are hard for people to understand.

The rapid rise of these companies, with their global customer bases and vast revenues, has been unprecedented. Perhaps the closest parallel is that of the Roman Catholic Church in the Middle Ages and Renaissance. The Catholic Church likewise held both spiritual and temporal powers over vast swathes of the globe, with massive financial interests. Its authority was held in a single individual, albeit one who worked within a power structure that gave immense authority to a relatively small number of people. A commonly held belief system, together with a common language, enabled their global authority to be maintained and to grow. Facebook today boasts of its 'single global community', and the statistics show that Google has the overwhelming market share of online search and consequently the largest share of 'adtech', the data used to track the behaviour of users of these services, which is then sold to online advertisers (and others).[4] The large tech companies in China, like Tencent and Alibaba, have billions of users, who interact with the platform many times a day. All of the companies offer free online hosting of images, messages, music and other content for their users, taking up vast amounts of storage using cloud technologies (Amazon is now the world's largest provider of data storage through its subsidiary Amazon Web Services). We have become used to clicking 'like' or engaging with posts and adverts created by other social media users or advertisers. The power that these companies now hold has made historian Timothy Garton Ash refer to them as 'private superpowers'.[5] And the way these companies operate has been termed 'surveillance capitalism'.[6]

At the end of 2019 the photo-sharing site Flickr, struggling to keep pace with competition from the likes of Instagram, announced that it was reducing the amount of free storage for its account holders. After February 2019 users of free accounts were limited to 1,000 photos and videos and any excess was automatically deleted by the company. Millions of Flickr users found that much of their content had been permanently removed. What happened at Flickr shows us that 'free' services aren't really free at all. Their business model is based on the (often unacknowledged) trading of user data, and as market share is lost to competitors, 'free' services have to make way for paid premium (freemium) services. Storage is not the same as preservation.[7]

The problem that the Flickr case throws up is one of trust in the companies that now control knowledge online. Active users will have known about the coming changes, and were perhaps able to move their data on to other platforms. Others who did not move fast enough perhaps lost images of their loved ones or a photographic record of their adventures. Gone in the blink of an eye. Consumers have had similar experiences with other 'free' platforms such as Myspace and Google+, both of which were also closed down in 2019 with little advance notice. YouTube destroyed thousands of hours of videos documenting the Syrian Civil War in 2017.[8] Precious information was lost, much of it gone for ever.[9] These sites, and the companies that maintain them, are driven by commercial gain and are (for the most part) answerable to shareholders. They have no public benefit mission, and any knowledge that they store is kept only to support their commercial operations.

Libraries and archives are trying to engage with this new information order and to play a positive role in the preservation of digital knowledge, but the tasks are complex and expensive. The Library of Congress, for example, announced a groundbreaking partnership with social media giant Twitter in 2010, with the library's aspiration to develop a complete archive of all of Twitter, past, present and future, since its launch in March 2006. The Library of Congress has been one of the leading institutions working with digital preservation; as the national library of the richest nation on earth it would seem natural for it to form a partnership with a technology company at the forefront of the social media revolution.

Unfortunately, owing to funding shortfalls the arrangement ceased in 2017, with the library now only preserving tweets 'on a selective basis'.[10] Given the power of social media platforms like Twitter and Facebook, and the use made of them by leading individuals and organisations involved in politics and other aspects of public life, the lack of any preserved systematic record cannot be good for the health of an open society.

We increasingly play out our lives on social media so we need to find ways for libraries and archives to help society remain open. As the political sphere has embraced digital information we have seen the rise of 'fake news' and 'alternative facts'. Preserving knowledge in order to inform citizens and to provide transparency in public life is becoming a critical issue in the future of democracy. The behaviour of tech companies, especially the social media firms, and data corporations who have been employed in political campaigning, is coming under increasing scrutiny. Archives can be vital to providing evidence of their behaviour.

Libraries and archives that preserve the web (in 'web archives') have become particularly important as they are able to provide permanent bases for a huge range of the human endeavours documented online in websites, blogs and other web-based resources. The public statements of political candidates, office holders and government officials (often to their embarrassment) appear on the web, and there is an increasing sentiment that they should be preserved so that the public, the media and, eventually, voters can call their representatives to account for those statements.

Web archiving is still a relatively new tool. The UK Web Archive, for example, is a collaborative effort of the six copyright libraries in the United Kingdom and the Republic of Ireland.[11] They have enjoyed 'legal deposit' privilege, whereby printed publications have been required to be deposited in designated libraries since the Licensing Acts of 1662 and the Copyright Act of Queen Anne in 1710.[12] The archiving of the UK web domain was begun in 2004 as a British Library initiative, with its collecting of carefully selected websites undertaken through a voluntary 'permissions-based' approach, where the sites were selected for capture, and each website owner was contacted and had to grant explicit permission before the site could be added to this archive. All the preserved sites were then openly accessible to the public, online. In 2013 the legal deposit legislation was updated when the 'Non-Print Legal Deposit Regulations' were passed into law. These regulations transferred this voluntary system to one mandated by law and harnessed to the six legal deposit libraries, which now co-fund the vast enterprise.[13]

Archiving the web is a complex task, as the targets are constantly moving. Many websites disappear or change address frequently. The UK Web Archive shows an astonishing rate of attrition of sites it has captured over time. Of the websites preserved in any one year, within two years around half of them have gone from the open web, or cannot be found for some reason (in technical terms, their web addresses are not resolvable). After three years this becomes 70 per cent or so. Despite these problems, the web archive is growing. In 2012 it held regular archived copies of around 20,000 websites. At the end of the last complete 'crawl' of the UK web, in 2019 (the crawls take almost a year to complete), the archive contained copies of over six million websites, which archive over 1.5 billion web resources. The archive also holds deeper, more regular collections of over nine thousand curated 'special collections' websites, which our curatorial teams have identified as being of more significant research value. These are crawled much more frequently: monthly, weekly or even daily, and they make up 500 million web resources as the sites are regularly re-crawled.[14]

One of the UK Web Archive's special collections of blogs and websites has captured 10,000 sites relating to the 2016 referendum on European Union (EU) membership known as Brexit, as well as the political aftermath of the vote. In April 2019 the Vote Leave campaign deleted a great deal of content from their public website, including references to that campaign's promise to spend £350 million a week on the National Health Service (NHS) if Britain left the EU, a promise that by 2019 had become increasingly controversial. Fortunately the UK Web Archive had captured the website before that content was deleted.

Access to knowledge on the web is now a social necessity. However, in 2007 Harvard scholars Jonathan Zittrain, Kendra Albert and Lawrence Lessig discovered that more than 70 per cent of the websites referenced in articles in the *Harvard Law Review* and other legal journals and, even more importantly, 50 per cent of URLs in the public website for the US Supreme Court, were broken, suffering from what is called in the digital preservation community 'linkrot'. These websites are of huge social importance: how can society behave unless it knows what the laws of the land are?[15]

The growth of digital information has moved faster than libraries and archives have been able to keep pace with, and other players have moved in to try to fill the gaps. The uber-web archive of them all, the Internet Archive, is a good example of this kind of private archiving initiative. Founded by internet pioneer Brewster Kahle in 1996, it is based in San Francisco. The archive's strapline 'Universal Access to All Human Knowledge' is typical of the bold thinking you encounter in this part of California. Since it was founded, through its key service called the Wayback Machine, it has captured more than 441 billion websites. The sites are publicly viewable through the internet and the tool has been developed entirely through the use of web-crawlers, which 'scrape' data from the public web and capture it. No permissions are sought and there is no explicit legal basis for their activity that would form the equivalent of the legal deposit regulations in the UK.

The Internet Archive has itself become subject to attempts to destroy the knowledge it holds. In June 2016 a massive DDoS was launched on the Internet Archive from groups angry that the site hosted websites and videos created by members of the extremist organisation ISIS and its supporters, but it failed. What the incident highlights is the relatively fine line between legitimate acquisition and provision of access to knowledge and censorship of knowledge that is either offensive to the majority of citizens, or being used as propaganda tools by groups that have been legitimately banned for their violent or illegal views.[16]

What concerns me most about the Internet Archive is its long-term sustainability. It is a small organisation, with a board to oversee its activities, but it operates with a modest funding base. It has no parent body to look after it – perhaps this is why it has been able to achieve what it has so quickly – but this could provide it with a greater capacity for longevity. At some point it must become part of, or allied to, a larger institution, one which shares its long-term goals to preserve the world's knowledge and make it available. I have used the Internet Archive many times and it is incredibly valuable. When my family and I moved to Oxford in 2003 we had to fight a case with the Local Education Authority to make it possible for our two children to attend the same local primary school. We were able to prove that the authority's public information about its policy changed on a certain date by accessing the preserved copies of their website through the Wayback Machine.

The Internet Archive is a reminder that there are some areas of public life where archives and libraries are not keeping up with the needs of society. They tend to be cautious institutions and slow to act. In many ways this has been one of their strengths, as the structures they have built have tended to be resilient. My sense is that the Internet Archive is now an 'organised body of knowledge' of huge importance for global society, but it is one that is 'at risk' in its current independent state. The international community of libraries and archives needs to come together to develop new ways of supporting the Internet Archive's mission.

The work of the Internet Archive is one example of what I would like to call 'public archiving', or 'activist archiving', initiatives that emerge from concerned members of the public who have taken tasks on themselves, independently of the 'memory organisations' like libraries and archives. Sometimes these public archiving activities can move faster than the institutionally bound ones, particularly with the rise of 'fake news', where again public archiving has had to step in.

One of the features of political life in the United States under the Trump administration has been the presidential use of social media – Donald Trump has an astonishing 73.1 million followers on Twitter as of 28 February 2020 (equating to 22 per cent of the US population), and 17.9 million followers on Instagram. Such an enormous following gives him the ability to reach out directly to the voting public of America. His statements on social media therefore have a powerful impact, with potentially profound consequences for the whole world. The organisation Factbase has been keeping track of the presidential Twitter feed and its deletions. Since the president joined Twitter in 2009 up to 28 February 2020, he has tweeted an astonishing 46,516 times, and a small number – 777 – of those have been deleted, presumably either by the president himself or by members of his staff. Under the rigours of the Presidential Records Act, eventually the presidential Twitter feed should become part of the Presidential Archive, and if that turns out to be the case it would become the responsibility of the National Archives and Records Administration.[17]

The Presidential Records Act depends on trust between the presidential office and the National Archives. The archivist of the United States cannot realistically force the president or his team to comply with the Act. The Act requires the president to 'take all such steps as may be necessary to assure that the activities, deliberations, decisions, and policies that reflect the performance of the President's constitutional, statutory, or other official or ceremonial duties are adequately documented, and that such records are preserved and maintained as Presidential records', but the president also has discretion to 'dispose of those Presidential records of such President that no longer have administrative, historical, informational, or evidentiary value'. The Act states that such disposals can only happen if the advice of the archivist of the United States is sought, but the president is not bound by law to adhere to this advice. As such, during the tenure of office of a US President, the archivist has limited ability to take any steps to preserve presidential records, beyond seeking the advice of two congressional committees.

Although Donald F. McGahn II, the White House Counsel to the President, issued a memorandum to all White House personnel in February 2017 on their obligation to maintain presidential records (as defined by the Presidential Records Act), expressly referring to electronic communication, it remains to be seen whether the administration, or indeed the president himself is complying with the Act. The Act has no teeth because of its inherent assumption that all presidents would honour the system. The use of technologies such as encrypted messaging apps (WhatsApp is, for example, known to be widely used by the president's inner circle of advisers), which allow for messages to be automatically deleted after a period of time that can be pre-set by the user, social networks and other 'internet-based means of electronic communication to conduct official business' are expressly prohibited without the approval of the Office of the White House.[18] The use of such technologies ought to have provided an opportunity for advice to be sought from the archivist of the United States, and numerous commentators have claimed that use of such technologies violates the Presidential Records Act.[19]

Prior to becoming president, Donald Trump maintained a video log (vlog) from 2011–14, which was mounted on the Trump Organization's YouTube channel. He deleted most of it prior to 2015 (only 6 of the original 108 original entries are still to be found on YouTube), but Factbase maintains a record of it on their website, in order to add it to the public record. One of the sections of the website covers media interviews that the president has undertaken during his term of office. The dominance of his interviews given to media outlets owned and controlled by Newscorp is one of the revealing pieces of data that Factbase makes available to the public:

36.4 per cent of all his interviews have been given to Newscorp organisations. Factbase has sourced, captured, transcribed and made all of these searchable, but it is not the only tool designed to document the president's online behaviour; a website called Trump Twitter Archive also attempts to track these tweets in a similar way.[20]

The work that Factbase, Trump Twitter Archive and others have done is to make the public utterances of the president available for public scrutiny in a way that no other president has been subject to before, at least not during his term of office. This 'public knowledge' is essential for the health of an open democratic system, particularly one where the incumbent of the most powerful political office in the world uses public media channels extensively to promote his political agenda. This work is made even more important when the president or his aides are prone to deleting these public utterances. The work relies on screenshots of the Trump tweets, which are then followed up by automated routines to transcribe the tweets, add metadata and place them in a database for further analysis.

Another example of public archiving has been developed by an independent organisation in the UK called Led By Donkeys. Operating in the public sphere, both online and in the physical setting of billboards and other public places in major cities, Led By Donkeys (the name originates in a phrase used during the First World War, when British infantrymen were often described as 'lions led by donkeys', giving a sense of what the men on the front thought of their generals) has been preserving statements by leading politicians that are now different from their stated policy position and making them public – essentially holding those politicians to account.[21]

These public archiving activities reveal the importance of preserving information that can call politicians to account for their comments. Political discourse has often been a battleground between truth and falsehood but the digital arena amplifies the influence that political falsehoods can have on the outcomes of elections. Public archiving initiatives like Factbase and Led By Donkeys seem to me to be filling a void where public institutions could, and should, be saving this kind of information more systematically.

★

One of the most heavily used 'organised bodies of knowledge' in the present day is the online encyclopaedia Wikipedia. Founded in 2000, it grew rapidly adding its millionth entry within six years. Despite its many critics and undoubted limitations, it is now a huge and heavily used resource with around 5,000 to 6,000 hits a second on any of its 6 million entries. Libraries and archives, far from feeling threatened by it, have from the outset chosen to work with it.

The knowledge held in Wikipedia is subject to attack. Public relations companies have, for instance, been paid to edit or remove material which their clients find uncomfortable. A popular beverage, the beer Stella Artois used to be nicknamed the 'wife-beater'. This is a verifiable fact backed up by sources and included in the Wikipedia article about Stella Artois. Such a nickname is no longer tolerated in Western society and at one point this was deleted. The account that did this turned out to belong to the PR company Portland Communications. Members of the Wikipedia community restored the deleted references.[22]

Politicians have deleted unwelcome references in Wikipedia to the so-called 'expenses scandal' (a series of revelations made by the *Daily Telegraph* and other newspapers relating to illegal expense claims made by Members of Parliament). By analysing the IP addresses of computers that made changes to the biographies of those MPs, the journalist Ben Riley-Smith uncovered the fact that the references, although verifiably in the public domain, were deleted by staff within the Palace of Westminster.[23]

Wikipedia is built on a culture of openness. Any entry has all the changes made to it tracked and these are openly viewable. The nature of the content deleted (or changed), the date and time it was done and which account made the change can all be seen. Wikipedia organises teams of 'watchers' who regularly read a number of pre-identified entries that they know will be subject to unwarranted malicious deletion or incorrect editing. Anyone with an account can elect to 'watch' any selection of pages, so they notice any change made in their area of interest.

Every contributor also has a contributions record that is openly viewable, so if someone is only making edits about certain individuals or topics, that information is also visible to other users. Although there is a human layer of 'watchers' they are supported by a technological layer of software tools (or 'bots') that do some large-scale automated 'watching'.

Wikipedia itself monitors the entire site. Their bots can detect events such as a significant part of an article being deleted, or a homophobic or racial slur being added. When a large amount of text is added they can automatically Google-search sentences from the article to detect any plagiarism. When the staff of a politician deletes material, various bots and human editors flag it up, can see the pattern of edits made by the same account or computer and restore the deleted material with one click. Sometimes attempts to delete or censor Wikipedia has generated its own media story, which then gets cited in the article.

The shift in the creation of knowledge to digital form is posing challenges for administrators who, facing the digital deluge, struggle to cope with the burden of dealing with large quantities of digital information. In December 2018 the state government in Maine revealed that it had suffered a catastrophic loss of public documents from the administrations of governors Angus King and John Baldacci with most state government emails sent before 2008 being irretrievably lost and many other kinds of documents destroyed by state officials before they reached the Maine State Archives. Not only has information for future historians gone but these emails could also contain documentation of vital information in high-profile legal cases, as the work done by lawyers like Larry Chapin on the Libor scandal of 2012 has shown – email records when pieced together can tell a story in enough detail to help secure a conviction or prevent a defendant from going to jail.[24]

There are other areas of life where future access to knowledge will be of critical importance, and where commercial interests would not necessarily be beneficial. A good example is the nuclear industry. As a society we need to be sure long into the future – not just five to ten years, but hundreds and even thousands of years hence – exactly where we have stored nuclear waste, what material it consists of, when it was placed there, what kind of container it was stored in, and so on. This data exists today but the challenge facing the Nuclear Decommissioning Authority and other players in the nuclear world is how we can be sure that property developers, mining companies, water suppliers, as well as local authorities and governments, in say five hundred years' time have guaranteed access to all this information. We need to know where to find the information, that the format the information is stored in can be accessed and that we can make sense of it when we need to. When businesses have turned bad, as in the case of Enron in the early years of the present century, litigation could have been made much easier if digital preservation solutions had been more available in the corporate world – as Enron employees deleted vast numbers of emails and other digital information, hampering the ability of its auditors to know what was going on, and making the job of litigation harder and more costly.

The preservation of knowledge is fundamentally not about the past but the future. The ancient libraries of Mesopotamia contained a preponderance of texts concerning the prediction of the future: astrology, astronomy and divination. Rulers wanted to have information to help them decide when was the optimal time to go to war. Today, the future continues to be dependent on access to the knowledge of the past and will be even more so as digital technology changes the way we can predict what will happen. It will also be contingent on how the knowledge created by our digital lives is harnessed for political and commercial gain by a number of organisations that are becoming increasingly powerful.

The tech industry is now pouring huge investment into 'the internet of things', where many domestic devices, such as fridges, are connected to the internet, operating by the passage of data from sensors. The internet of things is moving into the field of wearable devices, such as watches and jewellery. These are designed to monitor our health, generating massive amounts of biometric data. The volume of data will reach a point where medics will be able to make accurate predictions of our future health. This will help in the prevention of disease, but it will also open up major ethical issues as well. Who will own this data? We may be happy to share this material with our doctor, but would we be happy sharing it with our health insurer? It may be that libraries and archives could play a much stronger role in providing secure access to personal digital information, where the citizen can control who has access to it, but where anonymised aggregated use of that information could be facilitated by libraries for the purposes of public health. If this knowledge were to be destroyed it could have profound consequences for the health of individuals, as we become tied more tightly than ever to digital health systems.

In June 2019 Microsoft announced that it was taking offline a huge database of images of human faces, over 10 million images in all, relating to 100,000 individuals, that has been used to train AI facial recognition systems around the world. The images were collected without permission by being 'scraped' from the open web.[25] Other similar databases, openly available on the web, were discovered by researcher Adam Harvey whose work has resulted in a number of other facial recognition datasets being identified, including examples created by Duke and Stanford universities. They even include a dataset scraped from postings from transgender groups on YouTube, which was used to train facial recognition AI for transgender people.[26]

Until recently worries about the gathering of data generated by users of online services were centred around the invasion of privacy and the risk of monetisation of this data. The concerns are now shifting to broader areas. Where so much political campaigning takes place in the realm of social media, how can we be sure that our feeds are not being manipulated unlawfully, and that online campaigning is being done openly and fairly, and with the consent of individuals, unless the data collected by those companies can be archived for open scrutiny?

Through 2017 and 2018 it became clear that the data generated by users of Facebook had been used, almost certainly illegally, by a private company, Cambridge Analytica, to create targeted political advertising. At the same time one of the major credit agencies, Equifax, had compromised over 147 million users' financial information through an inadvertent data breach.[27] These issues have raised concerns about having the information of individuals owned by private companies, under weak or non-existent legislative frameworks. It has also been alleged that a number of governments have used the manipulation of these platforms for their own political advantage.

The Cambridge Analytica website has long since disappeared but fortunately several web archives captured the site before it went offline. On 21 March 2018 it was describing itself as 'Data drives all we do: Cambridge Analytica uses data to change audience behaviour.' People were then invited to 'visit our Commercial or Political divisions to see how we can help you'. With offices in New York, Washington, London, Brazil and Kuala Lumpur, Cambridge Analytica were digital mercenaries, aiming to put the global society at the service of anyone willing to pay, no matter what the political or commercial intent. The site claimed that they had gathered 5,000 data points on each American voter who uses the internet.

The web archives of their site seem to be the only archival traces of their behaviour, but the company had access to the data of a staggering 87 million Facebook users without their consent. The full scope of their activities remains unclear, and the full details of what went on are still being uncovered. 'Nobody has seen the Facebook data set for the Trump campaign,' Carole Cadwalladr, whose investigative journalism for the *Guardian* has worked to uncover this, commented on Twitter. 'Nobody has seen the ad archive. Nobody knows what Cambridge Analytica did. Nobody knows what worked. ★If anything★. It's why we need the evidence.'[28]

Archiving the datasets created by the big tech companies, such as the advertisements on Facebook, the posts on Twitter, or the 'invisible' user data harvested by the adtech companies is, I believe, one of the major challenges facing the institutions charged with the preservation of knowledge. Libraries and archives are only able to make relatively modest inroads into an area where the volumes of data are vast. But society needs such archives to exist and to be able to understand what our culture is doing today, and what role is played by key individuals, corporations and others in the way society is changing.

The problem of archiving social media sites is daunting and we have seen, in the case of Twitter, that the preservation of an entire social media platform digitally is a challenge greater than even the largest library in the world can face. These sites are dynamic, they change every second, and are presented to each user in a unique and personalised way. We need to archive the communications on the platform itself, and the data transmission that underpins it. The messages are one thing but the 'likes', the 'nudges' and other social tools that the platforms put in place can tell us a great deal about social behaviour, culture, politics, health and so much more. In my view preserving the great social media and adtech platforms is becoming one of the critical issues of the current period.

There are, however, some approaches to archiving social media beginning to emerge. In the summer of 2019 the National Library of New Zealand announced a project asking New Zealanders to donate their Facebook profiles to its Alexander Turnbull Library. As Jessica Moran, digital service team leader at the library, explains in her blog:

> We hope to collect a representative sample of Facebook archives. We want to build a collection that future researchers may use to understand what we saved and how we used social media platforms like Facebook, but also to better understand the rich context of early 21st Century digital culture and life. In return for your donation, we can offer potential donors a trusted digital repository that is committed to preserving these digital archives into the future.[29]

The National Library of New Zealand has highlighted two key issues. Firstly, the memory institutions must begin to archive the information held in the major social media platforms: the future needs to know what happened in the past and if this cannot be done at the platform level (there are currently over 2.5 billion monthly active users of Facebook worldwide) it must be done by tackling smaller chunks at a time. A sample of users in a relatively small country like New Zealand is a very good way to approach such a large problem. Secondly, they know that some current users of Facebook are interested in having their own histories preserved by a trusted public institution, one that will do most of the work, and bear the cost, on their behalf. Crucially the National Library also makes very clear statements about respecting the privacy of anyone who donates their Facebook material.

Society has been too slow to catch up with the commercial realities that the world of big data and ubiquitous computing have created.

Our laws and institutions have not been able to keep pace with an industry now incredibly rich and with very smart people working inside it. As data scientist Pedro Domingos has said: 'whoever has the best algorithms and the most data wins'.[30] The construction of the platforms and the 'data industry' around them has created what Shoshana Zuboff terms a 'private knowledge kingdom', although 'kingdoms' might be a better analogy. All of this data and technology has been created 'for the purposes of modification, prediction, monetization, and control'.[31] The warning sounded by Zuboff and other writers who have studied the growth of surveillance capitalism is that a disproportionate amount of the world's memory has now been outsourced to tech companies without society realising the fact or being fully able to comprehend the consequences.

At the heart of the current relationship between the public and the major tech companies is the problem of trust. We all use their services, partly because we have become reliant on them, but increasingly the public does not trust them. Society has created a huge bank of knowledge but has privatised its ownership, management and use, even though the knowledge was created freely by individuals around the world. Arguably the owners of the companies are beginning to be viewed by the public with a sense of dystopian fear and suspicion.

A 2016 study by Pew Research reported that 78 per cent of American adults regarded libraries as guiding them to information that is trustworthy and reliable. The figure is even higher among the 18–35 age group (so-called 'Millennials'). There are no long-term studies that allow us to plot this trend over time but the Pew researchers regard these levels of trust as increasing among adults, in stark contrast to the levels of trust in financial companies and social media organisations.[32] And even governments.

Given that the public trust in libraries and archives is high (and growing), perhaps they could become the place where individuals could store their personal data? Perhaps society is beginning to enter into an era that will challenge the dominance of the 'private superpowers' and bring the interests of society to the fore. Can we conceive of a future where the data of individuals is placed in the hands of public institutions, as trusted stewards of public data?

Certain conditions would need to be fulfilled. Firstly, there would have to be legislation to establish the facilities and to put regulation in place.[33] The public should be consulted and involved in the development of the policies, and the way the system was established. Such laws would need to be harmonised across geopolitical boundaries. Secondly, there would need to be significant levels of funding to allow the libraries to undertake the task. This could be derived from a 'memory tax' on the same tech companies.[34]

Existing bodies, such as the Digital Preservation Coalition, would be key players in supporting digital preservation, and national bodies like the British Library, National Archives and their sister organisations in Scotland, Wales and Northern Ireland could work in collaboration to achieve this. There are models for such a modus operandi – such as the shared responsibilities for legal deposit, which as we have seen were extended in 2013 to digital publications. While not perfect, the legislation and the system that has been built by the six legal deposit libraries works.

This would not in itself be sufficient. A new data architecture for the internet is required that allows the individual to control who has access to their data.[35] The General Data Protection Regulations (GDPR), which came into force in the UK as the Data Protection Act 2018, have gone a long way in Europe to increasing the protection of individuals' data.

The move of society's knowledge from the personal domain to the commercial has brought with it massive issues that society must address. The rights of individuals are certainly at stake. In other areas of life there is a notion of 'duty of care', where companies and institutions have to follow standards in, for example, the design and operation of public buildings. This notion could and should be applied to the digital world.[36] If we do not archive the data that is being exploited we will never properly understand the full extent of that exploitation, and the effect it has had. Until we have a full archive of the Facebook political adverts, we will not be able to assess how electorates were influenced. Without this information, to enable analysis, study and interrogation of these organisations, and the advertisements on their platforms, we will never know.

A hundred years from now, historians, political scientists, climate scientists and others will be looking for the answer to how the world in 2120 has come to be the way it is. There is still time for libraries and archives to take control of these digital bodies of knowledge in the early twenty-first century, to preserve this knowledge from attack, and in so doing, to protect society itself.

John Milton, aged twenty-one, by William Marshall.

14

Paradise Lost?

THE RENEWAL OF the Bodleian Library by Sir Thomas Bodley followed the destruction of the earlier university library in the 1550s. On two occasions, in the aftermath of a bloody civil war, official orders were proclaimed by convocation, the university's assembly, for the books written by John Milton to be burned in the quadrangle of the Old Schools, outside the library, along with the works of other religious writers associated with the losing Puritan cause such as John Knox, John Goodwin and Richard Baxter. According to Anthony Wood, on 16 June 1660, books by Milton and Goodwin were 'called in and burnd' after having been 'taken out of those libraryes where they were'.[1]

Milton had been a great supporter of the Bodleian, sending a special copy of his *Poems* (1645), bound together with other pamphlets, to his friend John Rous who was the second Bodley's librarian. The volume contained a poem especially written by Milton in praise of the librarian and the library, expressing his satisfaction that his poems would find 'an unmolested happy home' there.[2] Milton had also, famously, written an eloquent defence of free speech in his *Areopagitica* (1644). In 1683 the Bodleian found itself in a particularly difficult position: should it bow to the pressure of the university authorities and relinquish this special volume, or should it preserve the volumes of the defender of free speech? The independently minded Bodleian – established as a 'reference only' library at its foundation, which had famously refused to loan a book to King Charles I when he was resident in Oxford in 1645 during the Civil War (despite Parliament establishing themselves in the library)[3] – took the dangerous decision to defy the authorities and hid the volumes away, but a handwritten note kept in the librarian's personal copy of the Bodleian's catalogue shows that they had been carefully omitted from the public catalogue in order to maintain the secret of their existence.[4] As a result, they can still be consulted today.[5] As the case studies explored in this book have shown, librarians and archivists have played a vital role in preserving knowledge from attack, across many centuries.

Throughout this book I have tried to convey the long history of attacks on knowledge and the impact that the destruction of libraries and archives has had on communities and on society as a whole. Yet knowledge is still being attacked today. Ignorance about this history generates complacency of a kind that allowed the slow decline of the Library of Alexandria, and created a vulnerability that led to some libraries during the Reformation, including the University of Oxford's, to be destroyed.

Complacency takes many forms. It almost certainly encouraged Home Office officials in their destruction of the Windrush landing records, as they assumed that the information was held elsewhere. We are being complacent today by not adequately preserving knowledge in digital form, and complacency is leading governments to reduce funding.

Archivists and librarians have developed strategies and techniques to protect the knowledge in their care. As individuals they have often shown astonishing levels of commitment and courage in saving things from destruction, whether they were the men and women of the Paper Brigade in Vilna in the 1940s, or Aida Buturović, who was killed in Sarajevo in 1992, or Kanan Makiya and his colleagues in the Iraq Memory Foundation in Baghdad in the 2000s.

'There is no political power without power over the archive,' wrote Jacques Derrida, the great French critic, in his classic work *Archive Fever*.[6] This message has been learned by authoritarian regimes and major technology companies, the 'private superpowers' across the globe, who have taken control of the archive as it has moved into the digital realm (and in many cases where it has not). The complacency of society has meant lack of regulation, control and privacy surrounding the most powerful bodies of knowledge ever seen: the social media platforms and adtech datasets of the digital era, as I have tried to show in the previous chapter. As Orwell warned us in *Nineteen Eighty-Four*: 'the past was erased, the erasure was forgotten, the lie became truth.'

★

In the last few decades the library profession has undertaken what has been called 'a service turn'.[7] When I first began as a librarian a change was taking place, with the needs of users placed ahead of the priorities of the library staff. This has been a necessary strategy, and the profession has become much better because of it. As a result, however, we have become less concerned with preservation. Even as librarians and archivists have become very adept at using new technology, we have struggled to direct sufficient funding towards digital preservation.

As society begins to face the new digital age, we need to reprioritise. Preservation must be seen as a service to society. Ultimately, the funding that the 'memory organisations' receive from governments and other funding bodies is the most critical factor in enabling 'preservation as a service' to adapt to the changing nature of knowledge in the age of digital data. Funding for libraries has been reduced by political leaders in America, who have often assumed that online information has made libraries redundant. The reality is quite the reverse; libraries are so heavily used in the United States that they are being overwhelmed.[8] We need our communities to tell their elected officials to prioritise libraries and archives, as they did in Columbus, Ohio in 2016, where the electorate voted to pay increased taxes in order to sustain their public library system.

Our professional bodies need to have louder voices, and our communities need to be encouraged to add their voices on our behalf. The preservation of knowledge has critically relied on people. Staffing levels are essential to ensuring that the fundamental tasks of those organisations can be undertaken. A theorist of libraries in the seventeenth century, Gabriel Naudé, declared that a pile of books was no more a library than a crowd of soldiers was an army.[9] It is the library staff who turn the pile of books into 'an organised body of knowledge'. They are guardians of the truth, collecting knowledge in both analogue and digital form. Without them, with their mixture of skills, dedication and passion for preservation, we will continue to lose knowledge.

In November 2018, Professor Philip Alston, United Nations special rapporteur on extreme poverty and human rights, published a powerful statement on the condition of British society. 'Digital assistance has been outsourced to public libraries and civil society organizations. Public libraries are on the frontline of helping the digitally excluded and digitally illiterate who wish to claim their right to Universal Credit.'[10]

One of the ways libraries are facing the challenges of funding and the shift to digital is to work more collaboratively. The preservation of knowledge now depends on this collaboration; as the scale of the challenges is so large not one institution can do it alone. In many ways this has always been the case – after the Reformation the books from the medieval libraries of Europe were preserved by hundreds of different libraries, ranging from the Bodleian (with thousands of medieval books) to Shrewsbury School Library, which holds just a handful. This idea of a distributed collection was never explicit, but as early as 1600 my predecessor Thomas James compiled a catalogue listing all the manuscripts in the libraries of Oxford and Cambridge. A much more broadly conceived catalogue was published in 1696 by Edward Bernard, an academic at Oxford, which listed all the manuscripts in institutional and private libraries in Britain.[11] Scholars recognised the need to share the preservation of knowledge early on. Informal networks have expanded over time and have become more formal. A good example of this is the British and Irish Legal Deposit Libraries, who share the responsibility and the cost of legal deposit through multi-layered collaboration.

Libraries are increasingly sharing the storage of knowledge as well. In New Jersey, the massive RECAP facility is a shared store of printed materials and archives, co-funded and co-managed by Princeton University, Columbia University and the New York Public Library. The costs of operating great facilities like these are high, and if they can be shared then everyone benefits. In the digital sphere, coordinated action has been developed to distribute the burden of preservation. The CLOCKSS project is based on a very traditional model, one derived from the print world and applied to digital preservation by staff at Stanford University Library. The core concept they developed is simple and appealing: 'Lots of Copies Keeps Stuff Safe' (LOCKSS), but it relies on libraries volunteering spare computing power in their operations. Collaboration and trust are key to the success of CLOCKSS, which applies the LOCKSS concept to preserving scholarly journals and now preserves over 33 million journal articles.[12]

Preserving knowledge has never been inexpensive. Funding is at the heart of a sustainable and successful library. Sir Thomas Bodley recognised this in the sixteenth century, suggesting that he would personally provide a 'standing annual rent', what we would today call an endowment, to give his new library funds, 'in buying of books . . . officers stipends, and other pertinent occasions'. He thought that the reason the medieval library was destroyed was because of a lack of funding and a lack of staff.[13]

In the digital world knowledge is becoming inherently unstable and its durability depends on the institutions that keep it. Libraries and archives in the UK have found it hard to face the challenges of 'austerity' imposed on the public sector by the government in response to the global financial crisis of 2007–8. In local authorities, which are responsible for public libraries and for local record offices, funding for these services has to compete with schools, hospitals and collecting domestic refuse.

In South Africa, the task of archiving the Truth and Reconciliation Commission was given to the National Archives of South Africa, but the effectiveness of their work was severely hampered by lack of funds. The problem was simple – they didn't have enough staff to do the work. This impacted on the process of transferring records from government departments to the archivists, resulting in backlogs of unprocessed records. Individuals were unable to access this 'shared memory', and the process of national healing was less effective. These are political decisions and the passing of legislation to require openness in government and to support the rights of citizens is one thing, but the allocation of resources to enable the legislation to be meaningful is another.[14]

Support for libraries and archives across the globe is under extreme pressure. In Nigeria historians have recently raised concerns that the National Archives of Nigeria are 'in a very sorry state' and need reinvigorating in order to understand Nigeria's place in Africa. They have called for the federal government to 'inject more life into the records and services of the National Archives of Nigeria'.[15] In July 2019 the National Archives of Australia's advisory council warned that, having been overlooked by the government, their archives were 'in jeopardy', having lost 10 per cent of their budget each year since 2014.[16] The chairman of the advisory council said that 'the digital archival records of the Commonwealth are currently fragmented across hundreds of separate systems and government entities exposed to compromise, obsolescence or loss'.[17]

Libraries and archives need to hold large amounts of physical material – books, manuscripts, maps and so on – as well as dealing with rapidly growing digital collections that are often costly to maintain. The challenge of the 'hybrid' collection means hiring additional staff with the right skills, experience and mindset (such as digital archivists or electronic-records managers). It also means investing in technical systems and workflow processes that comply with industry standards. For now it is librarians and archivists, the custodians of the past, who are the advance guards of the future. They have worked with open approaches to software development, data practices and scholarly communication for years.

One way that governments could tackle the funding problem is through taxing the major technology companies. The 'private super-powers', with their transnational ways of working, have been adept at avoiding tax. I have previously suggested that a 'memory tax' might be one way of dealing with the funding problem.[18] The tech companies that earn so much from us all and pay so little in terms of regular business taxes could be asked to fund the very area they are undermining with their operations: social memory. A small levy, perhaps 0.5 per cent of their profits, might provide a serious fund that the public memory institutions could call on to support their work.

If other countries passed similar legislation in terms of taxation, a network could be formed to address the challenge of archiving the vast array of knowledge hosted by the social media companies. I have already shown that libraries and archives collaborate very effectively. They could do more, especially if given additional funds. As we have seen, archiving Twitter has proven to be too great a challenge even for the Library of Congress, and the challenges of archiving Facebook, WeChat, Weibo, Tencent or some of the other social media platforms could be even greater. Yet the longer we go on without a sustained attempt to archive the great social media platforms the weaker our society will be. We will lose a sense of the richness of human interaction and we will not be able to understand how our society has been influenced and affected by social media.

Modern life has become increasingly obsessed with the short-term. Investors look to gain instant returns, and trading has become automated to such an extent that billions of trades are made every hour in stock exchanges. This fixation with the short-term is evident in many walks of life. Long-term thinking has become unfashionable. The memory of mankind, the knowledge it has created in all its myriad forms, from cuneiform tablets to digital information, is never of purely short-term use. It may be cheaper, more convenient, easier and faster to destroy knowledge than to appraise, catalogue, preserve and make it available but to abandon knowledge for the sake of short-term expediency is a sure route to weakening society's grip on truth.

The ancient libraries of Mesopotamia were filled with texts containing predictions for the future, using techniques we now call astrology, astronomy and divination. Rulers wanted to have information that would help them to decide the optimal time to go to war, plant or harvest a crop, and so on. Today the future continues to be dependent on access to knowledge of the past – and will be even more so as digital technology changes the ways we are able to predict what comes next.

As knowledge and truth continue to be targets of attack we must continue to put faith in our archives and libraries. Preservation should be seen as a service to society, for it underpins integrity, a sense of place and ensures diversity of ideas, opinions and memory. Libraries and archives are highly trusted by the general public, yet they are experiencing declining levels of funding. This is happening when the preservation of knowledge held in digital form is a major requirement for open, democratic societies. There is no time for complacency, the next attack on knowledge is about to happen, but if we can give libraries, archives and the people who work in them enough support they will continue to protect knowledge and make it available for everyone.

Shelves of paper files in the Stasi Museum, Berlin, August 2013.

Coda

Why We Will Always Need Libraries and Archives

I WOULD LIKE to highlight five functions of libraries and archives that we lose when they are lost or destroyed. Librarians and archivists do their jobs, and advocate for their funding but the power often lies elsewhere. It is to the holders of power that these five functions of libraries and archives are addressed. This is what we lose when those institutions are destroyed or starved of funds.

- Firstly, they support the education of society as a whole and of specific communities within it.
- Secondly, they provide a diversity of knowledge and ideas.
- Thirdly, they support the well-being of citizens and the principles of the open society through the preservation of key rights and through encouraging integrity in decision-making.
- Fourthly, they provide a fixed reference point, allowing truth and falsehood to be judged through transparency, verification, citation and reproducibility.
- Finally, they help root societies in their cultural and historical identities through preserving the written record of those societies and cultures.

First, education. The educational role of libraries and archives is truly powerful. Libraries provide opportunities to enable critical thinking and they allow exploration of new ideas in a supportive setting. For most libraries access is free of charge, or at very low cost, and patrons are treated equally no matter what their background or purpose of study. In the 1990s the National and University Library of Bosnia and Herzegovina in Sarajevo supported the education not just of the students and researchers in the main university of the region but of the entire nation. Attacking it severely damaged the education of a generation. Today university and college libraries around the globe continue to serve huge populations of students and researchers. In the 2017–18 academic year alone there were more than 40 million interactions with the Bodleian's collections, ranging from downloads of journal articles to calling up medieval manuscripts from the stacks. The academic community in the University of Oxford reading this material (or running programmes to data-mine it) was less than 30,000 individuals. Multiply these figures across the hundred and thirty or so universities in the UK, or the thousands in the United States, and then across the globe, and you get a sense of the centrality of libraries and the impetus they give to the improvement of society.

Public library systems and local archives are similarly crucial for the communities they serve. The work they do is expanding all the time, as the needs of their communities change and evolve. Millions of books are borrowed every year in the UK alone. The reality of funding for these institutions is extremely challenging. In the UK in 2017–18, funding for public libraries fell by £30 million, over a hundred and thirty libraries closed and five hundred more were run by volunteers rather than professional librarians.[1] Given the importance of public libraries in education, this will undoubtedly exacerbate social inequality and reduce social mobility. We read with horror how the public library of Jaffna was deliberately targeted in an attack aimed at damaging the educational opportunities of a community there, yet all around us public libraries are closing, their funding being cut.

In the 'era of austerity' public libraries in many countries have found themselves in the front line of supporting their communities. Public libraries have responded in innovative ways. The New York Public Library has begun to 'loan' articles of clothing like ties and briefcases to help individuals who cannot afford to look conventionally 'smart' to attend job interviews. In the UK, as government has moved so many of its services to digital platforms, so public libraries have responded with targeted services for those excluded by the digital divide.

The preservation of knowledge can have a profound educational role. The issue of climate change is perhaps the most urgent facing the world and an important recent study analyses climate data contained in an extraordinary archival record, one that details the grape harvests in Beaune, the wine capital of Burgundy, between 1354 and 2018. There is an incredibly rich set of climate data in these records, going back in an unbroken run, perhaps the longest continuous set of climate records in Europe. Climate scientists have found that they can use this data to show that the frequencies of extreme weather in earlier centuries were outliers, but that these extremes have become the norm, since an observable shift in the climate since 1988.[2] The records were created by some of the greatest vineyards in the world, but are latent with potential for other uses than the ones they were originally created for. We do not always know the value of the knowledge we are losing when it is destroyed or allowed to decay.

Secondly, libraries and archives provide a diversity of knowledge and ideas. They make it possible to face the present and the future through deepening an understanding of the past. The ideas we encounter, the histories that we understand and the culture that we engage with help make us who we are. But we need this pool of ideas and information to be constantly refreshed if we are to be creative and innovative. This is true not just in the case of, say, the creative fields of art, music and literature, but more generally. The democracy that we have in Britain relies on the free circulation of ideas in order to breathe life into the questioning spirit of our democratic processes. This means, in part, the freedom of the press, but citizens need to have access to knowledge of all shades of opinion. Libraries acquire all kinds of content and this resource allows our views to be challenged and for citizens to inform them-selves, following John Stuart Mill's insistence in *On Liberty* that 'only through diversity of opinion is there, in the existing state of human intellect, a chance of fair play to all sides of the truth.'[3]

In 1703 Henry Aldrich, the dean of Christ Church, suggested to the great astronomer Edmund Halley that he should work on ancient Greek scientific works, following his appointment as Savilian Professor of Geometry at Oxford. One of the projects Halley began was to continue the work of a great scholar of languages, Edward

Bernard, who had consulted an Arabic manuscript of the Greek scientist Apollonius of Perga's important work of geometry 'On the division of a ratio' in the Bodleian. Halley, in completing Bernard's work, translated and published the text in 1706.[4] As Isaac Newton, Halley's friend and collaborator, famously said: 'If I have seen further it is by standing on the shoulders of Giants.' Generations of librarians and collectors had preserved these ancient texts from destruction so that they could provide the diverse knowledge that could spark new discoveries.

This diversity can be rejected by oppressive regimes, closing down the opportunity for learning and for testing ideas and opinions. In Turkey, the regime of Recep Tayyip Erdoğan in August 2019 began the destruction of books associated with their opponent, Fethullah Gülen. So far 300,000 copies of books have been removed from schools and libraries. Publishing houses have also been attacked, prompting criticism from bodies like International PEN. It is hard to see what the destruction of the books in libraries will achieve other than making the texts more desirable.

Unless libraries and archives are allowed to operate without interference from government their role in providing access to knowledge that may challenge authorities or received views will be eroded. In Guatemala's long internal conflict, the role of the police in state oppression of its citizens and the abuse of human rights was highly controversial. Human rights groups saved the historical archive of the national police from destruction. Access to these records was helping Guatemalans come to terms with their recent history, but in March 2019 the staff were made redundant and access to the papers was stopped. Calls have since been made for these archives to be protected from damage and political interference and for copies to be made and lodged in Switzerland and in the Library of the University of Texas at Austin.[5] As with the Zaydi libraries in Yemen, attacks on knowledge seek to eradicate diverse opinion and ideas, but the international community of scholarship can use digital technologies to preserve the material.

Thirdly, libraries and archives support the well-being of citizens and the principles of an open society through the preservation of key rights and encouraging integrity in decision-making. Archives can be, in the words of historian Trevor Aston, 'fortifications for the defence of one's rights'.[6] These rights can be abused when archival material is missing, as in the case of the former Yugoslavia, where records were destroyed by the Serbian militia, a deliberate attempt to deprive Muslim citizens of their rights and to eradicate the memory of Muslim presence in Bosnia-Herzegovina.

Over the last three decades the role played by archives to support the rights of citizens to know what happened in their country in states like East Germany and South Africa has been of critical importance in the re-establishment of democracy. Thousands of sacks of shredded material was found in the Stasi office in Berlin-Lichtenberg, which 'testified to the zeal of those fearful of the typewritten evidence of their activities', according to Joachim Gauck, the first Federal Commissioner for the Records of the State Security Service of the former German Democratic Republic (known more colloquially as the Gauck Authority).[7] The process of opening up the Stasi files has been enormously important for the former communist countries in central and eastern Europe. The way the state operated its regime of control has been made transparent, down to allowing people access to their own files.[8] By the end of June 1994, just five years after the fall of the Berlin Wall, over 1.85 million requests had been made to access files in the Gauck Authority.[9]

The shift in the documentation of everyday life, business and government to the digital world brings with it complex issues. Digital preservation is becoming one of the biggest problems we face: if we do not act now our successors in future generations will rue our inaction. The archiving of the web, and of social media, is a particularly pressing concern. In 2012, computer scientists Hany SalahEldeen and Michael Nelson examined a large sample of social media posts regarding major events, such as Barack Obama's Nobel Peace Prize, the death of Michael Jackson, the Egyptian revolution and the Syrian uprising. Their studies revealed a shocking rate of loss: 11 per cent of posts had disappeared from the sites within a year and the rate of attrition has continued. As we have seen with websites relating to the EU referendum in the UK, and with the record of other key contemporary events on the web, preserving these websites will become increasingly important for openness in our political and social lives.

Libraries and archives are developing web archiving as part of their preservation activities, sometimes supported by legal deposit legislation (as in the UK). There needs to be a much bolder push to develop legally supported and properly funded national domain-based web archiving. The Internet Archive continues to provide leadership and it is the memory institutions that must lead on archiving the web as a key part of social memory.

Fourthly, libraries and archives provide a fixed reference point allowing truth and falsehood to be held to account through verification, citation and reproducibility. The idea of keeping knowledge may have begun with the administration of taxes in the ancient world, but it should be placed squarely in the modern age with notions of accountability. 'Every record has been destroyed or falsified . . . every date altered . . . And the process is continuing day by day. Nothing exists except an endless present in which the Party is always right,' wrote Orwell in *Nineteen Eighty-Four*.[10] To avoid this situation we need to preserve records and make them accessible.

The summer of 2019 witnessed mass protests against the Hong Kong government, some of the largest non-violent protests in modern history, and although these have been marred by occasional acts of violence for the most part they show widespread concern by the citizens of Hong Kong that the independence of their society is threatened by the People's Republic of China. Hong Kong's public records are not subject to any legislation that controls what is kept or what rights the citizens have to access their own history or that of the city's government. In 2018 official reports suggest that 4,400 metres of records were destroyed (roughly half the height of Mount Everest) by the Government Records Service. There is concern that sensitive records, such as the treatment of the 2014 Occupy Protests, or those of the much more broadly supported protests in 2019, have been destroyed, and campaigners call for laws to bind government officials to be more transparent in their record-keeping, allowing the government to be held to account. An editorial in the *South China Morning Post* put it eloquently in April 2019 (before the wave of protests was underway): 'Proper archives and open access are hallmarks of good governance.'[11] Passing archives legislation is not going to solve the problems facing Hong Kong but it would be a big step towards openness and integrity in government.

Archives and libraries support their communities by providing infrastructure that supports accountability. Accountability has become important in contemporary science. 'Reproducibility of science' and 'research ethics' are the buzzwords in the scientific community but they boil down to the same thing: can the public access the underlying data so that the claims made by scientists can be verified (or the result of experiments reproduced) by other scientists? This process requires the data to be held independently so that it can be openly accessed – some of the research funders in the UK (like the Environmental and Physical Sciences Research Council) now require researchers to deposit the data connected to research that they have funded in recognised data repositories.

The volume of scientific papers has massively increased in recent decades, partly fuelled by the pressure on scientists to publish their findings quickly – often in order to be ahead of competing research groups. Scientific journals have also been complicit in encouraging scientists to bring out high profile papers that announce important science. The rush to publish, and the competitive nature of publishing, has led to some notable instances of 'fake science' where scientific discoveries have been announced that have essentially been made up, and where the results cannot be replicated by other researchers. A recent paper on 'fake science', published by the Royal Society in London (one of the oldest and most respected scientific bodies in the world), urged that 'it is especially important that the scientific world as a whole upholds the highest standards of ethical behaviour, honesty and transparency, aiming to sustain the gold standards of research integrity and validated information', and the authors admitted that 'Sadly, a range of forces are working counter to this aspiration. People in the world of science are not immune from the personal ambitions and prevailing pressures that drive behaviour in general.'[12]

In order to combat these trends, there has been an increased focus on research ethics in the academic world, bringing forward the notion of 'reproducibility of research', which means being able to obtain consistent scientific results using the same input data, methodologies, code and conditions of analysis. And publishing research data in open access form can help to rebuild trust and transparency. Libraries are key to this process, as they typically host institutional repositories of open access research papers and research data on behalf of scientific communities. Staff help guide researchers through this process, supporting the drafting of data management plans at the point of applying for funding to undertake the research, and through giving advice on technical aspects such as metadata.

Finally, libraries and archives help root societies in their cultural and historical identities through preserving the written record of those societies. The idea that they are key to helping communities appreciate their 'sense of place' and 'common memory' is nothing new. I first became aware of it as a teenager when I discovered that the Deal public library had a local history section, full of obscure books, pamphlets and newspapers (as well as special indexes and catalogues). Thousands of citizens in Deal have used the collection over the years to research the history of their home or an incident in the town's past, but especially their family history. Libraries, record offices and local history centres have wonderfully rich collections where often very rare and obscure materials are acquired (often by donation) and gifted to the local 'memory institution'. This work often goes uncelebrated and is often very poorly funded. A renewal of emphasis on local history might help our communities develop a greater sense of their own place, helping to bind them together, encouraging more understanding of who we are and where we come from.

People's culture and sense of identity have often been targeted. Nazi attacks on Jewish and 'un-German' literature were a warning sign of their policy of genocide against the People of the Book. In Bosnia the Serb attacks on archives and the destruction of the National and University Library were born of the desire to wipe out the memory of Muslim participation in Bosnian history and culture. We should all see attacks on books as an 'early warning' signal that attacks on humans cannot be far behind.

There are a multitude of accounts of the deliberate destruction of knowledge as a routine aspect of colonialism and empire. As we have seen, the issue of 'displaced and migrated archives' is becoming increasingly visible. These materials play an important role in shaping historical narratives for recently independent states, especially now that we are entering the period where some of these countries will celebrate anniversaries of their independence. Part of being happy to be seventy-five, sixty, fifty years of age may often include celebrating the history of achievement since the date of independence. But it may also reflect further back in time, to the former colonial periods, sometimes comparing 'now and then', sometimes addressing historic injustices, sometimes simply relating history. Colonial-era history is dependent on colonial-era archives and publications. Access to this history can become politically sensitive. 'What's burned won't be missed' is a comment uttered by a British official in 1963 instructing his staff on the appraisal of records in North Borneo prior to independence.[13]

The return of knowledge can help societies to understand their own place in the world and to come to terms with the past, especially when the past has been difficult, as we have seen with Iraq, Germany and South Africa. In November 2018, a controversial report on the restitution of cultural artefacts written by Bénédicte Savoy and Felwine Sarr was published in France. The Savoy-Sarr report has provoked major discussions in the international museum community over the treatment of collections acquired during the colonial era, calling for the complete and unconditional return of African artefacts. The report simply comments that: 'In Africa, all of our interlocutors insisted not only on the restitution of cultural heritage objects held in French museums but also on the need for a serious reflection on the question of archives.'[14]

These five functions are not intended to be comprehensive, but merely a way of highlighting the value of the preservation of knowledge to society. Libraries and archives take the long view of civilisation in a world that currently takes the short-term view. We ignore their importance at our peril.

Acknowledgements

THIS IDEA FOR this book emerged somewhat out of the blue, in the spring of 2018, following an op-ed I had published in the *Financial Times* concerning the place of archives in the Windrush Scandal. For some time I had been concerned about the need to raise public consciousness of the importance of the preservation of knowledge, and the Windrush issues showed that looking at the nature of attacks on knowledge could be a useful way to approach the problem. I was greatly assisted in developing the idea by my agent, Catherine Clarke at Felicity Bryan Associates, who has been an enormous support throughout the project.

My first thanks must go to all my colleagues in the Bodleian. In the course of researching this book I have used the collections of the Social Science Library, the Leopold Muller Memorial Library, the Radcliffe Camera, the Sackler Library, the Bodleian Law Library, the Weston Library, the Upper and Lower Reading Rooms in the Old Bodleian, and I have called countless books, documents and maps from the Book Storage Facility or the stacks of the Weston, asked for documents to be photographed in the imaging studio, made heavy use of our digital resources and services. All the hard-working, loyal and dedicated staff of the Bodleian deserve equal thanks. My tireless, efficient and cheerful directorate staff, led by the unflappable Rosemary Rey, have organised my professional life and made the research for, and writing of, this book possible. I received expert advice from a number of my curatorial colleagues, and would like to thank especially Chris Fletcher, Martin Kauffman, Chrissie Webb, Mike Webb, Mamtimyn Sunuodola, Mai Musié, and César Merchan-Hamann. Martin Poulter, then Wikimedian in residence at the Bodleian, was hugely illuminating about the work of Wikipedia.

An Oxford college is an extraordinary resource for any intellectual

ACKNOWLEDGEMENTS

endeavour, allowing multiple perspectives on almost any issue to be accessed with great efficiency. My Balliol colleagues have been enormously supportive and encouraging, patiently listening to my often very naive questions. I would especially like to thank John-Paul Ghobrial, Seamus Perry, Rosalind Thomas, Enrico Prodi, Tom Melham, Andy Hurrell, and especially Phil Howard, who was also greatly helpful wearing his hat as head of the Oxford Internet Institute. Balliol colleagues who attended my Research Consilium in May 2019 gave valuable comments. Two Balliol graduate students, Avner Ofrath (now a postdoc at the University of Bremen) and Olivia Thompson, worked with me as research assistants on the book, and I would not have been able to complete it without their industrious scholarship and their many important insights.

Other friends and colleagues in Oxford who have given generously of their advice and expertise: Jonathan Bate, Christian Sahner, Sir Noel Malcolm, James Willoughby, Meg Bent, Sandy Murray, Piet van Boxel, Paul Collins, Andrew Martin, Cécile Fabre, George Garnett, Alan Rusbridger, Paul Slack, Sir Keith Thomas, Steve Smith, Adam Smith, Sir Nigel Shadbolt, Anne Trefethen, Julia Walworth and Henry Woudhuysen. I benefited greatly from attending Richard Sharpe's wonderful Lyell Lectures in Oxford in May 2019 on the highly relevant topic of the medieval libraries of Great Britain. His sudden death, while this book was being copyedited, is a major blow to me, and to medieval scholarship. Stephanie Dalley saved me from many blunders.

I was greatly assisted by Andrea Dautović at the National Museum of Bosnia Herzegovina, Claire Weatherall at the Hull History Centre and by Ashley Gilbertson. Sara Baxter, Hattie Cooke and Emma Cheshire helped clear rights from the Society of Authors and Faber for use of the quotes by Philip Larkin.

Some friends and colleagues have been particularly generous and without them I would not have been able to write this book at all. Heading this list is Joseph Sassoon who shared his deep knowledge of the recent history of Iraq and introduced me to Kanan Makiya, who was incredibly helpful, allowing me to interview him, and who in turn introduced me to Hassan Mneimneh, Haider Hadi and Eric Wakin at the Hoover Institution. I have also appreciated Joseph's advice and support more broadly in writing this book, and he and Helen Jackson showed me wonderful hospitality in Washington. Timothy Garton Ash discussed at length both the place of archives in national remembering (and forgetting) and the dangers of the 'private superpowers' in the digital realm, and his own writing has been a continuing source of inspiration.

David Ferriero, archivist of the United States, and Jeff James, CEO of the National Archives of the United Kingdom, were both founts of wisdom on the current issues facing archives on both sides of the Atlantic, and William Waung shared his knowledge of the situation in Hong Kong. András Riedlmayer's knowledge of the fate of libraries and archives in Bosnia is without peer, but his generosity in sharing his knowledge was typical of the best of librarians. His own role in the War Crimes Tribunals deserves wider appreciation in my profession.

Other colleagues around the world who were immensely helpful were Ismail Serageldin, who talked with me about the modern Library of Alexandria, Sabine Schmidtke shared details of her work with the Zaydis, Jon Taylor was helpful with the cuneiform collections at the British Museum, and Helen Hockx-Yu, Brewster Kahle, Andy Jackson at the British Library gave me the benefit of their vast knowledge of web archiving. John Y. Cole and Jane Aikin were wonderful resources at the Library of Congress, especially for allowing me to see Jane's important work on the history of the library while still in draft. David Rundle shared the fruits of his research on the library of Duke Humfrey. Bryan Skib helped me with sources at the University of Michigan and Vint Cerf was a central node for many digital issues. John Simpson shared his memories of Bosnia. The Led By Donkeys team, especially James Sadri, interrupted their campaigning to talk with me. One of the most extraordinary 'discoveries' that I made personally was of the amazing institution known as YIVO in New York, and I would like to pay a special tribute to Jonathan Brent, Stefanie Halpern and Shelly Freeman there, who were wonderfully generous with explaining the background to contemporary operations of their unique and special organisation. They also introduced me to David Fishman at the Jewish Theological Seminary in New York, who spent several hours talking about the Paper Brigade with me. I have relied heavily on David's own work on those inspirational individuals in Vilna.

Robert Saunders shared his thoughts on the link between public knowledge and democracy. Pierre Delsaerdt and James Keating checked references for me at the last minute. My three oldest friends, David Pearson, Bill Zachs and Rev. Michael Suarez SJ, were fountains of good advice, clever ideas and solid support.

I would like to thank several editors for publishing and for vastly improving several pieces which form the earliest expressions of parts of this book: Lionel Barber and Jonathan Derbyshire at the *Financial Times*, Lorien Kite at the *Financial Times Weekend*, Kenn Cukier at *The Economist* and Kenneth Benson at the *Carnegie Reporter*.

I owe a huge debt to my editor at John Murray, Georgina Laycock, who has been, with her assistant editor Abigail Scruby, instrumental in shaping the book: through their careful and detailed editorial advice they have transformed my prose. Martin Bryant's insightful copy-editing greatly improved the book, Howard Davies made important improvements through his meticulous proofreading and Caroline Westmore steered the book through production with great skill. Lucy Morton did a wonderful job on the index. I would also like to pay tribute to Sharmila Sen at Harvard University Press for her support throughout the project.

The biggest debt of all is due to my family: my daughters Caitlin and Anna, but especially to my long-suffering wife Lyn, without whom this book would have been an unthinkable project to contemplate, let alone complete. I owe her everything.

Richard Ovenden
Oxford, June 2020

Picture Credits

Introduction: Nazi book-burnings in Berlin, 10 May 1933. (Scherl/ Süddeutsche Zeitung Photo/Alamy Stock Photo)

Chapter 1: Austen Henry Layard sketching at Nimrud. (From *Discoveries Among the Ruins of Nineveh and Babylon* (New York, 1859), Getty Institute, 84-B9374. Reproduced by Permission of the Getty Institute.)

Chapter 2: The poet Virgil holding a scroll, from a manuscript, early fifth century. (Bibliotheca Apostolica Vaticana, MS. Vat. Lat 3225, fol. 14r. De Agostini Picture Library/Bridgeman Images)

Chapter 3: St Dunstan kneeling at the foot of Christ, from St Dunstan's Classbook, late tenth century. (Bodleian Library, MS. Auct F.4.32 fol. 1 recto. Reproduced by Permission, Bodleian Libraries, University of Oxford.)

Chapter 4: Sir Thomas Bodley (1545–1613), portrait by an unknown artist, *c.*1590s. (Bodleian Library, LP 71. Reproduced by Permission, Bodleian Libraries, University of Oxford.)

Chapter 5: Rear Admiral Sir George Cockburn at the burning of Washington, painted by John James Halls, engraved by C. Turner, 1819. Mezzotint. (Library of Congress, PGA – Turner–Sir George Cockburn. (D size) [P&P]. Reproduced courtesy of the Library of Congress.)

Chapter 6: Franz Kafka, photograph by Atelier Jacobi, Prague, 1906. Silver gelatin print. (Bodleian Library, MS. Kafka 55, fol 4r. Reproduced by Permission, Bodleian Libraries, University of Oxford.)

Chapter 7: Louvain University Library, before the burning in 1914. (From Karel Sluyterman, *La Belgique monumentale: 100 planches en phototypie tirées. Intérieurs anciens en Belgique* (Le Haye: Martin Nijhoff, 1915). Chronicle/Alamy Stock Photo)

Chapter 8: YIVO materials being unpacked in New York, 1947.

Silver gelatin print. (From the Archives of the YIVO Institute for Jewish Research, New York.)

Chapter 9: Philip Larkin at All Souls, 1970, possibly a self-portrait. Silver gelatin print. (Hull History Centre, Larkin Photographs, U DLV/3/190(7))

Chapter 10: Esau coming back from the hunt, and Jacob's ladder from the Sarajevo Haggadah, c.1350. fol. 10r. (Courtesy of the National Museum of Bosnia Herzegovina.)

Chapter 11: One of the Bodleian's Ethiopian manuscripts with members of the Ethiopian and Eritrean communities, August 2019. (MS. Aeth.c.2, Gospels, fifteenth century. Photograph by Ian Wallman.)

Chapter 12: Kanan Makiya and Hassan Mneimneh examining Ba'ath Party files in the Iraq Memory Foundation offices, Baghdad, November 2003. (Ashley Gilbertson/VII/Redux/eyevine)

Chapter 13: Photograph of Led by Donkeys' banner, April 2019. (By permission of Led by Donkeys.)

Chapter 14: John Milton, aged twenty-one, by William Marshall. (Frontispiece to *Poems of Mr John Milton, Both English and Latin* (London, 1645). Bodleian Library, Arch.g.f.17. Reproduced by Permission, Bodleian Libraries, University of Oxford.)

Coda: Shelves of paper files in the Stasi Museum, Berlin. (Jason Langer/Glasshouse Images/Alamy Stock Photo)

Notes

Introduction

1   Rydell, *The Book Thieves*, p. 9, and Ritchie, 'The Nazi Book-Burning'. For the Institute of Sexual Studies, see Bauer, *The Hirschfeld Archives*, pp. 78–101.

2   Orwell, *Nineteen Eighty-Four*, p. 247.

3   Trump made initial claims about his crowd size at a speech at the CIA Headquarters in Langley, Virginia on 21 January 2017. In his first televised White House interview, also on 21 January 2017, then White House Press Secretary Sean Spicer stated, 'This was the largest audience to ever witness an inauguration – period – both in person and around the globe.' A comparison of images of the Mall during the inauguration of Trump and that of Barack Obama in 2009, including those released by Reuters (taken by photographers Lucas Jackson and Stelios Varias), does not back up this claim. Keith Still suggested in an analysis for the *New York Times* that Trump's crowd size was about a third of Obama's (Tim Wallace, Karen Yourish and Troy Griggs, 'Trump's Inauguration vs. Obama's: Comparing the Crowds', *New York Times*, 20 January 2017).

Figures also contradict Spicer's statement. Nielsen reported that 30.6 million viewers tuned in for Friday's ceremonies, 19 per cent below the 37.8 million viewers who watched in 2009, while the record audience for an inauguration is Ronald Reagan's, which drew 41.8 million. Lastly, according to WMATA, the Washington area transit authority, 193,000 trips had been taken on the Washington Metro system by 11 a.m. on the day of Trump's inauguration; at the same time on the day of Obama's inauguration in 2009 that number was 513,000. Figures for the whole day from opening at 4 a.m. until closing were 570,557 rides on Trump's inauguration day in 2017 and 1.1 million on Obama's in 2009. Kellyanne Conway, Counselor to the President, dismissed such evidence as 'alternative facts' in a Meet the Press interview with Chuck Todd on NBC, on 22 January 2017. It was later revealed that Trump's inauguration photos were additionally doctored at his command (Swaine, 'Trump inauguration photos were edited after he intervened', *Guardian*, 6 September 2018). President Trump himself remained preoccupied with the issue on 3 November 2018, tweeting a supporter's video of a queue at a rally in Montana, with the comment, 'Landing in Montana now – at least everybody admits that my lines and crowds are far bigger than Barack Obama's . . .' (Source: factba. se/search#%2Bin%@Bmontana)

4 Gentleman, 'Home Office Destroyed Windrush Landing Cards Says Ex-Staffer'.

5 Subsequent investigations showed that some of the same information was held in different record series in the National Archives; see Wright, et al., 'Windrush Migrants'.

6 Ovenden, 'The Windrush Scandal'.

7 For a general introduction see Posner, *Archives in the Ancient World*, and Pedersén, *Archives and Libraries in the Ancient Near East*.

8 Metadata is a term used for data that describes other forms of data, typically digital data.

9 See Pedersén, *Archives and Libraries in the Ancient Near East*, pp. 237–82, and the essays in König, et al., *Ancient Libraries*.

10 The lists survives in a fragment of papyrus excavated at Oxyrhynchus, and now in the library of Trinity College Dublin; see Hatzimachili, 'Ashes to Ashes? The Library of Alexandria after 48 BC', pp. 173–4.

11 Burke, *A Social History of Knowledge*, p.138; Weiss, 'Learning from Loss; Digitally-Reconstructing the Trésor des Chartes at the Sainte-Chapelle', pp. 5–8.

12 Naisbitt, *Megatrends*, p. 24.

13 Rosenzweig, 'Scarcity or Abundance?'.

14 Winters and Prescott, 'Negotiating the Born-Digital', pp. 391–403

15 On the foundation of the Bodleian see Clapinson, *A Brief History of the Bodleian Library*. For an introduction to the Bodleian's collections see Hebron, *Marks of Genius* and Vaisey, *Bodleian Library Treasures*.

16 Hansard, House of Commons Debates, 13 March 1850, 109: cc838–50. See the essays in Black and Hoare, *Cambridge History of Libraries*, III: *Part One*, and Max, 'Tory Reaction to the Public Libraries Bill, 1850', pp. 504–24.

17 Alsop, 'Suffrage Objects'.

18 Black, 'The People's University', p. 37.

19 Travers, 'Local Government'.

20 Busby, Eleanor, 'Nearly 800 Public Libraries Closed Since Austerity Launched in 2010'.

21 Asmal, Asmal, and Roberts, *Reconciliation Through Truth*, p. 6.

22 Garton Ash, 'True Confessions', p. 1.

23 Truth and Reconciliation Commission, *Final Report*, pp. 201–43.

24 Thomas Jefferson to Isaac Macpherson, 13 August 1813. See Lipscomb and Bergh (eds), *The Writings of Thomas Jefferson*, 13, pp. 333–5.

Chapter 1: Cracked Clay Under the Mounds

1 Although some scholars now doubt whether he actually made the journey.

2 Xenophon, *Anabasis*, 3.4.7–12.

3 Xenophon's slightly older predecessor, Herodotus, names the Assyrians when he mentions the sacking of Nineveh (*Histories*, 1.106). As Xenophon was at least partially acquainted with Herodotus' work, his ignorance of the Assyrians has puzzled scholars. Xenophon's detail of the storm, however, is reminiscent of the prophet Nahum's description of the fall of Nineveh (Nahum 2:6–7), and the later historian Diodorus of Sicily mentioned an oracle stating that no one would be able to capture Nineveh unless first the river turned against it (Diodorus, 21.26.9). The implication, then, is that local memory of the Assyrians had been so successfully expunged by their enemies that he could not identify them as the inhabitants of these once-great cities. See Haupt, 'Xenophon's Account of the Fall of Nineveh', pp. 99–107.

4 Buckingham, *Travels in Mesopotamia*, II, 211.

5 Rich, *Narrative of a Residence in Koordistan, and on the Site of Ancient Nineveh*, I, p. 2.

6 Ibid., p. xxii.

7 Lloyd, *Foundations in the Dust*, p. 9.

8 Ibid., p. 108.

9 Reade, 'Hormuzd Rassam and His Discoveries', pp. 39–62.

10 Robson, E., 'The Clay Tablet Book in Sumer, Assyria, and Babylonia', p. 74.

11 Layard, *Discoveries in the Ruins of Nineveh and Babylon*, pp. 344–5.

12 Ibid., p. 345.

13 Finkel, 'Ashurbanipal's Library'. Irving Finkel has done the most work to understand the significance of Ashurbanipal's library.

14 Ibid., p. 80.

15 Robson, 'The Clay Tablet Book', pp. 75–7.

16 Finkel, 'Ashurbanipal's Library', p. 82.

17 *Cuneiform Texts from Babylonian Tablets in the British Museum* 22,1 (BM 25676 = 98-2-16, 730 and BM 25678 = 98-2-16, 732). Translation adapted from Finkel, 'Ashurbanipal's Library', p. 82, and Frame and George, 'The Royal Libraries of Nineveh', p. 281.

18 Frame and George, 'The Royal Libraries of Nineveh', pp. 265–83.

19 Parpola, 'Assyrian Library Records', 4ff.

20 MacGinnis, 'The Fall of Assyria and the Aftermath of the Empire', p. 282.

21 See especially ibid.

22 Robson and Stevens, 'Scholarly Tablet Collections in First-Millennium Assyria and Babylonia, *c.*700–200 BCE', p. 335.

23 Posner, *Archives in the Ancient World*, p. 56; Pedersén, *Archives and Libraries in the Ancient Near East*, pp. 241–4.

Chapter 2: A Pyre of Papyrus

1 Bagnall, 'Alexandria: Library of Dreams', p. 349.

2 Strabo, *Geography*, 17.1.8, quoted in Hatzimichali, 'Ashes to Ashes? The Library of Alexandria after 48 BC', p. 170, n.7.

3 McKenzie, Gibson and Reyes, 'Reconstructing the Serapeum in Alexandria', pp. 79–81.

4 Ammianus Marcellinus, *History*, 22.16.12.

5 Roger Bagnall makes the most convincing argument on this point. Bagnall, 'Alexandria: Library of Dreams', pp. 351–6, with discussion of the sources.

6 Quoted in Rajak, *Translation and Survival*, p. 45. For a translation of the full passage see McKenzie, Gibson and Reyes, 'Reconstructing the Serapeum in Alexandria', pp. 104–5.

7 Suetonius, *Lives of the Caesars*, 8.3.20; Bagnall, 'Alexandria: Library of Dreams', p. 357.

8 Ammianus Marcellinus, *History*, 22.16.13, quoted in Barnes, 'Cloistered Bookworms in the Chicken-Coop of the Muses', p. 71.

9 Dio Cassius, *Roman History*, 42.38, quoted in Casson, *Libraries in the Ancient World*, p. 46.

10 This is most vividly recounted by Gibbon, in *Decline and Fall*, III, pp. 284–5.

11 Ibid., p. 83.

12 Bagnall, 'Cloistered Bookworms in the Chicken-Coop of the Muses', pp. 71–2; Jacob, 'Fragments of a History of Ancient Libraries', p. 65.

13 McKenzie, Gibson and Reyes, 'Reconstructing the Serapeum in Alexandria', pp. 86, 98–9. The date of the 181 CE fire is given by Jerome in his version of Eusebius' Chronicle (see McKenzie, Gibson and Reyes, p. 86, with references). The Christian writer Tertullian, writing in 197 CE, describes seeing the books of the Septuagint in the library in the Serapeum (*Apologeticum*, 18.8); this is the first reference to a library there. As he was writing so soon after the fire of 181 CE, this might suggest that the fire did not destroy the library. Dio (*Roman History Epitome*, 79.7.3) reports a fire in 217 CE, that miraculously did not damage the temple.

14 Aurelian's destruction of the Broucheion (royal quarter) is narrated by Ammianus Marcellinus, *History*, 22.16.15.

15 Gibbon, *Decline and Fall*, III, p. 285.

16 Ibid., pp. 284–5.

17 On this fire and Galen's account, see Tucci, 'Galen's Storeroom, Rome's Libraries, and the Fire of A.D. 192'.

18 Plutarch, *Aemilius Paulus* 28.6, recounts the seizure of the library. See Affleck, 'Priests, Patrons, and Playwrights', pp. 124–6.

19 Houston, 'The Non-Philodemus Book Collection in the Villa of the Papyri', p. 183.

20 Posner, *Archives in the Ancient World*, pp. 71–2.

21 Strabo, *Geography*, 13.1.54; Coqueugniot, 'Where Was the Royal Library of Pergamum?', p. 109.

22 Bagnall, 'Alexandria: Library of Dreams', p. 352.

23 Casson, *Libraries in the Ancient World*, pp. 52–3.

24 Hatzimichali, 'Ashes to Ashes?', p. 173.

25 MacLeod, 'Introduction: Alexandria in History and Myth', p. 4.

26 See Pfeiffer, *Politics, Patronage and the Transmission of Knowledge*; Burnett, 'The Coherence of the Arabic-Latin Translation Program in Toledo in the Twelfth Century'; Gutas, *Greek Thought, Arabic Culture*.

27 The image is reproduced in Clark, J. W., *The Care of Books*, p. 41.

28 Reynolds and Wilson, *Scribes & Scholars*, pp. 81–3.

29 Ibid., p. 54.

30 Breay and Story (eds), *Anglo-Saxon Kingdoms*, pp. 126–9.

31 This is discussed further in chapter 8. See also Stroumsa, 'Between "Canon" and Library in Medieval Jewish Philosophical Thought'.

32 Bloom, *Paper Before Print*, pp. 48–9.

33 Ibid., pp. 119–21.

34 Cited in Biran, 'Libraries, Books and Transmission of Knowledge in Ilkhanid Baghdad', pp. 467–8.

35 See Hirschler, *Medieval Damascus*, and Hirschler, *The Written Word in the Medieval Arabic Lands*; Biran, 'Libraries, Books and Transmission of Knowledge in Ilkhanid Baghdad'.

36 Thomson, 'Identifiable Books from the Pre-Conquest Library of Malmesbury Abbey'; Gameson, *The Earliest Books of Canterbury Cathedral: Manuscripts and Fragments to c.1200*; Lapidge, *The Anglo-Saxon Library*, Chapter 2, 'Vanished libraries of Anglo-Saxon England'.

37 Meehan, *The Book of Kells*, p. 20.

38 Gameson, 'From Vindolanda to Domesday', pp. 8–9.

39 Ganz, 'Anglo-Saxon England', pp. 93–108.

40 Ibid., p. 103.

41 Bodley, *The Life of Sir Thomas Bodley*, sig. A2v.

Chapter 3: When Books Were Dog Cheap

1 Leland, *De uiris illustribus*, p. xxii.

2 Ibid., p. liii.

3 Harris, O., 'Motheaten', p. 472. Harrison, *The Description of Britain* (1587), p. 63, quoted in Harrison and Edelen, *The Description of England*, p. 4.

4 Bodleian, MS. Top. Gen. c. 3, p. 203. Leland's entire journey has been reconstructed in Leland, *De uiris illustribus*, pp. lxi–xcv.

5 The medieval library has been analysed in great detail by Bruce Barker-Benfield, *St Augustine's Abbey, Canterbury*.

6 Leland, *De uiris illustribus*, pp. 67, 69.

7 Ibid., pp. 315, 321.

8 Ibid., p. 66.

9 Ibid., p. 386.

10 The shelf-mark in the Bodleian today is MS. Auct.F.4.32.

11 See the entry in the Bodleian's online catalogue *Medieval Manuscripts in Oxford Libraries*, http://medieval.bodleian.ox.ac.uk/catalog/manuscript_675 (Accessed: 29 February 2020)

12 There is a moving account in Knowles, *The Religious Orders in England*, pp. 348–9.

13 Ibid., p. 381.

14 Wood, *History and Antiquities of the University of Oxford*, 1, p. 141.

15 Dixon, 'Sense of the Past in Reformation Germany', pp. 184–6.

16 Leland, *The laboryouse journey*, sig. Bi.

17 See Ker, *Pastedowns in Oxford Bindings*; Pearson, *Oxford Bookbinding 1500–1640*.

18 See Watson, *A Descriptive Catalogue of the Medieval Manuscripts of All Souls College Oxford*, pp. 28–30; Ker, *Pastedowns in Oxford Bindings*, p. xi.

19 Duffy, *The Stripping of the Altars*, pp. 181–3.

20 Carley, 'The Dispersal of the Monastic Libraries', pp. 284–7.

21 Watson, 'Thomas Allen of Oxford', p. 287.

22 Ovenden, 'The Manuscript Library of Lord William Howard of Naworth', p. 306.

23 The manuscript is now in the British Library, MS. Royal 1.A.xviii, see *Libraries of King Henry VIII*, p. xlv.

24 The manuscript is now in the British Library, MS. Royal 2.C.x, see *Libraries of King Henry VIII*, p. xxxix.

25 *Libraries of King Henry VIII*, pp. xliii–xlvi.

26 Quoted in Leland, *The Itinerary of John Leland*, II, p. 148.

27 The largest group of manuscripts to leave these shores were the 250 manuscripts from Dominican houses that were sent to Cardinal Cervini in Rome and are now in the Vatican Library. See Ker, 'Cardinal Cervini's Manuscripts from the Cambridge Friars'; Carley, 'John Leland and the Contents of English Pre-Dissolution Libraries: The Cambridge Friars', pp. 90–100.

28 This account of John Leland relies on the awesome scholarship of James Carley. Leland, *The laboryouse journey*, sig. Biiiv.

29 Leland, *De uiris illustribus*, p. xxiv.

30 Ibid., p. xliii.

31 Wood, *The Life of Anthony à Wood from 1632 to 1672, written by himself*, p. 107.

32 The best account is Vincent, N., *The Magna Carta*.

33 Ovenden, 'The Libraries of the Antiquaries', p. 528.

Chapter 4: An Ark to Save Learning

1 Quoted by Philip, *The Bodleian Library in the Seventeenth and Eighteenth Centuries*, pp. 2–3.

2 Ker, 'Oxford College Libraries before 1500', pp. 301–2.

3 Parkes, 'The Provision of Books', pp. 431–44, 456–7.

4 The history of the medieval libraries of Oxford is best told by Parkes, 'The Provision of Books' and Ker, 'Oxford College Libraries before 1500'.

5 See Rundle, 'Habits of Manuscript-Collecting: The Dispersals of the Library of Humfrey, Duke of Gloucester', pp. 106–16; *Duke Humfrey's Library & the Divinity School, 1488–1988*, p. 46.

6 See *Duke Humfrey's Library & the Divinity School, 1488–1988.*

7 Personal communication from Dr David Rundle.

8 Quoted in *Duke Humfrey's Library & the Divinity School, 1488–1988*, p. 123.

9 Ibid., pp. 18–49.

10 The most recent account of Bodley's early life is Goldring, *Nicholas Hilliard*, pp. 40–59.

11 Bodley, *The Life of Sir Thomas Bodley*, p. 15.

12 *Letters of Sir Thomas Bodley to the University*, pp. 4–5.

13 Peterson, *The Kelmscott Press*, pp. 45–7.

14 This effectively meant that all books published in England would come to the library, as the Company had a near monopoly on printing and publishing. The story is best told by Barnard, 'Politics, Profits and Idealism'.

15 See Clapinson, *A Brief History of the Bodleian Library*, pp. 20–2.

16 Reproduced in Burke, *A Social History of Knowledge*, pp. 104–5.

17 Naudé, *Advice on Establishing a Library*, pp. 17, 67–8.

18 Bodley, *Reliquiae Bodleianae*, p. 61.

19 Ovenden, 'Catalogues of the Bodleian Library and Other Collections', p. 282.

20 Southern, 'From Schools to University', p. 29.

21 Slack, 'Government and Information in Seventeenth-Century England', p. 38.

22 Tyacke, 'Archives in a Wider World', p. 216.

23 Ovenden, 'Scipio le Squyer'.

24 Slack, 'Government and Information in Seventeenth-Century England', pp. 42–3, quoting John Graunt.

25 Slack, *The Invention of Improvement*, pp. 116–20.

26 Buck, 'Seventeenth-Century Political Arithmetic', p. 71.

27 Pepys, *The Diary of Samuel Pepys*, 5, p. 142.

28 Webster, *The Great Instauration*, p. 194.

29 Rozenberg, 'Magna Carta in the Modern Age'.

30 Prest, *William Blackstone*, p. 165.

31 This is a much-quoted passage, here taken from Ovenden, 'The Libraries of the Antiquaries', p. 528.

32 Bepler, 'The Herzog August Library in Wolfenbüttel', p. 18.

33 Quoted by Philip, *The Bodleian Library in the Seventeenth and Eighteenth Centuries*, pp. 6–7.

Chapter 5: Spoil of the Conqueror

1 Gleig, *A Narrative of the Campaigns of the British Army at Washington and New Orleans*, p. 128.
2 Ibid., pp. 127, 134.
3 Madison, *The Papers of James Madison*, 1, p. 269.
4 Ostrowski, *Books, Maps, and Politics*, pp. 39–72.
5 Ibid., pp. 12–14.
6 See Beales and Green, 'Libraries and Their Users'; Carpenter, 'Libraries'; Ostrowski, *Books, Maps, and Politics*, pp. 14–19.
7 Quoted in Johnston, *History of the Library of Congress*, p. 23.
8 Ibid., p. 19.
9 McKitterick, *Cambridge University Library*, pp. 418–19; Ostrowski, *Books, Maps, and Politics*, pp. 44–5.
10 Quoted in Johnston, *History of the Library of Congress*, p. 38.
11 Ibid., p. 517.
12 Fleming, et al., *History of the Book in Canada*, p. 313.
13 Vogel, '"Mr Madison Will Have to Put on His Armor"', pp. 144–5.
14 The story is told in Johnston, *History of the Library of Congress*, pp. 65–6. For Caldwell, see Allen C. Clark, 'Sketch of Elias Boudinot Caldwell', p. 208.
15 Gleig, *A Narrative of the Campaigns of the British Army at Washington and New Orleans*, p. 129.
16 Thanks to the suggestion of John Y. Cole, Jane Aikin very generously shared the drafts of her new history of the Library of Congress with me.
17 Gleig, *A Narrative of the Campaigns of the British Army at Washington and New Orleans*, p. 132.
18 Ibid., p. 124. Rosenbach's gift is recounted in the *Annual Report of the Librarian of Congress for the fiscal year ended June 30, 1940*, p. 202. Rosenbach himself tells the story of the book in *A Book Hunter's Holiday*, pp. 145–6.
19 Quoted in Johnston, *History of the Library of Congress*, pp. 69–71.
20 Ibid., p. 71.
21 Ostrowski, *Books, Maps, and Politics*, pp. 74–8.
22 Ibid., p. 75.
23 Quoted in Johnston, *History of the Library of Congress*, pp. 86, 90.

24 Ibid., p. 97.

25 Ibid., p. 168.

26 Fox, *Trinity College Library Dublin*, pp. 90, 121; McKitterick, *Cambridge University Library*, p. 152; Harris, P. R., *A History of the British Museum Library*, p. 47.

27 Ostrowski, *Books, Maps, and Politics*, pp. 81–3.

28 Johnston, *History of the Library of Congress*, p. 154.

29 Conaway, *America's Library*, p. 68.

Chapter 6: How to Disobey Kafka

1 MacCulloch, *Thomas Cromwell*, pp. 1–3.

2 Quoted in Krevans, 'Bookburning and the Poetic Deathbed: The Legacy of Virgil', p. 198.

3 Letter to Thomas Love Peacock, 10 August 1821. *Letters of Percy Bysshe Shelley* (ed. F. L. Jones), II, p. 330.

4 Frederick Locker-Lampson, 'Tennyson on the Romantic Poets', pp. 175–6.

5 The best overview of John Murray the firm is the great Humphrey Carpenter's *The Seven Lives of John Murray*.

6 Carpenter, *Seven Lives*, pp. 128–9.

7 Hobhouse's journal, British Library Add. MS 56548 ff. 73v–87v, transcribed by Peter Cochran and quoted in ibid., p. 132.

8 *Journal of Thomas Moore*, (ed.) W. S. Dowden, II, p. 731 (15 May 1824), quoted in Carpenter, *Seven Lives*, p. 132.

9 My account of the burning is drawn from Carpenter's synthesis of the various sources in *Seven Lives*, pp. 128–48, and from Fiona MacCarthy's *Byron: Life and Legend*, pp. 539–43.

10 Quoted in Balint, *Kafka's Last Trial*, p. 128.

11 Stach, *Kafka*, pp. 542–3.

12 Ibid., p. 642.

13 Ibid., pp. 402–3.

14 Ibid., pp. 475–6.

15 Murray, *Kafka*, pp. 39–43.

16 Balint, *Kafka's Last Trial*, p. 135.

Chapter 7: The Twice-Burned Library

1 Coppens, et al., *Leuven University Library 1425–2000*, p. 160. He was executed by a German firing squad for writing this note.

2 J. de le Court, *Recueil des ordonnances des Pays-Bas autrichiens. Troisième série: 1700–1794*, pp. 276–7.

3 Coppens, et al., *Leuven University Library 1425–2000*, pp. 52–5, 73–4.

4 The best account of the library is in *Leuven University Library 1425–2000*.

5 'A Crime Against the World', *Daily Mail*, 31 August 1914, p. 4.

6 Toynbee, *The German Terror in Belgium*, p. 116; *La Croix*, 30 August 1914.

7 Schivelbusch, *Die Bibliothek von Löwen*, pp. 27–31.

8 Ibid., pp. 27–8.

9 Ibid., pp. 36–9.

10 Coppens, et al., *Leuven University Library 1425–2000*, p. 190.

11 Mercier, *Pastoral Letter of His Eminence Cardinal Mercier*, pp. 1–2.

12 *Illustrated London News*, 30 July 1921.

13 Guppy, *The Reconstitution of the Library of the University of Louvain*, p. 19.

14 Proctor, 'The Louvain Library', pp. 156–63.

15 Ibid., pp. 163–6.

16 'Nazis Charge, British Set Fire to Library', *New York Times*, 27 June 1940, p. 12.

17 'Librarian of Louvain Tells of War Losses', *New York Times*, 17 April 1941, p. 1.

18 'News Reel Shows Nazi Bombing', *Daily Mail*, 28 May 1940, p. 3.

19 Schivelbusch, *Die Bibliothek von Löwen*, p. 19.

Chapter 8: The Paper Brigade

1 Rose, 'Introduction', p. 1.

2 The story of the Cairo Geniza is brilliantly told by Adina Hoffman and Peter Cole in *Sacred Trash*. See pp. 12–16 for the phenomenon of the genizah more generally.

3 The original text of the letter is in the Helen Keller Archive, held by the American Foundation for the Blind. It is available online at: https://www.afb.org/HelenKellerArchive?a=d&d=A-HK02-B210-F03-001&e=------en-20--1--txt--------3-7-6-5-3--------------0-1 (Accessed: 10 April 2020)

4 'Mr H. G. Wells on Germany', *The Times*, 22 September 1933, p. 14.

5 von Merveldt, 'Books Cannot Be Killed By Fire', pp. 523–7.

6 Ibid., p. 528. The collections of the American Library of Banned Books are now preserved in the Library of the Jewish Theological Seminary in New York.

7 Hill, 'The Nazi Attack on "Un-German Literature"'.

8 Ibid., p. 32.

9 Ibid., pp. 12–14.

10 Lustig, 'Who Are to Be the Successors of European Jewry?', p. 523.

11 Piper, *Alfred Rosenberg*, pp. 462–508.

12 Sutter, 'The Lost Jewish Libraries of Vilna', pp. 220–3.

13 Hill, 'The Nazi Attack on "Un-German Literature"', pp. 29–32.

14 Steinweis, *Studying the Jew*, pp. 115–16.

15 Ibid., p. 117.

16 Matthäus, 'Nazi Genocides', pp. 167–73.

17 van Boxel, 'Robert Bellarmine Reads Rashi: Rabbinic Bible Commentaries and the Burning of the Talmud', pp. 121–3.

18 Grendler, *The Roman Inquisition and the Venetian Press, 1540–1605*, pp. 93–102.

19 Beit-Arié, *Hebrew Manuscripts of East and West*, pp. 9–10.

20 Shamir, 'Johannes Pfefferkorn and the Dual Form of the Confiscation Campaign'.

21 Goodman, *A History of Judaism*, p. 440.

22 Kuznitz, *YIVO and the Making of Modern Jewish Culture*, p. 3.

23 Ibid., p. 18; Fishman, 'Embers Plucked from the Fire', pp. 66–8.

24 Kuznitz, *YIVO and the Making of Modern Jewish Culture*, p. 51.

25 Goodman, *A History of Judaism*, pp. 387–9.

26 For the account of the Paper Brigade in Vilna, I am indebted to the scholarship, generosity and advice of David Fishman; Fishman, *The Book Smugglers*, pp. 13–22.

27 Ibid., p. 17.

28 The history of the Strashun is brilliantly told in Dan Rabinowitz, *The Lost Library*.

29 Sutter, 'The Lost Jewish Libraries of Vilna', p. 224.

30 Fishman, *The Book Smugglers*, p. 21.

31 Kuznitz, *YIVO and the Making of Modern Jewish Culture*, pp. 73–6.

32 Ibid., pp. 182–5.

33 The account is detailed in Sutter, 'The Lost Jewish Libraries of Vilna', pp. 224–5 and Fishman, *The Book Smugglers*, pp. 25–30.

34 Fishman, *The Book Smugglers*, pp. 55, 61–3, 71.

35 Fishman, 'Embers Plucked from the Fire', pp. 69–70.

36 Ibid., p. 69.

37 Sutter, 'The Lost Jewish Libraries of Vilna', p. 228.

38 Fishman, 'Embers Plucked from the Fire', p. 70.

39 Ibid., p. 71; Fishman, *The Book Smugglers*, p. 97.

40 Fishman, *The Book Smugglers*, p. 114.

41 The history of the Vilna Ghetto Library is told by Dina Abramowicz herself in 'The Library in the Vilna Ghetto', and by Herman Kruk, 'Library and Reading Room in the Vilna Ghetto, Strashun Street 6'.

42 In New York, YIVO was one of the first organisations to bring word of the unfolding catastrophe to the American public, publishing an account of the Warsaw Ghetto in 1940, and a brochure on the ghetto uprising four years later.

43 Roskies (ed.), *Voices from the Warsaw Ghetto*, pp. 62–3.

44 Ibid., p. xxv.

45 Quoted in Fishman, *The Book Smugglers*, pp. 138–9.

46 Ibid., pp. 65 (biographical details), 140.

47 Ibid., pp. 145–52; Fishman, 'Embers Plucked from the Fire', p. 73.

48 The best account in English is told in Fishman, *The Book Smugglers*, pp. 244–8, but the story deserves to be told in even greater depth.

49 Goodman, *A History of Judaism*, pp. 387–9.

50 https://vilnacollections.yivo.org/Discovery-Press-Release

51 The process of returning looted books and documents has been extensively studied, most notably by Harvard scholar Patricia Kennedy Grimsted. Her article 'The Postwar Fate of Einsatztab Reichsleiter Rosenberg Archival and Library Plunder, and the Dispersal of ERR Records' is a good place to start.

52 The visitor was Lucy Dawidowicz, quoted in Gallas, *'Das Leichenhaus der Bücher': Kulturrestitution und jüdisches Geschichtsdenken nach 1945*, pp. 11–14.

53 Ibid., pp. 60–4; Lustig, 'Who Are to Be the Successors of European Jewry?', p. 537.

54 Esterow, 'The Hunt for the Nazi Loot Still Sitting on Library Shelves'.

55 *Trial of the Major War Criminals Before the International Military Tribunal, Nuremberg, 14 November 1945–1 October 1946*, I, pp. 293–6, II, pp. 493, 585.

Chapter 9: To Be Burned Unread

1 Larkin, *Letters to Monica* (22 May 1964), p. 335.

2 Larkin, 'A Neglected Responsibility', p. 99.

3 Motion, *Philip Larkin*, pp. xv–xviii.

4 Ibid., p. 522.

5 Ibid., pp. 522, 552.

6 Larkin, *Letters to Monica*, pp. 278–83.

7 Larkin, *Selected Letters of Philip Larkin*, p. 600.

8 Selections of which have been printed as Philip Larkin, *Letters Home 1936–1977*.

9 Bate, *Ted Hughes*, p. 385.

10 Brain, 'Sylvia Plath's Letters and Journals', p. 141. Sylvia Plath's archive is now dispersed among several repositories in North America: the Mortimer Rare Book Collection at Neilsen Library of Smith College (Plath's alma mater), the Lilly Library which is the special collections library of the University of Indiana in Bloomington, and some materials that are held within the major tranche of the Ted Hughes Archive held at the Stuart A. Rose Manuscript, Archives, and Rare Book Library at Emory University in Atlanta, Georgia. Most of the Plath journals are among the Plath Papers in Smith College, and they have been meticulously edited by Karen Kukil, the former Archivist at Smith.

11 See Frieda Hughes's introduction to the restored edition of Plath's collection *Ariel* (2004). In a letter to Andrew Motion, Ted Hughes wrote:

> The main problem with S.P.'s biographers is that they fail . . . to realise that the most interesting and dramatic part of S.P.'s life is only ½ S.P. – the other ½ is *me*. They can caricature and remake S.P. in the image of their foolish fantasies, and get away with it – and assume, in their brainless way, that it's perfectly O.K. to give me the same treatment. Apparently forgetting that I'm still here, to check, and that I've no intention of feeding myself to their digestions and submitting myself to their reconstitution, if I can help it. (Quoted in Malcolm, *The Silent Woman*, p. 201.)

12 Plath, *Journals of Sylvia Plath*, p. xi.

13 Brain, 'Sylvia Plath's Letters and Journals', p. 144. These journals were published in 2000 by Karen Kukil in her edition of *The Unabridged Journals of Sylvia Plath: 1950–1962*. It was a prodigious feat of scholarship, as the journals were highly miscellaneous in nature. Some were in the form of bound or spiral-bound notebooks, some typed or written on individual sheets of paper, some of them just scraps, and many difficult to date.

14 Ted Hughes, *Winter Pollen*.

15 Erica Wagner, 'Ted Hughes Archive Opened at Emory University', *The Times*, 10 April 2000, consulted in the version at http://ericawagner. co.uk/ted-hughess-archive-opened-at-emory-university/ (Accessed: 10 November 2019)

16 Cited by Brain, 'Sylvia Plath's Letters and Journals', p. 154.
17 Bate, *Ted Hughes*, pp. 305–6.
18 Read, *Letters of Ted Hughes*, pp. 366–7.
19 Brain, 'Sylvia Plath's Letters and Journals', p. 152.

Chapter 10: Sarajevo Mon Amour

1 Kalender, 'In Memoriam: Aida (Fadila) Buturovic (1959–1992)', p. 73.
2 Riedlmayer, '*Convivencia* Under Fire', p. 274.
3 Quoted in Huseinovic and Arbutina, 'Burned Library Symbolizes Multiethnic Sarajevo'.
4 Donia, *Sarajevo*, pp. 72, 314.
5 The best summary of the political, religious and cultural background to the events described in this chapter can be found in Noel Malcolm, *Bosnia*, pp. 213–33.
6 Dunford, *Yugoslavia: The Rough Guide*, p. vii.
7 Quoted in ibid., p. 257.
8 For an overview of the richness of libraries and archives of Bosnia see Riedlmayer, '*Convivencia* Under Fire'; Riedlmayer, 'The Bosnian Manuscript Ingathering Project'; and Stipčević, 'The Oriental Books and Libraries in Bosnia during the War, 1992–1994'.
9 Schork, 'Jewel of a City Destroyed by Fire', p. 10.
10 'Jewel of a City Destroyed by Fire' ran the headline in *The Times* on 27 August by Kurt Schork, although only on page ten of the newspaper. A larger piece by Roger Boyes, 'This is Cultural Genocide', on 28 August, eventually uncovered the broader implications of the attack.
11 Riedlmayer, '*Convivencia* Under Fire', pp. 289–90.
12 Malcolm, 'Preface', in Koller and Karpat (eds), *Ottoman Bosnia*, p. vii.
13 Riedlmayer, *Destruction of Cultural Heritage in Bosnia-Herzegovina, 1992–1996*, p. 18.
14 Riedlmayer, '*Convivencia* Under Fire', p. 274.
15 Riedlmayer, 'Crimes of War, Crimes of Peace', p. 114.
16 Riedlmayer, '*Convivencia* Under Fire', p. 276
17 Walasek, 'Domains of Restoration', p. 72.
18 Ibid., p. 212.
19 Riedlmayer, '*Convivencia* Under Fire', p. 274.
20 Riedlmayer, 'Foundations of the Ottoman Period in the Balkan Wars of the 1990s', p. 91.
21 Walasek, 'Cultural Heritage, the Search for Justice, and Human Rights', p. 313.

22 Personal communication, August 2019.

23 See Walasek, 'Cultural Heritage, the Search for Justice, and Human Rights'.

24 *The Prosecutor vs. Ratko Mladić: 'Prosecution Submission of the Fourth Amended Indictment and Schedule of Incidents'*.

25 Quoted by Riedlmayer, '*Convivencia* Under Fire', p. 274.

26 Ibid., p. 276.

27 Ibid., p. 288.

28 Sambandan, 'The Story of the Jaffna Public Library'.

29 Wheen, 'The Burning of Paradise'.

30 Moldrich, 'Tamils Accuse Police of Cultural Genocide'.

31 Sahner, 'Yemen's Threatened Cultural Heritage'.

32 Riedlmayer, 'The Bosnian Manuscript Ingathering Project'.

33 Ahmed, 'Saving Yemen's Heritage'; Schmidtke, 'The History of Zaydī Studies', p. 189.

Chapter 11: Flames of Empire

1 See especially the Savoy and Sarr *Report on the Restitution of African Cultural Heritage*.

2 The best accounts are Purcell, 'Warfare and Collection-Building', and Pogson, 'A Grand Inquisitor and His Books'.

3 Philip, *The Bodleian Library in the Seventeenth and Eighteenth Centuries*, pp. 9–10.

4 Ovenden, 'Catalogues of the Bodleian Library and Other Collections', p. 283.

5 Mittler (ed.), *Bibliotheca Palatina*, p. 459.

6 Engelhart, 'How Britain Might Have Deliberately Concealed Evidence of Imperial Crimes'.

7 See Banton, 'Record-Keeping for Good Governance and Accountability in the Colonial Office', pp. 76–81.

8 Hampshire, '"Apply the Flame More Searingly"', p. 337.

9 W. J. Watts, Ministry of External Defence, to Private Secretary to High Commissioner, July 1956, folio 2, FCO 141/7524, National Archives; see Hampshire, p. 337.

10 Hampshire, '"Apply the Flame More Searingly"', p. 340.

11 Ibid., p. 341.

12 Anderson, 'Deceit, Denial, and the Discovery of Kenya's "Migrated Archive"', p. 143.

13 Ibid., p. 146.

14 Karabinos, 'Displaced Archives, Displaced History', p. 279.

15 Archives nationales d'outre-mer: History, http://archivesnationales. culture.gouv.fr/anom/en/Presentation/Historique.html (Accessed: 28 February 2020)

16 Shepard, '"Of Sovereignty"', pp. 871–2.

17 McDougall, *A History of Algeria*, pp. 224–31.

18 Shepard, '"Of Sovereignty"', pp. 875–6.

19 Ibid., p. 873.

20 Chifamba, 'Rhodesian Army Secrets Kept Safe in the UK'.

21 Matthies, *The Siege of Magdala*, p. 129.

22 This was led by Dr Mai Musié, now the Bodleian's Public Engagement Manager.

23 Gnisci (ed.), *Treasures of Ethiopia and Eritrea in the Bodleian Library*.

Chapter 12: An Obsession with Archives

1 Große and Sengewald, 'Der chronologische Ablauf der Ereignisse am 4. Dezember 1989'.

2 This account relies heavily on the work of Joseph Sassoon, especially his magisterial *Saddam Hussein's Ba'ath Party*.

3 See Sassoon, 'The East German Ministry for State Security and Iraq, 1968–1989', and Dimitrov and Sassoon, 'State Security, Information, and Repression'.

4 Sassoon, 'The East German Ministry for State Security and Iraq, 1968–1989', p. 7.

5 Tripp, *A History of Iraq*, pp. 239–45.

6 See the Hoover Institution Archival Finding Aid, Register of the Hizb al-Ba'th al-'Arabī al-Ishtirākī in Iraq [Ba'th Arab Socialist Party of Iraq] Records, http://oac.cdlib.org/findaid/ark:/13030/c84j0cg3 (Accessed: 3 June 2019)

7 Quoted in Makiya, *Republic of Fear*, p. 22.

8 I am grateful to Kanan Makiya for giving me the time to interview him at length.

9 Filkins, 'Regrets Only?'.

10 Roberts recounts this period, and the discovery of the archives in an interview: Stephen Talbot, 'Saddam's Road to Hell', 24 January 2006, https://www.pbs.org/frontlineworld/stories/iraq501/audio_index.html (Accessed: 24 November 2019)

11 Gellman and Randal, 'U.S. to Airlift Archive of Atrocities out of Iraq'.

12 See Montgomery, 'The Iraqi Secret Police Files', pp. 77–9.

13 A transcript of the interview of Kanan Makiya by Bill Moyers, *PBS: Now Special Edition*, 17 March 2003, https://www.pbs.org/now/transcript/transcript031703_full.html (Accessed: 17 March 2019). See also Filkins, 'Regrets Only?'.

14 Gravois, 'A Tug of War for Iraq's Memory'.

15 Burkeman, 'Ancient Archive Lost in Baghdad Library Blaze', *Guardian*, 15 April 2003.

16 *Salam Pax: The Baghdad Blogger*, 19 March 2003, https://salampax. wordpress.com/page/22/ (Accessed: 17 March 2019); Tripp, *A History of Iraq*, pp. 267–76.

17 Makiya, 'A Model for Post-Saddam Iraq', p. 5.

18 Gravois, 'A Tug of War for Iraq's Memory'.

19 The exact size of the archive is subject to varying accounts, one statement from the Society of American Archivists, quoting the IMF website in April 2008, describes the archive as being 3 million pages: https://www2.archivists.org/statements/acasaa-joint-statement-on-iraqi-records (Accessed: 28 February 2020)

20 Montgomery, 'Immortality in the Secret Police Files', pp. 316–17.

21 Quoted by Caswell, '"Thank You Very Much, Now Give Them Back"', p. 231.

22 Montgomery, 'The Iraqi Secret Police Files', pp. 69–99.

23 Montgomery and Brill, 'The Ghosts of Past Wars Live on in a Critical Archive'.

24 Interview with Kanan Makiya, June 2019.

25 Makiya, 'A Personal Note', p. 317.

26 Garton Ash, 'Trials, Purges and History Lessons', in *History of the Present*, p. 294.

27 Gauck, 'State Security Files', p. 72.

28 Tucker and Brand, 'Acquisition and Unethical Use of Documents Removed from Iraq by *New York Times* Journalist Rukmini Callimachi'.

Chapter 13: The Digital Deluge

1 Rosenzweig, 'Scarcity or Abundance?'.

2 Desjardins, 'What Happens in an Internet Minute in 2019'.

3 Halvarsson, 'Over 20 Years of Digitization at the Bodleian Libraries'.

4 See Binns, et al., 'Third Party Tracking in the Mobile Ecosystem'.

5 Garton Ash, *Free Speech*, p. 47.

6 See especially Zuboff, *The Age of Surveillance Capitalism*.

7   Hern, 'Flickr to Delete Millions of Photos as it Reduces Allowance for Free Users'.

8   Hill, E., 'Silicon Valley Can't Be Trusted with Our History'.

9   For more examples see SalahEldeen and Nelson, 'Losing My Revolution'.

10 Bruns, 'The Library of Congress Twitter Archive'.

11 This grouping includes the Bodleian, the British Library, the National Libraries of Scotland and Wales, Cambridge University Library and the Library of Trinity College Dublin.

12 See Feather, *Publishing, Piracy and Politics*.

13 In the spirit of full disclosure I should reveal that as Bodley's Librarian I am part of the governance structure of this whole system, sitting on the Legal Deposit Directors Group, and on the Joint Committee for Legal Deposit (alongside the other library directors and representatives of the publishing industry). Since 2014 I have also chaired the group charged with the implementation of the whole system of digital legal deposit.

14 I am particularly grateful to Andy Jackson at the British Library for sharing his deep knowledge and expertise in web archiving with me.

15 Zittrain, Albert and Lessig, 'Perma', pp. 88–99.

16 'Internet Archive is Suffering from a DDoS attack'; Jeong, 'Anti-ISIS Hacktivists are Attacking the Internet Archive'.

17 As cited on https://factba.se/trump (Accessed: 28 February 2020)

18 'The White House. Memorandum for All Personnel . . .'.

19 McClanahan, 'Trump and the Demise of the Presidential Records Honor System'.

20 The relevant websites can be found at: https://factba.se/ and http://trumptwitterarchive.com/

21 Sherwood, 'Led By Donkeys Reveal Their Faces at Last'.

22 Wright, O., 'Lobbying Company Tried to Wipe Out "Wife Beater" Beer References'.

23 Riley-Smith, 'Expenses and Sex Scandal Deleted from MPs' Wikipedia Pages by Computers Inside Parliament'.

24 Woodward, 'Huge Number of Maine Public Records Have Likely Been Destroyed'.

25 Murgia, 'Microsoft Quietly Deletes Largest Public Face Recognition Data Set'.

26 Harvey, https://megapixels.cc/; Vincent, 'Transgender YouTubers had Their Videos Grabbed to Train Facial Recognition Software'.

27 Coulter and Shubber, 'Equifax to Pay almost $800m in US Settlement Over Data Breach'.

28 https://twitter.com/carolecadwalla/status/1166486817882947586?s=20 (Accessed: 28 August 2019)

29 Moran, 'Is Your Facebook Account an Archive of the Future?'.

30 Quoted in Zuboff, *The Age of Surveillance Capitalism*, p. 191.

31 Ibid., pp. 351–2.

32 https://www.pewresearch.org/fact-tank/2017/08/30/most-americans-especially-millennials-say-libraries-can-help-them-find-reliable-trustworthy-information/ (Accessed: 29 February 2020)

33 Perhaps through amending laws such as (in the UK) either the Public Records Act 1958, or the Public Libraries and Museums Act 1964.

34 Ovenden, 'Virtual Memory'.

35 Sir Nigel Shadbolt has argued elsewhere for a different approach to web governance which he describes as 'Architectures for Autonomy'.

36 I am grateful to Sir Nigel Shadbolt for this suggestion.

Chapter 14: Paradise Lost?

1 See Wood, *Life and Times of Anthony Wood, Antiquary, of Oxford, 1632–1695*, I, p. 319.

2 Philip, *The Bodleian Library*, pp. 42–3.

3 The request is still preserved: MS. Clarendon 91, fol. 18.

4 This act of defiance would later inspire a moving passage in Philip Pullman's novel *La Belle Sauvage* (2017), where the Librarian of the Bodleian in Pullman's fictional world refused to give up the Alethiometer to the Consistorial Court of Discipline, even to the point of facing a firing squad: 'The Librarian refused, saying that he had not taken up his office in order to give away the contents of the library, and that he had a sacred duty to conserve and protect them for scholarship.' Pullman, *La Belle Sauvage*, pp. 62–3.

5 The copy of the 1645 edition of Milton's *Poems* with his personal dedication to Rous is now shelf-marked: Arch.G.e.44(1). See also Achinstein, *Citizen Milton*, pp. 5–7.

6 Derrida, *Archive Fever*, p. 4.

7 The phrase was coined by Lorcan Dempsey, 'The Service Turn . . .' http://orweblog.oclc.org/The-service-turn/ (Accessed: 5 January 2020)

8 Klinenberg, *Palaces for the People*, p. 32.

9 Naudé, *Advice on Establishing a Library*, p. 63.

10 Alston, 'Statement on Visit to the United Kingdom'.

11 See Ovenden, 'Catalogues of the Bodleian Library'.

12 For more information see: https://www.clockss.org

13 *Letters of Sir Thomas Bodley to the University of Oxford 1598–1611*, p. 4.

14 Kenosi, 'Preserving and Accessing the South African Truth and Reconciliation Commission Records'.

15 Ojo, 'National Archives in a "Very Sorry State"'.

16 Koslowski, 'National Archives May Not Survive Unless Funding Doubles, Warns Council'.

17 Ibid.

18 See Ovenden, 'Virtual Memory' and 'We Must Fight to Preserve Digital Information'.

Coda: Why We Will Always Need Libraries and Archives

1 *CIPFA Annual Library Survey*, 2017–18.

2 Labbé, et al., 'The Longest Homogeneous Series of Grape Harvest Dates'.

3 Mill, *On Liberty*, p. 47.

4 Hamilton, 'The Learned Press', pp. 406–7; Carter, *A History of the Oxford University Press*, pp. 240–3.

5 Doyle, 'Imminent Threat to Guatemala's Historical Archive of the National Police'.

6 Aston, 'Muniment Rooms', p. 235.

7 Gauck and Fry, 'Dealing with a Stasi Past', pp. 279–80; Maddrell, 'The Revolution Made Law', p. 153.

8 With the exception of the Foreign Ministry files. Garton Ash argues that this was because they would reveal 'sycophantic conversations' between the leaders of East and West Germany, and that as a result, 'west German politicians have thus fearlessly spared nobody – except themselves'. Garton Ash, 'Trials, Purges and History Lessons', in *History of the Present*, p. 309.

9 Gauck and Fry, 'Dealing with a Stasi Past', p. 281.

10 Orwell, *Nineteen Eighty-Four*, p. 178.

11 'Time to Press Ahead with Archive Law'.

12 Hopf, et al., 'Fake Science and the Knowledge Crisis', p. 4.

13 Quoted in Hampshire, '"Apply the Flame More Searingly"', p. 343.

14 Savoy and Sarr, *Report on the Restitution of African Cultural Heritage*, pp. 42–3.

Bibliography

Abramowicz, Dina, 'The Library in the Vilna Ghetto', in Jonathan Rose (ed.), *The Holocaust and the Book: Destruction and Preservation* (Amherst, MA: University of Massachusetts Press, 2001), pp. 165–70

Achinstein, Sharon, *Citizen Milton* (Oxford: Bodleian Library, 2007)

Affleck, Michael, 'Priests, Patrons, and Playwrights: Libraries in Rome Before 168 BC', in Jason König, Katerina Oikonomopolou and Greg Woolf (eds), *Ancient Libraries* (Cambridge: Cambridge University Press, 2013), pp. 124–36

Ahmed, Amel, 'Saving Yemen's Heritage, "Heart and Soul of Classical Islamic Tradition"', *Al Jazeera America*, 5 February 2016, http://america. aljazeera.com/articles/2016/2/5/american-professor-in-race-to-save-yemens-cultural-heritage.html (Accessed: 17 November 2019)

Allen, P. S., 'Books Brought from Spain in 1596', *English Historical Review*, 31 (1916), pp. 606–8

Alsop, Ben, 'Suffrage Objects in the British Museum', *British Museum Blog*, 23 February 2018, https://blog.britishmuseum.org/suffrage-objects-in-the-british-museum/ (Accessed: 17 September 2019)

Alston, Philip, 'Statement on Visit to the United Kingdom, by Professor Philip Alston, United Nations Special Rapporteur on Extreme Poverty and Human Rights', 17 November 2018, https://www.ohchr.org/Documents/Issues/Poverty/EOM_GB_16Nov2018.pdf (Accessed: 3 September 2019)

Ammianus Marcellinus, *History*, (ed.) John Carew Rolfe, 3 vols (Harvard, MA: Harvard University Press, 1986)

Anderson, David M., 'Deceit, Denial, and the Discovery of Kenya's "Migrated Archive"', *History Workshop Journal*, 80 (2015), pp. 142–60

Annual Report of the Librarian of Congress for the Fiscal Year Ended June 30, 1940 (Washington: United States Government Printing Office, 1941)

Archi, Alfonso, 'Archival Record-Keeping at Ebla 2400–2350 BC', in Maria Brosius (ed.), *Ancient Archives and Archival Traditions: Concepts of Record-Keeping in the Ancient World* (Oxford: Oxford University Press, 2003), pp. 17–26

Asher-Schapiro, Avi, 'Who gets to tell Iraq's history?', *LRB Blog*, 15 June 2018, https://www.lrb.co.uk/blog/2018/06/15/avi-asher-schapiro/who-gets-to-tell-iraqs-history/

Asmal, Kaider, Asmal, Louise, and Roberts, Ronald Suresh, *Reconciliation Through Truth: A Reckoning of Apartheid's Criminal Governance*, 2nd edn (Cape Town: David Philip Publishers, 1997)

Aston, Trevor, 'Muniment Rooms and Their Fittings in Medieval and Early Modern England', in Ralph Evans (ed.), *Lordship and Learning: Studies in Memory of Trevor Aston* (Woodbridge: Boydell Press, 2004), pp. 235–47

Al-Tikriti, Nabil, '"Stuff Happens": A Brief Overview of the 2003 Destruction of Iraqi Manuscript Collections, Archives and Libraries', *Library Trends* (2007), pp. 730–45

Bagnall, Roger S., 'Alexandria: Library of Dreams', *Proceedings of the American Philosophical Society*, 146 (2002), pp. 348–62

Balint, Benjamin, *Kafka's Last Trial: The Case of a Literary Legacy* (London: Picador, 2018)

Banton, Mandy, '"Destroy? Migrate? Conceal?" British Strategies for the Disposal of Sensitive Records of Colonial Administrations at Independence', *Journal of Imperial and Commonwealth History*, 40 (2012), pp. 321–35

——, 'Record-Keeping for Good Governance and Accountability in the Colonial Office: An Historical Sketch', in James Lowry and Justus Wamukoya (eds), *Integrity in Government Through Records Management: Essays in Honour of Anne Thurston* (Farnham: Ashgate, 2014), pp. 73–84

Barker-Benfield, B. C. (ed.), *St Augustine's Abbey, Canterbury* (*Corpus of British Medieval Library Catalogues 13*), 3 vols (London: British Library in association with the British Academy, 2008)

Barnard, John, 'Politics, Profits and Idealism: John Norton, the Stationers' Company and Sir Thomas Bodley', *Bodleian Library Record*, 17 (2002), pp. 385–408

Barnes, Robert, 'Cloistered Bookworms in the Chicken-Coop of the Muses: The Ancient Library of Alexandria', in Roy MacLeod (ed.), *The Library of Alexandria: Centre of Learning in the Ancient World* (London: I. B. Tauris, 2000), pp. 61–77

Bate, Jonathan, *Ted Hughes: The Unauthorised Life* (London: William Collins, 2015)

Bauer, Heiker, *The Hirschfeld Archives: Violence, Death and Modern Queer Culture* (Philadelphia, PA: Temple University Press, 2017)

Beales, Ross W., and Green, James N., 'Libraries and Their Users', in

Hugh Amory and David D. Hall (eds), *A History of the Book in America*, 1: *The Colonial Book in the Atlantic World* (Cambridge: Cambridge University Press/American Antiquarian Society, 2000), pp. 399–403

Beit-Arié, Malachi, *Hebrew Manuscripts of East and West: Towards a Comparative Codicology* (London: British Library, 1993)

Belgium, Ministry of Justice, *War Crimes Committed During the Invasion of the National Territory, May, 1940: The Destruction of the Library of the University of Louvain* (Liège: [Ministère de la justice] 1946)

Bélis, Mireille, 'In search of the Qumran Library', *Near Eastern Archaeology*, 63 (2000), pp. 121–3

Bepler, Jill, 'The Herzog August Library in Wolfenbüttel: Foundations for the Future', in *A Treasure House of Books: The Library of Duke August of Brunswick-Wolfenbüttel* (Wiesbaden: Harrasowitz, 1998), pp. 17–28

——, 'Vicissitudo Temporum: Some Sidelights on Book Collecting in the Thirty Years War', *Sixteenth Century Journal*, 32 (2001), pp. 953–68

La bibliothèque de Louvain: séance commémorative du 4ᵉ anniversaire de l'incendie (Paris: Librairie académique, 1919)

Binns, Reuben, Lyngs, Ulrik, van Kleek, Max, Jun Zhao, Libert, Timothy, and Shadbolt, Nigel, 'Third Party Tracking in the Mobile Ecosystem', *WebSci '18: Proceedings of the 10th ACM Conference on Web Science*, May 2018, pp. 23–31, https://doi.org/10.1145/3201064.3201089

Biran, Michal, 'Libraries, Books and Transmission of Knowledge in Ilkhanid Baghdad', *Journal of the Economic and Social History of the Orient*, 62 (2019), pp. 464–502

Black, Alistair, 'The People's University: Models of Public Library History', in Alistair Black and Peter Hoare (eds), *The Cambridge History of Libraries in Britain and Ireland*, III: *1850–2000* (Cambridge: Cambridge University Press, 2006), pp. 24–39

——, and Hoare, Peter (eds), *The Cambridge History of Libraries in Britain and Ireland*, III: *1850–2000* (Cambridge: Cambridge University Press, 2006)

Bloom, Jonathan M., *Paper Before Print: The History and Impact of Paper in the Islamic World* (New Haven, CT: Yale University Press, 2001)

Bodley, Sir Thomas, *The Life of Sir Thomas Bodley, The Honourable Founder of the Publique Library in the University of Oxford* (Oxford: Printed by Henry Hall, 1647)

——, *Reliquiae Bodleianae* (London: John Hartley, 1703)

Bond, W. H., and Amory, Hugh (eds), *The Printed Catalogues of the Harvard College Library 1723–1790* (Boston, MA: Colonial Society of Massachusetts, 1996)

Boraine, Alex, 'Truth and Reconciliation Commission in South Africa Amnesty: The Price of Peace', in Jon Elster (ed.), *Retribution and Repatriation in the Transition to Democracy* (Cambridge: Cambridge University Press, 2006), pp. 299–316

Boxel, Piet van, 'Robert Bellarmine Reads Rashi: Rabbinic Bible Commentaries and the Burning of the Talmud', in Joseph R. Hacker and Adam Shear (eds), *The Hebrew Book in Early Modern Italy* (Philadelphia, PA: University of Pennsylvania Press, 2011), pp. 121–32

Boyes, Roger, 'This is Cultural Genocide', *The Times*, 28 August 1992, p.12

Brain, Tracy, 'Sylvia Plath's Letters and Journals', in Jo Gill (ed.), *Cambridge Companion to Sylvia Plath* (Cambridge: Cambridge University Press, 2006), pp. 139–55

Brammertz, S., et al., 'Attacks on Cultural Heritage as a Weapon of War', *Journal of International Criminal Justice*, 14 (2016), pp. 1143–74

Breay, Claire, and Harrison, Julian (eds), *Magna Carta: Law, Liberty, Legacy* (London: British Library, 2015)

Breay, Claire, and Story, Joanna (eds), *Anglo-Saxon Kingdoms: Art, Word, War* (London: British Library, 2018)

Brent, Jonathan, 'The Last Books', *Jewish Ideas Daily*, 1 May 2013, http://www.jewishideasdaily.com/6413/features/the-last-books/

Brosius, Maria (ed.), *Ancient Archives and Archival Traditions: Concepts of Record-Keeping in the Ancient World* (Oxford: Oxford University Press, 2003)

Bruns, Axel, 'The Library of Congress Twitter Archive: A Failure of Historic Proportions', *Medium.com*, 2 January 2018, https://medium.com/dmrc-at-large/the-library-of-congress-twitter-archive-a-failure-of-historic-proportions-6dc1c3bc9e2c (Accessed: 2 September 2019)

Bryce, Trevor, *Life and Society in the Hittite World* (Oxford: Oxford University Press, 2002)

Buck, Peter, 'Seventeenth-Century Political Arithmetic: Civil Strife and Vital Statistics', *Isis*, 68 (1977), pp. 67–84

Buckingham, James Silk, *Travels in Mesopotamia*, 2 vols (London: Henry Colburn, 1827)

Burke, Peter, *A Social History of Knowledge II: From the Encyclopédie to Wikipedia* (Cambridge: Polity, 2012)

Burkeman, Oliver, 'Ancient Archive Lost in Baghdad Library Blaze', *Guardian*, 15 April 2003, https://www.theguardian.com/world/2003/apr/15/education.books (Accessed: 12 June 2019)

Burnett, Charles, 'The Coherence of the Arabic-Latin Translation Program in Toledo in the Twelfth Century', *Science in Context*, 14 (2001), pp. 249–88

Busby, Eleanor, 'Nearly 800 Public Libraries Closed Since Austerity Launched in 2010', *Independent*, 6 December 2019, https://www.independent. co.uk/news/uk/home-news/library-closure-austerity-funding-cuts-conservative-government-a9235561.html (Accessed: 4 April 2020)

'Cardinal Mercier in Ann Arbor', *Michigan Alumnus* (November 1919), pp. 64–6

Carley, James P., 'John Leland and the Contents of English Pre-Dissolution Libraries: The Cambridge Friars', *Transactions of the Cambridge Bibliographical Society*, 9 (1986), pp. 90–100

——, 'John Leland and the Contents of English Pre-Dissolution Libraries: Glastonbury Abbey', *Scriptorium*, 40 (1986), pp. 107–20

——, 'The Dispersal of the Monastic Libraries and the Salvaging of the Spoils', in Elisabeth Leedham-Green and Teresa Webber (eds), *The Cambridge History of Libraries in Britain and Ireland*, 1: *To 1640* (Cambridge: Cambridge University Press, 2006), pp. 265–91

Carpenter, Humphrey, *The Seven Lives of John Murray: The Story of a Publishing Dynasty 1768–2002* (London: John Murray, 2008)

Carpenter, Kenneth E., 'Libraries', in *A History of the Book in America*, 2: *Print, Culture, and Society in the New Nation, 1790–1840* (Chapel Hill, NC: University of North Carolina Press in association with the American Antiquarian Society, 2010), pp. 273–86

Carter, Harry, *A History of the Oxford University Press*, 1: *To the year 1780* (Oxford: Clarendon Press, 1975)

Casson, Lionel, *Libraries in the Ancient World* (New Haven, CT: Yale University Press, 2001)

Caswell, Michelle, '"Thank You Very Much, Now Give them Back": Cultural Property and the Fight over the Iraqi Baath Party Records', *American Archivist*, 74 (2011), pp. 211–40

Chifamba, Sarudzayi, 'Rhodesian Army Secrets Kept Safe in the UK', *Patriot*, 5 December 2013, https://www.thepatriot.co.zw/old_posts/rhodesian-army-secrets-kept-safe-in-the-uk/ (Accessed: 8 February 2020)

Choi, David, 'Trump Deletes Tweet after Flubbing Congressional Procedure After Disaster Relief Bill Passes in the House', *Business Insider*, 4 June 2019, https://www.businessinsider.com/trump-mistakes-congress-disaster-aid-bill-tweet-2019-6?r=US&IR=T (Accessed: 9 September 2019)

Clapinson, Mary, *A Brief History of the Bodleian Library* (Oxford: Bodleian Library, 2015)

Clark, Allen C., 'Sketch of Elias Boudinot Caldwell', *Records of the Columbia Historical Society, Washington, D.C.*, 24 (1992), pp. 204–13

Clark, John Willis, *The Care of Books: An Essay on the Development of Libraries and Their Fittings, From the Earliest Times to the End of the Eighteenth Century* (Cambridge: Cambridge University Press, 1909)

Clennell, William, 'The Bodleian Declaration: A History', *Bodleian Library Record*, 20 (2007), pp. 47–60

Conaway, James, *America's Library: The Story of the Library of Congress 1800–2000* (New Haven, CT: Yale University Press, 2000)

Conway, Paul, 'Preserving Imperfection: Assessing the Incidence of Digital Imaging Error in HathiTrust', *Digital Technology and Culture*, 42 (2013), pp. 17–30, https://deepblue.lib.umich.edu/bitstream/handle/2027.42/99522/J23%20Conway%20Preserving%20Imperfection%202013.pdf; sequence=1 (Accessed: 3 September 2019)

Coppens, Chris, Derez, Mark, and Roegiers, Jan (eds), *Leuven University Library 1425–2000* (Leuven: Leuven University Press, 2005)

Coqueugniot, Gaëlle, 'Where was the Royal Library of Pergamum?: An Institution Lost and Found Again', in Jason König, Katerina Oikonomopolou and Greg Woolf (eds), *Ancient Libraries* (Cambridge: Cambridge University Press, 2013), pp. 109–23

Coulter, Martin, and Shubber, Kadhim, 'Equifax to Pay almost $800m in US Settlement Over Data Breach', *Financial Times*, 22 July 2019, https://www.ft.com/content/dd98b94e-ac62-11e9-8030-530adfa879c2 (Accessed: 15 April 2020)

Cox, Joseph, 'These Bots Tweet When Government Officials Edit Wikipedia', *Vice.com*, 10 July 2014, https://www.vice.com/en_us/article/pgaka8/these-bots-tweet-when-government-officials-edit-wikipedia (Accessed 30: August 2019)

Craig, Barbara, *Archival Appraisal: Theory and Practice* (Munich: K. G. Sauer, 2014)

Cuneiform Texts from Babylonian Tablets &c., in the British Museum (London: British Museum, 1896–)

Darnton, Robert, 'The Great Book Massacre', *New York Review of Books*, 26 April 2001, pp. 16–19

Davison, Phil, 'Ancient treasures destroyed', *Independent*, 27 August 1992, https://www.independent.co.uk/news/world/europe/ancient-treasures-destroyed-1542650.html (Accessed: 18 February 2020)

de le Court, J. (ed.), *Recueil des ordonnances des Pays-Bas autrichiens. Troisième série: 1700–1794* (Brussels, 1894)

Deguara, Brittney, 'National Library Creates Facebook Time Capsule to

Document New Zealand's History', *stuff.co.nz*, 5 September 2019, https://www.stuff.co.nz/national/115494638/national-library-creates-facebook-time-capsule-to-document-new-zealands-history (Accessed: 6 September 2019)

Derrida, Jacques, *Archive Fever: A Freudian Impression* (Chicago: University of Chicago Press, 1998)

Desjardins, Jeff, 'What Happens in an Internet Minute in 2019', *Visualcapitalist.com*, 13 March 2019, https://www.visualcapitalist.com/what-happens-in-an-internet-minute-in-2019/ (Accessed: 5 June 2019)

Dimitrov, Martin K., and Sassoon, Joseph, 'State Security, Information, and Repression: A Comparison of Communist Bulgaria and Ba'thist Iraq', *Journal of Cold War Studies*, 16 (2014), pp. 3–31

Dixon, C. Scott, 'The Sense of the Past in Reformation Germany: Part II', *German History*, 30 (2012), pp. 175–98

Dolsten, Josefin, '5 Amazing Discoveries from a Hidden Trove', *Washington Jewish Week*, 30 November 2017, pp. 10–11

Donia, Robert J., *Sarajevo: A Biography* (London: Hurst & Co., 2006)

Doyle, Kate (ed.), 'Imminent Threat to Guatemala's Historical Archive of the National Police (AHPN)', *National Security Archive*, 30 May 2019, https://nsarchive.gwu.edu/news/guatemala/2019-05-30/imminent-threat-guatemalas-historical-archive-national-police-ahpn (Accessed: 2 June 2019)

Duffy, Eamon, *The Stripping of the Altars: Traditional Religion in England c.1400–c.1580* (New Haven, CT: Yale University Press, 1992)

Duke Humfrey's Library & the Divinity School, 1488–1988: An Exhibition at the Bodleian Library June–August 1988 (Oxford: Bodleian Library, 1988)

Dunford, Martin, *Yugoslavia: The Rough Guide* (London: Harrop Columbus, 1990)

Engelhart, Katie, 'How Britain Might Have Deliberately Concealed Evidence of Imperial Crimes', *Vice.com*, 6 September 2014, https://www.vice.com/en_us/article/kz55yv/how-britain-might-have-deliberately-concealed-evidence-of-imperial-crimes (Accessed: 28 February 2020)

Esterow, Milton, 'The Hunt for the Nazi Loot Still Sitting on Library Shelves', *New York Times*, 14 January 2019, https://www.nytimes.com/2019/01/14/arts/nazi-loot-on-library-shelves.html (Accessed: 12 February 2020)

Feather, John, *Publishing, Piracy and Politics: An Historical Study of Copyright in Britain* (London: Mansell, 1994)

Feingold, Mordechai, 'Oriental Studies', in Nicholas Tyacke (ed.), *The History of the University of Oxford*, 4: *Seventeenth-Century Oxford* (Oxford: Clarendon Press, 1997), pp. 449–504

Filkins, Dexter, 'Regrets Only?', *New York Times Magazine*, 7 October 2007, https://www.nytimes.com/2007/10/07/magazine/07MAKIYA-t. html (Accessed: 16 April 2019)

Finkel, Irving, 'Ashurbanipal's Library: Contents and Significance', in Gareth Brereton (ed.), *I am Ashurbanipal King of the World, King of Assyria* (London: Thames & Hudson/British Museum, 2018), pp. 88–97

Fishman, David E., 'Embers Plucked from the Fire: The Rescue of Jewish Cultural Treasures at Vilna', in Jonathan Rose (ed.), *The Holocaust and the Book: Destruction and Preservation* (Amherst, MA: University of Massachusetts Press, 2001), pp. 66–78

——, *The Book Smugglers: Partisans, Poets, and the Race to Save Jewish Treasures from the Nazis* (New York: Foredge, 2017)

Fleming, Patricia, Gallichan, Gilles, and Lamonde, Yves (eds), *History of the Book in Canada*, 1: *Beginnings to 1840* (Toronto: University of Toronto Press, 2004)

Flood, Alison, 'Turkish Government Destroys More Than 300,000 books', *Guardian*, 6 August 2019

Fox, Peter, *Trinity College Library Dublin: A History* (Cambridge: Cambridge University Press, 2014)

Frame, Grant, and George, A. R., 'The Royal Libraries of Nineveh: New Evidence for King Ashurbanipal's Tablet Collecting', *Iraq*, 67 (2005), pp. 265–84

Gallas, Elisabeth, *'Das Leichenhaus der Bücher': Kulturrestitution und jüdisches Geschichtsdenken nach 1945* (Göttingen: Vandenhoeck & Ruprecht, 2016)

Gameson, Richard, *The Earliest Books of Canterbury Cathedral: Manuscripts and Fragments to c.1200* (London: Bibliographical Society/ British Library/ Dean and Chapter of Canterbury, 2008)

——, 'From Vindolanda to Domesday: The Book in Britain from the Romans to the Normans', in Richard Gameson (ed.), *The Cambridge History of the Book in Britain*, 1: *c.400–1100* (Cambridge: Cambridge University Press, 2012), pp. 1–12

Ganz, David, 'Anglo-Saxon England', in Elisabeth Leedham-Green and Teresa Webber (eds), *The Cambridge History of Libraries in Britain and Ireland*, 1: *To 1640* (Cambridge: Cambridge University Press, 2006), pp. 91–108

García-Arenal, Mercedes, and Rodríguez Mediano, Fernando, 'Sacred History, Sacred Languages: The Question of Arabic in Early Modern Spain', in Jan Loop, et al. (eds), *The Teaching and Learning of Arabic in Early Modern Europe* (Leiden: Brill, 2017), pp. 133–62

Garton Ash, Timothy, *The File* (London: Atlantic Books, 1997)

——, 'True Confessions', *New York Review of Books*, 17 July 1997

——, *History of the Present: Essays, Sketches and Dispatches from Europe in the 1990s* (London: Allen Lane, 1999)

——, *Free Speech: Ten Principles for a Connected World* (London: Atlantic Books, 2016)

Gauck, Joachim, 'State Security Files', in Alex Boraine, Janet Levy and Ronel Sheffer (eds), *Dealing with the Past: Truth and Reconciliation in South Africa* (Cape Town: Institute for Democracy in South Africa, 1994), pp. 71–5

——, and Fry, Martin, 'Dealing with a Stasi Past', *Daedalus*, 123 (1994), pp. 277–84

Gellman, Barton, and Randal, Jonathan C., 'U.S. to Airlift Archive of Atrocities out of Iraq', *Washington Post*, 19 May 1992, p. A12

Gentleman, Amelia, 'Home Office Destroyed Windrush Landing Cards Says Ex-Staffer', *Guardian*, 17 April 2018, https://www.theguardian.com/uk-news/2018/apr/17/home-office-destroyed-windrush-landing-cards-says-ex-staffer (Accessed: 3 September 2019)

Gibbon, Edward, *The History of the Decline and Fall of the Roman Empire*, (ed.) David Womersely, 3 vols (London: Penguin Books, 1994–5)

Gleig, George Robert, *A Narrative of the Campaigns of the British Army at Washington and New Orleans, Under Generals Ross, Pakenham, and Lambert, in 1814 and 1815* (London: John Murray, 1821)

Gnisci, Jacopo (ed.), *Treasures of Ethiopia and Eritrea in the Bodleian Library, Oxford* (Oxford: Mana al-Athar, 2019)

Goldring, Elizabeth, *Nicholas Hilliard: Life of an Artist* (New Haven, CT: Published by the Paul Mellon Center for British Art by Yale University Press, 2019)

Goodman, Martin, *A History of Judaism* (London: Allen Lane, 2017)

Gordon, Martin K., 'Patrick Magruder: Citizen, Congressman, Librarian of Congress', *Quarterly Journal of the Library of Congress*, 32 (1975), pp. 153–71

Gravois, John, 'A Tug of War for Iraq's Memory', *Chronicle of Higher Education*, 54 (8 February 2008), pp. 7–10

Grendler, Paul F., *The Roman Inquisition and the Venetian Press, 1540–1605* (Princeton, NJ: Princeton University Press, 1977)

——, 'The Destruction of Hebrew Books in Venice in 1568', *Proceedings of the American Academy for Jewish Research*, 45 (1978), pp. 103–30

Grierson, Jamie, and Marsh, Sarah, 'Vital Immigration Papers Lost by UK Home Office', *Guardian*, 31 May 2018, https://www.theguardian.com/uk-news/2018/may/31/vital-immigration-papers-lost-by-uk-home-office (Accessed: 31 May 2018)

Grimsted, Patricia Kennedy, 'Displaced Archives and Restitution Problems on the Eastern Front in the Aftermath of the Second World War', *Contemporary European History*, 6 (1997), pp. 27–74

——, *Trophies of War and Empire: The Archival Heritage of Ukraine, World War II and the International Politics of Restitution* (Cambridge, MA: Harvard Ukrainian Research Institute, 2001)

——, 'The Postwar Fate of Einsatzstab Reichsleiter Rosenberg Archival and Library Plunder, and the Dispersal of ERR Records', *Holocaust and Genocide Studies*, 20, 2 (2006), pp. 278–308

Gross, Robert, and Kelley, Mary (eds), *A History of the Book in America, 2: An Extensive Republic: Print, Culture & Society in the New Nation 1790–1840* (Chapel Hill, NC: American Antiquarian Society and the University of North Carolina Press, 2010)

Große, Peter, and Sengewald, Barbara and Matthias, 'Der chronologische Ablauf der Ereignisse am 4. Dezember 1989', *Gesellschaft für Zeitgeschichte: Stasi-Besetzung*, 4.12.1989, http://www.gesellschaft-zeitgeschichte.de/geschichte/1-stasi-besetzung-1989-in-erfurt/der-4-dezember-1989-in-erfurt/ (Accessed: 6 June 2020)

Guppy, Henry, *The Reconstitution of the Library of the University of Louvain: Great Britain's Contribution 1914–1925* (Manchester: Manchester University Press, 1926)

Gutas, Dimitri, *Greek Thought, Arabic Culture: The Graeco-Arabic Translation Movement in Baghdad and Early Abbasid Society (2nd–4th/8th–10th centuries)* (London: Routledge, 2012)

Hacker, Joseph R., 'Sixteenth-Century Jewish Internal Censorship of Hebrew Books', in Joseph R. Hacker and Adam Shear (eds), *The Hebrew Book in Early Modern Italy* (Philadelphia, PA: University of Pennsylvania Press, 2011), pp. 109–20

Halvarsson, Edith, 'Over 20 Years of Digitization at the Bodleian Libraries', *Digital Preservation at Oxford and Cambridge*, 9 May 2017, http://www.dpoc.ac.uk/2017/05/09/over-20-years-of-digitization-at-the-bodleian-libraries/ (Accessed: 21 December 2019)

Hamel, Christopher de, *Syon Abbey: The Library of the Bridgettine Nuns and Their Peregrinations After the Reformation* (Otley: Printed for the Roxburghe Club, 1991)

——, 'The Dispersal of the Library of Christ Church Canterbury from the

Fourteenth to the Sixteenth Century', in James P. Carley and Colin C. G. Tite (eds), *Books and Collectors 1200–1700: Essays Presented to Andrew Watson* (London: British Library, 1997), pp. 263–79

Hamilton, Alastair, 'The Learned Press: Oriental Languages', in Ian Gadd (ed.), *The History of Oxford University Press*, 1: *Beginnings to 1780* (Oxford: Oxford University Press, 2013), pp. 399–417

Hampshire, Edward, '"Apply the Flame More Searingly"': The Destruction and Migration of the Archives of British Colonial Administration: A Southeast Asia Case Study', *Journal of Imperial and Contemporary History*, 41 (2013), pp. 334–52

Handis, Michael W., 'Myth and History: Galen and the Alexandrian Library', in Jason König, Katerina Oikonomopolou and Greg Woolf (eds), *Ancient Libraries* (Cambridge: Cambridge University Press, 2013), pp. 364–76

Harris, Oliver, 'Motheaten, Mouldye, and Rotten: The Early Custodial History and Dissemination of John Leland's Manuscript Remains', *Bodleian Library Record*, 18 (2005), pp. 460–501

Harris, P. R., *A History of the British Museum Library 1753–1973* (London: British Library, 1998)

Harrison, William, and Edelen, George, *The Description of England: The Classic Contemporary Account of Tudor Social Life* (Washington, DC: Folger Library and Dover Publications, 1994)

Harvey, Adam, *MegaPixels*: https://megapixels.cc/ (Accessed: 2 September 2019)

Hatzimachili, Myrto, 'Ashes to Ashes? The Library of Alexandria after 48 BC', in Jason König, Katerina Oikonomopolou and Greg Woolf (eds), *Ancient Libraries* (Cambridge: Cambridge University Press, 2013), pp. 167–82

Haupt, P., 'Xenophon's Account of the Fall of Nineveh', *Journal of the American Oriental Society*, 28 (1907), pp. 99–107

Hayner, Priscilla B., *Unspeakable Truths: Transitional Justice and the Challenge of Truth Commissions*, 2nd edn (New York: Routledge, 2011)

Hebron, Stephen, *Marks of Genius: Masterpieces from the Collections of the Bodleian Libraries* (Oxford: Bodleian Library, 2014)

——, and Denliger, Elizabeth C., *Shelley's Ghost: Reshaping the Image of a Literary Family* (Oxford: Bodleian Library, 2010)

Hern, Alex, 'Flickr to Delete Millions of Photos as it Reduces Allowance for Free Users', *Guardian*, 18 November 2018, https://www.theguardian.com/technology/2018/nov/02/flickr-delete-millions-photos-reduce-allowance-free-users (Accessed: 2 June 2019)

Hill, Evan, 'Silicon Valley Can't Be Trusted with Our History', *Buzzfeednews. com*, 29 April 2018, https://www.buzzfeednews.com/article/evanhill/ silicon-valley-cant-be-trusted-with-our-history (Accessed 1 July 2019)

Hill, Leonidas E., 'The Nazi Attack on "Un-German" Literature, 1933– 1945', in Jonathan Rose (ed.), *The Holocaust and the Book: Destruction and Preservation* (Amherst, MA: University of Massachusetts Press, 2001), pp. 9–46

Hirschler, Konrad, *The Written Word in the Medieval Arabic Lands: A Social and Cultural History of Reading Practices* (Edinburgh: Edinburgh University Press, 2012)

——, *Medieval Damascus: Plurality and Diversity in an Arabic Library: The Ashrafiyya Library Catalogue* (Edinburgh: Edinburgh University Press, 2016)

Hoffman, Adina, and Cole, Peter, *Sacred Trash: The Lost and Found World of the Cairo Genizah* (New York: Schocken, 2011)

Hopf, Henning, Krief, Alain, Mehta, Goverdhan, and Matlin, Stephen A., 'Fake Science and the Knowledge Crisis: Ignorance Can Be Fatal', *Royal Society Open Science*, 6 (2019), 1–7, https://doi.org/10.1098/ rsos.190161

Horrigan, John B., *Libraries 2016*, Pew Research Center, Washington, DC, September 2016, https://www.pewinternet.org/2016/09/09/libraries- 2016/ (Accessed: 8 September 2019)

Houston, George W., 'The Non-Philodemus Book Collection in the Villa of the Papyri', in Jason König, Katerina Oikonomopolou and Greg Woolf (eds), *Ancient Libraries* (Cambridge: Cambridge University Press, 2013), pp. 183–208

Hughes, Ted, *Winter Pollen: Occasional Prose*, (ed.) William Scammell (London: Faber & Faber, 1994)

Hunt, R. W. (ed.), *A Summary Catalogue of Western Manuscripts in the Bodleian Library at Oxford*, 1: *Historical Introduction and Conspectus of Shelf-Marks* (Oxford: Clarendon Press, 1953)

Huseinovic, Samir, and Arbutina, Zoran, 'Burned Library Symbolizes Multiethnic Sarajevo', *dw.com*, 25 August 2012, https://p.dw.com/p/15wWr (Accessed: 18 February 2020)

International Tribunal for the Prosecution of Persons Responsible for Serious Violations of International Humanitarian Law Committed in the Territory of the Former Yugoslavia Since 1991, *The Prosecutor vs. Ratko Mladić: 'Prosecution Submission of the Fourth Amended Indictment and Schedules of Incidents'*, Case Number: IT-09-92-PT, 16 December 2011, https://heritage.sense-agency.com/assets/sarajevo-national-library/sg-3-02-mladic-indictment-g-en.pdf (Accessed: 17 February 2020)

'Internet Archive is Suffering from a DDoS Attack', *Hacker News*, 15 June 2016, https://news.ycombinator.com/item?id=11911926 (Accessed: 2 June 2019)

'The *Irish Times* View: Neglect of the National Archives', *Irish Times*, 31 December 2019, https://www.irishtimes.com/opinion/editorial/the-irish-times-view-neglect-of-the-national-archives-1.4127639 (Accessed: 31 December 2019)

Jacob, Christian, 'Fragments of a History of Ancient Libraries', in Jason König, Katerina Oikonomopolou and Greg Woolf (eds), *Ancient Libraries* (Cambridge: Cambridge University Press, 2013), pp. 57–81

Jefferson, Thomas to Isaac Macpherson, 13 August 1813. Document 12 in Andrew A. Lipscomb and Albert Ellery Bergh (eds), *The Writings of Thomas Jefferson*, 13 (Washington, DC: Thomas Jefferson Memorial Association, 1905), pp. 333–5

Jenkinson, Hilary, and Bell, H. E., *Italian Archives During the War and at its Close* (London: HM Stationery Office, 1947)

Jeong, Sarah, 'Anti-ISIS Hacktivists are Attacking the Internet Archive', *Tech by Vice: Motherboard*, 15 June 2016, https://web.archive.org/web/20190523193053/https://www.vice.com/en_us/article/3davzn/anti-isis-hacktivists-are-attacking-the-internet-archive (Accessed: 1 September 2019)

Johnston, William Dawson, *History of the Library of Congress*, 1: *1800–1864* (Washington, DC: Government Printing Office, 1904)

Jones, Meg Leta, *Ctrl + Z: The Right to be Forgotten* (New York: New York University Press, 2016)

Kalender, Fahrudin, 'In Memoriam: Aida (Fadila) Buturovic (1959–1992)', *Bibliotekarstvo: godišnjak Društva bibliotekara Bosne i Hercegovine*, 37–41 (1992–6), p. 73

Karabinos, Michael Joseph, 'Displaced Archives, Displaced History: Recovering the Seized Archives of Indonesia', *Bijdragen tot de Taal-, Land- en Volkenkunde*, 169 (2013), pp. 279–94

Kenosi, Lekoko, 'Preserving and Accessing the South African Truth and Reconciliation Commission Records', in James Lowry and Justus Wamukoya (eds), *Integrity in Government Through Records Management: Essays in Honour of Anne Thurston* (Farnham: Ashgate, 2014), pp. 111–23

Ker, Neil R., *Pastedowns in Oxford Bindings With a Survey of Oxford Binding c.1515–1620* (Oxford: Oxford Bibliographical Society publications, new series 5, 1954)

——, 'Cardinal Cervini's Manuscripts from the Cambridge Friars', in Andrew G. Watson (ed.), *Books, Collectors and Libraries: Studies in the Medieval Heritage* (London: Hambledon Press, 1985), pp. 437–58

——, 'Oxford College Libraries before 1500', in Andrew G. Watson (ed.), *Books, Collectors and Libraries: Studies in the Medieval Heritage* (London: Hambledon Press, 1985), pp. 301–20

Klinenberg, Eric, *Palaces for the People: How to Build a More Equal and United Society* (London: Bodley Head, 2018)

Knowles, David, *The Religious Orders in England, 3: The Tudor Age* (Cambridge: Cambridge University Press, 1959)

Knuth, Rebecca, *Libricide: The Regime-Sponsored Destruction of Books and Libraries in the Twentieth Century* (Westport, CT: Praeger, 2003)

——, *Burning Books and Levelling Libraries: Extremist Violence and Cultural Destruction* (Westport, CT: Praeger, 2006)

Koller, Markus, and Karpat, Kemal H. (eds), *Ottoman Bosnia: A History in Peril* (Madison, WI: Publication of the Center for Turkish Studies, University of Wisconsin Press, 2004)

Kominko, Maja (ed.), *From Dust to Digital: Ten Years of the Endangered Archives Programme* (Cambridge: Open Book Publishers, 2015)

König, Jason, Oikonomopolou, Katarina, and Woolf, Greg (eds), *Ancient Libraries* (Cambridge: Cambridge University Press, 2013)

Koslowski, Max, 'National Archives May Not Survive Unless Funding Doubles, Warns Council', *Canberra Times*, 18 July 2019, https://www.canberratimes.com.au/story/6279683/archives-may-not-survive-unless-funding-doubles-warns-council/?cs=14350 (Accessed: 11 September 2019)

Krevans, Nita, 'Bookburning and the Poetic Deathbed: The Legacy of Virgil', in Philip Hardie and Helen Moore (eds), *Classical Literary Careers and Their Reception* (Cambridge: Cambridge University Press, 2010), pp. 197–208

Kruk, Herman, 'Library and Reading Room in the Vilna Ghetto, Strashun Street 6', in Jonathan Rose (ed.), *The Holocaust and the Book: Destruction and Preservation* (Amherst, MA: University of Massachusetts Press, 2001), pp. 171–200

Kuznitz, Cecile Esther, *YIVO and the Making of Modern Jewish Culture: Scholarship for the Yiddish Nation* (Cambridge: Cambridge University Press, 2014)

Labbé, Thomas, et al., 'The Longest Homogeneous Series of Grape Harvest Dates, Beaune 1354–2018, and its Significance for the Understanding of Past and Present Climate', *Climate of the Past*, 15 (2019), pp. 1485–1501, https://doi.org/10.5194/cp-15-1485-2019

Lapidge, Michael, *The Anglo-Saxon Library* (Oxford: Oxford University Press, 2008)

Larkin, Philip, 'A Neglected Responsibility: Contemporary Literary Manuscripts', in *Required Writing: Miscellaneous Pieces 1955–1982* (London: Faber & Faber, 1983), pp. 98–108

——, *Selected Letters of Philip Larkin 1940–1985*, (ed.) Anthony Thwaite (London: Faber & Faber, 1992)

——, *Letters to Monica*, (ed.) Anthony Thwaite (London: Faber & Faber in association with the Bodleian Library, 2010)

——, *Complete Poems*, (ed.) Archie Burnett (New York: Farrar, Straus & Giroux, 2012)

——, *Letters Home 1936–1977*, (ed.) James Booth (London: Faber & Faber, 2018)

Layard, Austen H., *Discoveries in the Ruins of Nineveh and Babylon* (London: John Murray, 1853)

Led By Donkeys: How Four Friends with a Ladder Took on Brexit (London: Atlantic Books, 2019)

Leland, John, *The laboryouse journey & serche . . . for Englandes antiquitees . . .*, (ed.) John Bale (London: S. Mierdman, 1549)

——, *The Itinerary of John Leland*, (ed.) Lucy Toulmin Smith, 5 vols (London: Centaur Press, 1964)

——, *De uiris illustribus. On famous men*, (ed.) James P. Carley (Toronto: Pontifical Institute of Medieval Studies/Oxford: Bodleian Library, 2010)

Letters of Sir Thomas Bodley to the University of Oxford 1598–1611, (ed.) G. W. Wheeler (Oxford: Printed for private circulation at Oxford University Press, 1927)

'Librarian of Louvain Tells of War Losses', *New York Times*, 17 April 1941, p. 1

Libraries Connected, 'Value of Libraries', https://www.librariesconnected. org.uk/page/value-of-libraries (Accessed: 25 August 2019)

The Libraries of King Henry VIII, (ed.) James P. Carley (*Corpus of British Medieval Library Catalogues* 7) (London: British Library in association with the British Academy, 2000)

Lieberman, S. J., 'Canonical and Official Cuneiform Texts: Towards an Understanding of Assurbanipal's Personal Tablet Collection', in Tzvi Abusch, John Huehnergard and Piotr Steinkeller (eds), *Lingering Over Words: Studies in Ancient Near Eastern Literature in Honor of William L. Moran* (Atlanta, GA: Scholars' Press, 1990), pp. 310–11

Lipstadt, Deborah, *Denying the Holocaust: The Growing Assault on Truth and Memory* (New York: Free Press, 1993)

Lloyd, Seton, *Foundations in the Dust: The Story of Mesopotamian Exploration* (London: Thames & Hudson, 1980)

Locker-Lampson, Frederick, 'Tennyson on the Romantic Poets', in Norman Page (ed.), *Tennyson: Interviews and Recollections* (Basingstoke: Macmillan, 1983)

Lor, Peter, 'Burning Libraries for the People: Questions and Challenges for the Library Profession in South Africa', *Libri* (2013), pp. 359–72

The Lorsch Gospels – Introduction by Wolfgang Braunfels (New York: George Braziller, 1967)

Lowndes, Susan, *Portugal: A Traveller's Guide* (London: Thornton Cox, 1989)

Lowry, James (ed.), *Displaced Archives* (London: Routledge, 2014)

Lustig, Jason, 'Who Are to Be the Successors of European Jewry? The Restitution of German Jewish Communal and Cultural Property', *Journal of Contemporary History*, 52 (2017), pp. 519–45

MacCarthy, Fiona, *Byron: Life and Legend* (London: John Murray, 2002)

McClanahan, Kel, 'Trump and the Demise of the Presidential Records Honor System', *JustSecurity*, 22 March 2019, https://www.justsecurity. org/63348/trump-and-the-demise-of-the-presidential-records-honor-system/ (Accessed: 13 August 2019)

McConica, James (ed.), *The History of the University of Oxford*, III: *The Collegiate University* (Oxford: Oxford University Press, 1986)

MacCulloch, Diarmaid, *Thomas Cromwell: A Life* (London: Allen Lane, 2018)

McDougall, James, *A History of Algeria* (Cambridge: Cambridge University Press, 2017)

MacGinnis, John, 'The Fall of Assyria and the Aftermath of the Empire', in Gareth Brereton (ed.), *I am Ashurbanipal King of the World, King of Assyria* (London: Thames & Hudson/British Museum, 2018), pp. 276–85

McKenzie, Judith S., Gibson, Sheila, and Reyes, A. T., 'Reconstructing the Serapeum in Alexandria from the Archaeological Evidence', *Journal of Roman Studies*, 94 (2004), pp. 73–121

McKitterick, David, *Cambridge University Library, A History: The Eighteenth and Nineteenth Centuries* (Cambridge: Cambridge University Press, 1986)

MacLeod, Roy, 'Introduction: Alexandria in History and Myth', in Roy MacLeod (ed.), *The Library of Alexandria: Centre of Learning in the Ancient World* (London: I. B. Tauris, 2000), pp. 1–15

MacMillan, Margaret, *The War That Ended Peace: How Europe Abandoned Peace for the First World War* (London: Profile, 2013)

Macray, William Dunn, *Annals of the Bodleian Library Oxford*, 2nd edn, Enlarged and Continued from 1868 to 1880 (Oxford: Clarendon Press, 1890)

Maddrell, Paul, 'The Revolution Made Law: The Work Since 2001 of the Federal Commissioner for the Records of the State Security Service of the Former German Democratic Republic', *Cold War History*, 4 (2004), pp. 153–62

Madison, James, *The Papers of James Madison*, (ed.) Henry Gilpin, 4 vols (New York: J. & H. G. Langley, 1841)

Makiya, Kanan, *Republic of Fear: The Politics of Modern Iraq* (Berkeley, CA: University of California Press, 1998)

——, 'A Model for Post-Saddam Iraq', *Journal of Democracy*, 14 (2003), pp. 5–12

——, 'A Personal Note', in *The Rope* (New York: Pantheon, 2016), pp. 297–319

Malcolm, Janet, *The Silent Woman: Sylvia Plath and Ted Hughes* (New York: Knopf, 1994)

Malcolm, Noel, *Bosnia: A Short History* (London: Macmillan, 1994)

——, 'Preface', in Markus Koller and Kemal H. Karpat (eds), *Ottoman Bosnia: A History in Peril* (Madison, WI: Publication of the Center for Turkish Studies, University of Wisconsin, 2004), pp. vii–viii

Matthäus, Jürgen, 'Nazi Genocides', in Richard J. Bosworth and Joseph A. Maiolo (eds), *The Cambridge History of the Second World War*, 2: *Politics and Ideology* (Cambridge: Cambridge University Press, 2015), pp. 162–80

Matthies, Volker, *The Siege of Magdala: The British Empire Against the Emperor of Ethiopia* (Princeton, NJ: Markus Wiener, 2012)

Max, Stanley M., 'Tory Reaction to the Public Libraries Bill, 1850', *Journal of Library History*, 19 (1974–87), pp. 504–24

Mayer-Schönberger, Viktor, *Delete: The Virtue of Forgetting in the Digital Age* (Princeton, NJ: Princeton University Press, 2009)

Meehan, Bernard, *The Book of Kells* (London: Thames & Hudson, 2012)

Mercier, Désiré-Félicien-François-Joseph, *Pastoral Letter of his Eminence Cardinal Mercier Archbishop of Malines Primate of Belgium Christmas 1914* (London: Burns & Oates Ltd, 1914)

Mill, John Stuart, *On Liberty, Utilitarianism, and Other Essays*, (eds) Mark Philp and Frederick Rosen (Oxford: Oxford University Press, 2015)

Mittler, Elmar (ed.), *Bibliotheca Palatina: Katalog zur Austellung vom. 8 Juli bis 2. Nov 1986, Heideliggeitskirche Heidelberg* (Heidelberg: Braus, 1986)

Moldrich, Donovan, 'Tamils Accuse Police of Cultural Genocide', *The Times*, 8 September 1984, p. 4

Montagne, Renée, 'Iraq's Memory Foundation: Context in Culture', *Morning Edition* (NPR), 22 March 2005, https://www.npr.org/templates/story/story.php?storyId=4554528 (Accessed: 16 April 2019)

Montgomery, Bruce P., 'The Iraqi Secret Police Files: A Documentary Record of the Anfal Genocide', *Archivaria*, 52 (2001), pp. 69–99

——, 'Immortality in the Secret Police Files: The Iraq Memory Foundation and the Baath Party Archive', *International Journal of Cultural Property*, 18 (2011), pp. 309–36

——, 'US Seizure, Exploitation, and Restitution of Saddam Hussein's Archive of Atrocity', *Journal of American Studies*, 48 (2014), pp. 559–93

——, and Brill, Michael P., 'The Ghosts of Past Wars Live on in a Critical Archive', *War on the Rocks*, 11 September 2019, https://warontherocks.com/2019/09/the-ghosts-of-past-wars-live-on-in-a-critical-archive/ (Accessed: 3 October 2019)

Moran, Jessica, 'Is Your Facebook Account an Archive of the Future?', *National Library of New Zealand Blog*, 30 August 2019, https://natlib.govt.nz/blog/posts/is-your-facebook-account-an-archive-of-the-future (Accessed: 6 September 2019)

Motion, Andrew, *Philip Larkin: A Writer's Life* (London: Faber & Faber, 1993)

Murgia, Madhumita, 'Microsoft Quietly Deletes Largest Public Face Recognition Data Set', *Financial Times*, 6 June 2019, https://www.ft.com/content/7d3e0d6a-87a0-11e9-a028-86cea8523dc2 (Accessed: 2 September 2019)

Murray, Nicholas, *Kafka* (London: Little Brown, 2004)

Myres, J. N. L., 'Recent Discoveries in the Bodleian Library', *Archaeologia*, 101 (1967), pp. 151–68

Naisbitt, John, *Megatrends* (London: Futura, 1984)

Naudé, Gabriel, *Advice on Establishing a Library*, with an Introduction by Archer Taylor (Berkeley, CA: University of California Press, 1950)

'Nazis Charge, British Set Fire to Library', *New York Times*, 27 June 1940, p. 12

'News Reel Shows Nazi Bombing', *Daily Mail*, 28 May 1940, p. 3

Now Special Edition, 17 March 2003, transcript, https://www.pbs.org/now/transcript/transcript031703_full.html (Accessed: 17 March 2019)

Oates, Joan, and Oates, David, *Nimrud: An Assyrian Imperial City Revealed* (London: British School of Archaeology in Iraq, 2001)

O'Brien, Hettie, 'Spy Stories: How Privacy is Informed by the Past', *Times Literary Supplement*, 16 August 2019, p. 11

O'Dell, Eoin, 'Not Archiving the .ie Domain, and the Death of New

Politics', *Cearta.ie: the Irish for Rights*, 17 May 2019, http://www.cearta. ie/2019/05/not-archiving-the-ie-domain-and-the-death-of-new-politics/ (Accessed: 18 May 2019)

Ojo, Oluseye, 'National Archives "in a Very Sorry State", Historians Warn', *Sunnewsonline*, 1 September 2019, https://www.sunnewsonline. com/national-archives-in-very-sorry-state-historians-warn/ (Accessed: 10 September 2019)

Orwell, George, *Nineteen Eighty-Four* (London: Penguin, 1989)

Ostrowski, Carl, *Books, Maps, and Politics: A Cultural History of the Library of Congress 1783–1861* (Amherst, MA: University of Massachusetts Press, 2004)

Ovenden, Richard, 'Scipio le Squyer and the Fate of Monastic Cartularies in the Early Seventeenth Century', *The Library*, 6th series, 13 (1991), pp. 323–37

——, 'The Libraries of the Antiquaries, 1580–1640 and the Idea of a National Collection', in Elisabeth Leedham-Green and Teresa Webber (eds), *The Cambridge History of Libraries in Britain and Ireland*, 1: *To 1640* (Cambridge: Cambridge University Press, 2006), pp. 527–61

——, 'Catalogues of the Bodleian Library and Other Collections', in Ian Gadd (ed.), *The History of Oxford University Press*, 1: *Beginnings to 1780* (Oxford: Oxford University Press, 2013), pp. 278–92

——, 'Virtual Memory: The Race to Save the Information Age', *Financial Times Weekend*, 21–22 May 2016, https://www.ft.com/content/907fe3a6-1ce3-11e6-b286-cddde55ca122 (Accessed: 22 November 2018)

——, 'The Manuscript Library of Lord William Howard of Naworth (1563–1640)', in James Willoughby and Jeremy Catto (eds), *Books and Bookmen in Early Modern Britain: Essays Presented to James P. Carley* (Toronto: Pontifical Institute of Medieval Studies, 2018), pp. 278–318

——, 'The Windrush Scandal Reminds Us of the Value of Archives', *Financial Times*, 25 April 2018, https://www.ft.com/content/5cc54f2a-4882-11e8-8c77-ff51caedcde6 (Accessed: 22 November 2018)

——, 'We Must Fight to Preserve Digital Information', *The Economist*, 21 February 2019, https://www.economist.com/open-future/2019/02/21/we-must-fight-to-preserve-digital-information

Pankhurst, Richard, 'The Removal and Restitution of the Third World's Historical and Cultural Objects: The Case of Ethiopia', *Development Dialogue*, 1–2 (1982), pp. 134–40

Pankhurst, Rita, 'The Library of Emperor Tewodros II at Maqdala', *Bulletin of the School of Oriental and African Studies*, 36 (1973), pp. 14–42

Parkes, M. B., 'The Provision of Books', in J. I. Catto and Ralph Evans (eds), *A History of the University of Oxford*, 2: *Late Medieval Oxford* (Oxford: Clarendon Press, 1992), pp. 407–84

Parpola, Simo, 'Assyrian Library Records', *Journal of Near Eastern Studies*, 42 (1983), pp. 1–23

——, 'Library of Assurbanipal', in Roger S. Bagnall, et al. (eds), *The Encyclopedia of Ancient History* (Oxford: Wiley-Blackwell, 2010)

Pearson, David, *Oxford Bookbinding 1500–1640* (Oxford: Oxford Bibliographical Society Publications, 3rd series, 3, 2000)

Pedersén, Olof, *Archives and Libraries in the Ancient Near East 1500–300 BC* (Bethesda, MD: CDL Press, 1998)

Pepys, Samuel, *The Diary of Samuel Pepys*, (eds) Robert Latham and William Matthews, 11 vols (London: G. Bell & Sons, 1970–83)

Peterson, William S., *The Kelmscott Press: A History of William Morris's Typographical Adventure* (Oxford: Oxford University Press, 1991)

Pfeiffer, Judith (ed.), *Politics, Patronage and the Transmission of Knowledge in 13th–15th Century Tabriz* (Leiden: Brill, 2013)

Philip, Ian, *The Bodleian Library in the Seventeenth and Eighteenth Centuries* (Oxford: Clarendon Press, 1983)

Piper, Ernst, *Alfred Rosenberg: Hitler's Chefideologe* (Munich: Karl Blessing Verlag, 2005)

Plath, Sylvia, *The Journals of Sylvia Plath*, Foreword by Ted Hughes (New York: Ballantyne Books, 1983)

——, *The Unabridged Journals of Sylvia Plath: 1950–1962*, (ed.) Karen V. Kukil (New York: Anchor, 2000)

Pogson, K. M., 'A Grand Inquisitor and His Books', *Bodleian Quarterly Record*, 3 (1920), pp. 239–44

Poole, Reginald Lane, *A Lecture on the History of the University Archives* (Oxford: Clarendon Press, 1912)

Posner, Ernst, 'The Effect of Changes in Sovereignty on Archives', *American Archivist*, 5 (1942), pp. 141–55

——, *Archives & the Public Interest: Selected essays by Ernst Posner*, (ed.) Ken Munden (Washington, DC: Public Affairs, 1967)

——, *Archives in the Ancient World* (Cambridge, MA: Harvard University Press, 1972)

Potts, D. T., 'Before Alexandria: Libraries in the Ancient Near East', in Roy MacLeod (ed.), *The Library of Alexandria: Centre of Learning in the Ancient World* (London: I. B. Tauris, 2000), pp. 19–33

Prest, Wilfred, *William Blackstone: Law and Letters in the Eighteenth Century* (Oxford: Oxford University Press, 2008)

Price, David H., *Johannes Reuchlin and the Campaign to Destroy Jewish Books* (Oxford: Oxford University Press, 2010)

Proctor, Tammy M., 'The Louvain Library and US Ambition in Interwar Belgium', *Journal of Contemporary History*, 50 (2015), pp. 147–67

Pullman, Philip, *The Book of Dust*, 1: *La Belle Sauvage* (London: David Fickling in association with Penguin, 2017)

Purcell, Mark, 'Warfare and Collection-Building: The Faro Raid of 1596', *Library History*, 18 (2013), pp. 17–24

Rabinowitz, Dan, *The Lost Library: The Legacy of Vilna's Strashun Library in the Aftermath of the Holocaust* (Waltham, MA: Brandeis University Press, 2019)

Rajak, Tessa, *Translation and Survival: The Greek Bible of the Ancient Jewish Diaspora* (Oxford: Oxford University Press, 2009)

Rankovic, Didi, 'The Internet Archive Risks Being Blocked in Russia Over Copyright Suits', *Reclaimthenet.org*, 24 August 2019, https://reclaimthenet.org/the-internet-archive-risks-blocked-isps/ (Accessed: 30 August 2019)

Raven, James (ed.), *Lost Libraries: The Destruction of Great Book Collections Since Antiquity* (London: Palgrave Macmillan, 2004)

——, 'The Resonances of Loss', in James Raven (ed.), *Lost Libraries: The Destruction of Great Book Collections Since Antiquity* (London: Palgrave Macmillan, 2004), pp. 1–40

Read, Christopher (ed.), *Letters of Ted Hughes* (London: Faber & Faber, 2007)

Reade, Julian, 'Archaeology and the Kuyunjik Archives', in Klaas R. Veenhof (ed.), *Cuneiform Archives and Libraries: Papers Read at the 30e Rencontre assyriologique internationale, Leiden, 3–8 July 1983* (Istanbul: Nederlands Historisch-Archaeologisch Instituut te Istanbul, 1986), pp. 213–22

——, 'Hormuzd Rassam and His Discoveries', *Iraq*, 55 (1993), pp. 39–62

Reynolds, L. D., and Wilson, N. G., *Scribes & Scholars: A Guide to the Transmission of the Greek & Latin Literature*, 3rd edn (Oxford: Clarendon Press, 1991)

Rich, Claudius James, *Narrative of a Residence in Koordistan, and on the Site of Ancient Nineveh* (London: James Duncan, 1836)

Riedlmayer, András, '*Convivencia* Under Fire: Genocide and Book Burning in Bosnia', in Jonathan Rose (ed.), *The Holocaust and the Book: Destruction and Preservation* (Amherst, MA: University of Massachusetts Press, 2001), pp. 266–91

——, 'The Bosnian Manuscript Ingathering Project', in Markus Koller and Kemal Karpat (eds), *Ottoman Bosnia: A History in Peril* (Madison, WI: Publication of the Center for Turkish Studies, University of Wisconsin Press, 2004), pp. 27–38

——, *Destruction of Cultural Heritage in Bosnia-Herzegovina, 1992–1996: A Post-War Survey of Selected Municipalities* (Milosevic Case No. IT-02-54, Exhibit P486, Date 08/-7/2003 and Krajisnik Case No. IT-00-39, Exhibit P732, Date: 23/05/2005)

——, 'Crimes of War, Crimes of Peace: Destruction of Libraries During and After the Balkan Wars of the 1990s', in Michèle Cloonan and Ross Harvey (eds), *Preserving Cultural Heritage, Library Trends*, 56 (2007), pp. 107–32

——, 'Foundations of the Ottoman Period in the Balkan Wars of the 1990s', in Mehmet Kurtoğlu (ed.), *Balkan'larda Osmanlı Vakıfları ve Eserleri Uluslararası Sempozyumu, İstanbul-Edirne 9-10-11 Mayıs 2012* (Ankara: T. C. Başbakanlık Vakıflar Genel Müdürlüğü, 2012), pp. 89–110

Riley-Smith, Ben, 'Expenses and Sex Scandal Deleted from MPs' Wikipedia Pages by Computers Inside Parliament', *Daily Telegraph*, 26 May 2015, https://www.telegraph.co.uk/news/general-election-2015/11574217/Expenses-and-sex-scandal-deleted-from-MPs-Wikipedia-pages-by-computers-inside-Parliament.html (Accessed: 29 August 2019)

Ritchie, J. C., 'The Nazi Book-Burning', *Modern Language Review*, 83 (1988), pp. 627–43

Robertson, J. C., 'Reckoning with London: Interpreting the *Bills of Mortality* Before John Graunt', *Urban History*, 23 (1996), pp. 325–50

Robson, Ann, 'The Intellectual Background to the Public Library Movement in Britain', *Journal of Library History*, 11 (1976), pp. 187–205

Robson, Eleanor, 'The Clay Tablet Book in Sumer, Assyria, and Babylonia', in Simon Eliot and Jonathan Rose (eds), *A Companion to the History of the Book* (Malden, MA: Blackwell Publishing, 2009), pp. 67–83

——, and Stevens, K., 'Scholarly Tablet Collections in First-Millennium Assyria and Babylonia, *c.*700–200 BCE', in Gojko Barjamovic and Kim Ryholt (eds), *Libraries Before Alexandria: Near Eastern Traditions* (Oxford: Oxford University Press, 2019), pp. 319–66

Rose, Jonathan, 'Introduction', in Jonathan Rose (ed.), *The Holocaust and the Book: Destruction and Preservation* (Amherst, MA: University of Massachusetts Press, 2001), pp. 1–6

Rosenbach, A. S. W., *A Book Hunter's Holiday: Adventures With Books and Manuscripts* (Boston: Houghton Mifflin, 1936)

Rosenzweig, Roy, 'Scarcity or Abundance? Preserving the Past in a Digital Era', *American Historical Review*, 108 (2003), pp. 735–62

Roskies, David G. (ed.), *Voices from the Warsaw Ghetto: Writing Our History* (New Haven, CT: Yale University Press, 2019)

Rossi, Valentina Sagaria, and Schmidtke, Sabine, 'The Zaydi Manuscript Tradition (ZMT) Project: Digitizing the Collections of Yemeni Manuscripts in Italian Libraries', *COMSt Bulletin*, 5/1 (2019), pp. 43–59

Rozenberg, Joshua, 'Magna Carta in the Modern Age', in Claire Breay and Julian Harrison (eds), *Magna Carta: Law, Liberty, Legacy* (London: British Library, 2015), pp. 209–57

Rundle, David, 'Habits of Manuscript-Collecting: The Dispersals of the Library of Humfrey, Duke of Gloucester', in James Raven (ed.), *Lost Libraries: The Destruction of Great Book Collections Since Antiquity* (London: Palgrave Macmillan, 2004), pp. 106–24

Rydell, Anders, *The Book Thieves: The Nazi Looting of Europe's Libraries and the Race to Return a Literary Inheritance* (New York: Viking, 2017)

Sahner, Christian C., 'Yemen's Threatened Cultural Heritage', *Wall Street Journal*, 26 December 2018, https://www.wsj.com/articles/yemens-threatened-cultural-heritage-11545739200 (Accessed: 4 January 2019)

SalahEldeen, Hany M., and Nelson, Michael L., 'Losing My Revolution: How Many Resources Shared on Social Media Have Been Lost?', in Panayiotis Zaphiris, George Buchanan, Edie Rasmussen and Fernando Loizides (eds), *Theory and Practice of Digital Libraries: Second International Conference, TPDL 2012, Paphos, Cyprus, September 23–27, 2012. Proceedings* (Berlin: Springer, 2012), pp. 125–37

Saleh, Maryam, 'Protection or Plunder: A U.S. Journalist Took Thousands of ISIS Files Out of Iraq, Reigniting a Bitter Dispute Over the Theft of Iraqi History', *Intercept*, 23 May 2018, https://theintercept.com/2018/05/23/isis-files-podcast-new-york-times-iraq/

Sambandan, V. S., 'The Story of the Jaffna Public Library', *Frontline*, 20, 15–28 March 2003, https://frontline.thehindu.com/magazine/archive (Accessed: 13 April 2019)

Sassoon, Joseph, *Saddam Hussein's Ba'ath Party: Inside an Authoritarian Regime* (Cambridge: Cambridge University Press, 2012)

——, 'The East German Ministry for State Security and Iraq, 1968–1989', *Journal of Cold War Studies*, 16 (2014), pp. 4–23

——, *Anatomy of Authoritarianism in the Arab Republics* (Cambridge: Cambridge University Press, 2016)

Savoy, Bénédicte, and Sarr, Felwine, *Report on the Restitution of African Cultural Heritage, Toward a New Relational Ethics* (Paris: Ministère de la Culture / CRNS-ENS Paris Saclay Université Paris Nanterre, 2018), http://restitutionreport2018.com/sarr_savoy_en.pdf (Accessed: 12 January 2019)

Schipper, Friedrich T., and Frank, Erich, 'A Concise Legal History of the Protection of Cultural Property in the Event of Armed Conflict and a Comparative Analysis of the 1935 Roerich Pact and the 1954 Hague Convention in the Context of the Law of War', *Archaeologies: Journal of the World Archaeological Congress*, 9 (2013), pp. 13–28

Schivelbusch, Wolfgang, *Die Bibliothek von Löwen: eine Episode aus der Zeit der Weltkriege* (Munich: Carl Henser Verlag, 1988)

Schmidt-Glintzer, Helwig, and Arnold, Helwig (eds), *A Treasure House of Books: The Library of Duke August of Brunswick-Wolfenbüttel* (Wiesbaden: Harrassowitz, 1998)

Schmidtke, Sabine, 'The History of Zaydī Studies: An Introduction', *Arabica*, 59 (2012), pp. 85–199

——, 'The Zaydi Manuscript Tradition: Preserving, Studying, and Democratizing Access to the World Heritage of Islamic Manuscripts', *IAS The Institute Letter* (Spring 2017), pp. 14–15

Schork, Kurt, 'Jewel of a City Destroyed by Fire', *The Times*, 27 August 1992, p. 10

Shamir, Avner, 'Johannes Pfefferkorn and the Dual Form of the Confiscation Campaign', in Jonathan Adams and Cordelia Heß (eds), *Revealing the Secrets of the Jews: Johannes Pfefferkorn and Christian Writings About Jewish Life and Literature in Early Modern Europe* (Munich: de Gruyter, 2017), pp. 61–76

Shelley, Percy Bysshe, *Letters of Percy Bysshe Shelley*, (ed.) F. L. Jones, 2 vols (Oxford: Clarendon Press, 1964)

Shepard, Todd, '"Of Sovereignty": Disputed Archives, "Wholly Modern" Archives, and the Post-Decolonisation French and Algerian Republics, 1962–2012', *American Historical Review* (2015), pp. 869–83

Sherwood, Harriet, 'Led by Donkeys Reveal Their Faces at Last: "No One Knew It Was Us"', *Observer*, 25 May 2019, https://www.theguardian.com/politics/2019/may/25/led-by-donkeys-reveal-identities-brexit-billboards-posters

Sider, Sandra, 'Herculaneum's Library in AD 79: The Villa of the Papyri', *Libraries & Culture* (1990), pp. 534–42

Slack, Paul, 'Government and Information in Seventeenth-Century England', *Past & Present*, 184 (2004), pp. 33–68

——, *The Invention of Improvement: Information and Material Progress in Seventeenth-Century England* (Oxford: Oxford University Press, 2015)

Southern, R. W., 'From Schools to University', in J. I. Catto (ed.), *The*

History of the University of Oxford, 1: *The Early Oxford Schools* (Oxford: Clarendon Press, 1984), pp. 1–36

Sroka, Marek, 'The Destruction of Jewish Libraries and Archives in Cracow During World War II', *Libraries & Culture*, 28 (2003), pp. 147–65

Stach, Reiner, *Kafka: The Years of Insight* (Princeton, NJ: Princeton University Press, 2008)

Steinweis, Alan E., *Studying the Jew: Scholarly Antisemitism in Nazi Germany* (Cambridge, MA: Harvard University Press, 2006)

Stevenson, Tom, 'How to Run a Caliphate', *London Review of Books*, 20 June 2019, pp. 9–10

Stipčević, Aleksandar, 'The Oriental Books and Libraries in Bosnia during the War, 1992–1994', *Libraries & Culture*, 33 (1998), pp. 277–82

Stroumsa, Sarah, 'Between "Canon" and Library in Medieval Jewish Philosophical Thought', *Intellectual History of the Islamicate World*, 5 (2017), pp. 28–54

Suetonius, *Lives of the Caesars*, (ed.) John Carew Rolfe, 2 vols (Cambridge, MA: Harvard University Press, 2014)

Sutter, Sem C., 'The Lost Jewish Libraries of Vilna and the Frankfurt Institut zur Erforschung der Judenfrage', in James Raven (ed.), *Lost Libraries: The Destruction of Great Book Collections Since Antiquity* (London: Palgrave MacMillan, 2004), pp. 219–35

Swaine, John, 'Trump Inauguration Crowd Photos Were Edited After He Intervened', *Guardian*, 6 September 2018, https://www.theguardian.com/world/2018/sep/06/donald-trump-inauguration-crowd-size-photos-edited (Accessed: 14 January 2020)

Sweney, Mark, 'Amazon Halved Corporation Tax Bill Despite UK Profits Tripling', *Guardian*, 3 August 2018, https://www.theguardian.com/technology/2018/aug/02/amazon-halved-uk-corporation-tax-bill-to-45m-last-year (Accessed: 11 September 2019)

Talbot, Stephen, 'Saddam's Road to Hell: Interview with the Filmmaker', *pbs.org*, 24 January 2006, https://www.pbs.org/frontlineworld/stories/iraq501/audio_index.html (Accessed: 24 November 2019)

Thielman, Sam, 'You Are Not What You Read: Librarians Purge User Data to Protect Privacy', *Guardian*, 13 January 2016, https://www.theguardian.com/us-news/2016/jan/13/us-library-records-purged-data-privacy (Accessed: 21 December 2019)

Thomson, Rodney, 'Identifiable Books from the Pre-Conquest Library of Malmesbury Abbey', *Anglo-Saxon England*, 10 (1981), pp. 1–19

'Time to Press Ahead with Archive Law', *South China Morning Post*,

30 April 2019, https://www.scmp.com/comment/insight-opinion/article/3008341/time-press-ahead-archive-law (Accessed: 12 July 2019)

'To Repair a War Crime: Louvain's Future Library', *Illustrated London News*, 30 July 1921, pp. 145–6

Toynbee, Arnold J., *The German Terror in Belgium* (London: Hodder & Stoughton, 1917)

Travers, Tony, 'Local Government: Margaret Thatcher's 11 Year War', *Guardian*, 9 April 2013, https://www.theguardian.com/local-government-network/2013/apr/09/local-government-margaret-thatcher-war-politics (Accessed: 18 January 2020)

Trecentale Bodleianum: A Memorial Volume for the Three Hundredth Anniversary of the Public Funeral of Sir Thomas Bodley March 29 1613 (Oxford: Clarendon Press, 1913)

Trial of the Major War Criminals Before the International Military Tribunal, Nuremberg, 14 November 1945–1 October 1946, 42 vols (Nuremberg: International Military Tribunal, 1947–9)

Tripp, Charles, *A History of Iraq*, 3rd edn (Cambridge: Cambridge University Press, 2007)

Truth and Reconciliation Commission of South Africa, *Final Report* (1998), http://www.justice.gov.za/trc/report/finalreport/Volume%201.pdf (Accessed: 21 September, 2019)

Tucci, Pier Luigi, 'Galen's Storeroom, Rome's Libraries, and the Fire of A.D. 192', *Journal of Roman Archaeology*, 21 (2008), pp. 133–49

Tucker, Judith E., and Brand, Laurie A., 'Acquisition and Unethical Use of Documents Removed from Iraq by *New York Times* Journalist Rukmini Callimachi', Communication from Academic Freedom Committee of the Middle Eastern Studies Association of North America, 2 May 2018, https://mesana.org/advocacy/committee-on-academic-freedom/2018/05/02/acquisition-and-unethical-use-of-documents-removed-from-iraq-by-rukmini-callimachi (Accessed: 17 March 2019)

Tyacke, Sarah, 'Archives in a Wider World: The Culture and Politics of Archives', in Wallace Kirsop (ed.), *The Commonwealth of Books: Essays and Studies in Honour of Ian Willison* (Monash: Centre for the Book, 2007), pp. 209–26

Vaisey, David, *Bodleian Library Treasures* (Oxford: Bodleian Library, 2015)

Vincent, James, 'Transgender YouTubers had Their Videos Grabbed to Train Facial Recognition Software', *Verge*, 22 August 2017, https://www.theverge.com/2017/8/22/16180080/transgender-youtubers-ai-facial-recognition-dataset (Accessed: 28 February 2020)

Vincent, Nicholas, *The Magna Carta* (New York, Sotheby's: 18 December 2007)

Vogel, Steve, '"Mr Madison Will Have to Put on His Armor": Cockburn and the Capture of Washington', in *America Under Fire: Mr Madison's War & the Burning of Washington City* (Washington, DC: David M. Rubinstein National Center for White House History, 2014), pp. 137–46

von Merveldt, Nikola, 'Books Cannot Be Killed By Fire: The German Freedom Library and the American Library of Nazi-Banned Books as Agents of Cultural Memory', *Library Trends*, 55 (2007), pp. 523–35

Walasek, Helen, 'Cultural Heritage, the Search for Justice, and Human Rights', in Helen Walasek (ed.), *Bosnia and the Destruction of Cultural Heritage* (Farnham: Ashgate, 2015), pp. 307–22

——, 'Domains of Restoration: Actors and Agendas in Post-Conflict Bosnia-Herzegovina', in Helen Walasek (ed), *Bosnia and the Destruction of Cultural Heritage* (Farnham: Ashgate, 2015), pp. 205–58

Watson, Andrew G., 'Thomas Allen of Oxford and His Manuscripts', in M. B. Parkes and Andrew G. Watson (eds), *Medieval Scribes, Manuscripts & Libraries: Essays Presented to N. R. Ker* (London: Scolar Press, 1978), pp. 279–313

——, *A Descriptive Catalogue of the Medieval Manuscripts of All Souls College Oxford* (Oxford: Oxford University Press, 1997)

Webster, Charles, *The Great Instauration: Science, Medicine, and Reform 1626–1660*, 2nd edn (Oxford: Peter Lang, 2002)

Weiss, Rachel, 'Learning From Loss: Digitally-Reconstructing the Trésor des Chartes at the Sainte-Chapelle', MA Dissertation, University of California, Los Angeles, 2016 (Ann Arbor, MI: Proquest Dissertations Publishing, 2016)

Wheen, Francis, 'The Burning of Paradise', *New Statesman*, 102, 17 July 1981, p. 13

'The White House. Memorandum for All Personnel, Through Donald F. McGahan II . . . Subject: Presidential Records Act Obligations', 22 February 2017, https://www.archives.gov/files/foia/Memo%20to%20WH%20Staff%20Re%20Presidential%20Records%20Act%20(Trump,%2002-22-17)_redacted%20(1).pdf (Accessed: 15 February 2020)

Winters, Jane, and Prescott, Andrew, 'Negotiating the Born-Digital: A Problem of Search', *Archives and Manuscripts*, 47 (2019), pp. 391–403

Wood, Anthony, *The Life of Anthony à Wood from 1632 to 1672, written by himself* (Oxford: Clarendon Press, 1772)

——, *The History and Antiquities of the University of Oxford*, (ed.) John Gutch, 2 vols (Oxford: Printed for the Editor, 1792–96)

——, *The Life and Times of Anthony Wood, Antiquary, of Oxford, 1632–1695 Described by Himself*, (ed.) Andrew Clark, 5 vols (Oxford: Oxford Historical Society, 1891–1900)

——, *The Life and Times of Anthony Wood in His Own Words*, (ed.) Nicolas K. Kiessling (Oxford: Bodleian Library, 2009)

Woodward, Colin, 'Huge Number of Maine Public Records Have Likely Been Destroyed', *Pressandherald.com*, 30 December 2018, https://www.pressherald.com/2018/12/30/huge-number-of-maine-public-records-have-likely-been-destroyed/ (Accessed: 17 September 2019)

Wright, C. E., 'The Dispersal of the Libraries in the Sixteenth Century', in Francis Wormald and C. E. Wright (eds), *The English Library Before 1700* (London: Athlone Press, 1958), pp. 148–75

Wright, Oliver, 'Lobbying Company Tried to Wipe Out "Wife Beater" Beer References', *Independent*, 4 January 2012, https://www.independent.co.uk/news/uk/politics/lobbying-company-tried-to-wipe-out-wife-beater-beer-references-6284622.html (Accessed 29 August 2019)

Wright, Robert, Cocco, Federica, and Ford, Jonathan, 'Windrush Migrants' Cases Backed by Records in National Archives', *Financial Times Weekend*, 21–2 April 2018, p. 1

Xenophon, *Anabasis*, (eds) Carleton L. Brownson and John Dillery (Cambridge, MA: Harvard University Press, 2001)

Zgonjanin, Sanja, 'The Prosecution of War Crimes for the Destruction of Libraries and Archives During Times of Armed Conflict', *Libraries & Culture* (2005), pp. 128–87

Zittrain, Jonathan, Albert, Kendra, and Lessig, Lawrence, 'Perma: Scoping and Addressing the Problem of Link and Reference Rot in Legal Citations', *Legal Information Management*, 88 (2014), pp. 88–99

Zuboff, Shoshana, *The Age of Surveillance Capitalism: The Fight for the Future at the New Frontier of Power* (London: Profile, 2019)

Index